Library of Southern Civilization
Lewis P. Simpson, Editor

THE MISSISSIPPI DELTA AND THE WORLD

THE MISSISSIPPI DELTA AND THE WORLD

The Memoirs of David L. Cohn

EDITED BY

James C. Cobb

Louisiana State University Press • *Baton Rouge and London*

Copyright © 1995 by Louisiana State University Press
All rights reserved
Manufactured in the United States of America
First printing
04 03 02 01 00 99 98 97 96 95   5 4 3 2 1

Designer: Amanda McDonald Key
Typeface: Bembo
Typesetter: Moran Printing, Inc.
Printer and Binder: Thomson–Shore, Inc.

Library of Congress Cataloging-in-Publication Data

Cohn, David L. (David Lewis), 1896–1960.
    The Mississippi Delta and the World :   the memoirs of David L. Cohn
  / edited by James C. Cobb.
        p.   cm. — (Library of Southern civilization)
    ISBN 0-8071-1991-1 (acid-free paper)
    1. Cohn David L. (David Lewis), 1896–1960. 2. Historians—
Mississippi—Delta (Region)—Biography, 3. Delta (Miss. : Region)—
Biography.   I. Cobb, James C. (James Charles), 1947– .
II. Title. III. Series.
F347.M6C64 1995
976.3' 306' 092—dc20
    [B]   94-24290
                                                                    CIP

All photographs are from the David L. Cohn Papers, University of Mississippi Library.

The paper in this book meets the guidelines for permanence and durability of the Committee on Production Guidelines for Book Longevity of the Council on Library Resources. ∞

Contents

Illustrations

Preface

The Mississippi Delta begins in the lobby of the Peabody Hotel in Memphis and ends on Catfish Row in Vicksburg.

—David L. Cohn
God Shakes Creation (1935)

Mississippi begins in the Lobby of a Memphis, Tennessee, hotel and extends south to the Gulf of Mexico.

—William Faulkner
"Mississippi," *Holiday* magazine (1954)

Few writers take kindly to having their gems of originality appropriated without attribution, although most would regard such treatment at the hands of William Faulkner as the supreme compliment. In the case of David Cohn, there was actually little choice in the matter. His succinct description of the geographic and cultural outlines of the Mississippi Delta proved so memorable and so apt that through the force of sheer repetition it passed almost immediately into the public domain.

No one knew the Delta more intimately or told its story more eloquently, but although he produced ten books and scores of articles, Cohn was not by any means the best-known writer to come out of an area that produced the richest array of literary talent—including Walker Percy, Shelby Foote, Elizabeth Spencer, Ellen Douglas, Ellen Gilchrist, and Willie Morris—of any definable subregion in the United States. Certainly, Cohn's modest insistence in his unpublished memoir that he would be content to write "one paragraph with high survival value" suggests that he probably would have been philosophical about his fate as the sometimes-forgotten author of a never-to-be-forgotten sentence. Writers, after all, are far more likely to achieve immortality through their prose then their personas. In Cohn's case, however, the latter was virtually inseparable from the former, and therein lay his importance as an author and essayist.[1]

Although his indelible southernness permeated his writing, David Cohn was

---

1. James C. Cobb, *The Most Southern Place on Earth: The Mississippi Delta and the Roots of Regional Identity* (New York, 1992), 306.

no simple provincial. Rather, he was an amazingly complex, thoroughly cosmopolitan one. His intellectual curiosity nurtured by influential teachers and friends including William Alexander Percy, Cohn vowed early in life to become "a rounded man." The pursuit of roundedness led him to rebel against what he saw as a lamentable trend toward overspecialization, and he showed no reluctance whatsoever in airing his views on an array of topics as diverse—but in his view, closely interrelated—as race and religion, free trade and internationalism, technology and culture, and materialism and matrimony, to name but a few.

Profoundly and obsessively interested in politics, Cohn was a "yellow dog" Democrat, who served as a trusted adviser to Adlai Stevenson, Lyndon Johnson, J. William Fulbright, and a host of others. Southern to the marrow and a sometimes critical but almost fanatically patriotic American, Cohn was also a Jew, and despite his aversion to religious orthodoxy, his quest for self-definition fueled his fascination with what fellow southerner Eli Evans described as "the Jew's involvement in history, his deep roots in the drama of man's struggle to understand deity and creation." On the other hand, whereas Evans admitted, "We were Jews; we were Southerners. I was never sure what either meant, nor how they came together," Cohn was more comfortable with who he was. A southerner, an American, and a Jew, he managed to integrate his identities rather than separate or suppress them.[2]

In order to appreciate Cohn's fascinating search for self-definition, we must first understand the personal and cultural backdrop upon which his southernness and his Americanness were imposed. His father, Herman Cohn, was born in 1862 in Cracow, a Russian village that would later become part of Poland. At age twenty-three, Cohn married Mary Witkowski, and shortly thereafter, the couple went to Greenville, Mississippi, with the apparent assistance of relatives who had preceded them to the United States.[3]

Herman Cohn worked first as a traveling salesman and then became a merchant. He and his wife eventually had two daughters and three sons, including David Lewis Cohn, who was born in 1894. The Cohn family prospered during David's childhood; Herman became the proprietor of The Fair, a dry goods and ready-to-wear clothing store, and the Cohns eventually moved from their home on Walnut Street, near the river, to a more fashionable house on Washington Avenue. As a family of some means, the Cohns were able to send David to study law at the University of Virginia and Yale University. A brief stint in the navy during World War I interrupted Cohn's stay at Yale, but he returned to complete the Master of Law program.[4]

2. Eli Evans, *The Provincials: A Personal History of Jews in the South* (New York, 1974), x, xi.
3. Lee Lewellyn Jordan, "A Biographical Sketch of David L. Cohn" (M.A. thesis, University of Mississippi, 1963), 1.
4. *Ibid.*, 1, 2. Jordan shows Cohn's birthdate as 1897. Official alumni records of the University of Virginia show it as 1894.

By this time, however, Cohn had already realized that a legal career held little appeal for him. Since adolescence, he had been fascinated with the literary world, but his family met with a series of financial reverses in 1917, and Cohn explained later that he "went into business instead of writing because my family went bust on a cotton plantation they had bought."[5]

Although he became a businessman by necessity rather than choice, Cohn displayed an immediate genius for marketing, management, and employee relations. Cohn's father died in 1924 and his mother in 1928, and he readily assumed responsibility for the well-being of his siblings. His financial success enabled him not only to do this but soon thereafter to abandon the business world entirely and begin at last to transform his passion for literature from an avocation to a career.[6]

As a writer, Cohn proved extraordinarily prolific. One of his greatest frustrations, however, was his inability to organize and prepare for publication the memoir that he began while recuperating from an illness in 1953. After Cohn's death, in 1960, these reminiscences and reflections became part of the David L. Cohn Collection at the University of Mississippi. Ole Miss historian James W. Silver, a close friend of Cohn's, sought a publisher for the memoirs, but the size of the manuscript and its apparent disorganization plus the difficulty of finding a suitable editor with the time to undertake the task ultimately stalled this effort. Although the memoirs became the primary source for Lee Lewellyn Jordan's excellent master's thesis on Cohn, the material lay otherwise untouched until 1985 when I ran across it in the course of my research for a book on the Mississippi Delta.[7]

Struck by Cohn's rich prose and even richer insights into Delta life, I was amazed that this material had never been published. Moreover, in the course of mining it for my book, I realized that rather than a seven-hundred-page manuscript, Cohn had actually produced a basic text of approximately half that length and had simply drafted several versions of some of the chapters. Heartened by this discovery and armed with the permission of the Cohn heirs, I proceeded to identify what I viewed as the most effective versions of the various chapters and to delete and rearrange the material in the interest of more effective organization. Readers familiar with William Alexander Percy's *Lanterns on the Levee* are likely to see certain similarities between Percy's memoir and this volume. Cohn certainly shared Percy's affection for the Delta and its people and, to some extent, his longing for the Delta as it was and would never be again. Yet, whereas Percy's nostalgia paralyzed him, Cohn drew on his heritage as a source of inspiration and perspective. Consequently, I have treated this manuscript not as a historical document but as a piece of literature and have sought to let the memoir convey to the reader, with minimal interruption and encumbrance, David Cohn's vision both of the Delta

5. *Ibid.*, 29, 35, 45–46.

6. *Ibid.*, 35.

7. Richard L. Wentworth to James W. Silver, September 10, 1964, in David L. Cohn Collection, J. D. Williams Library, University of Mississippi, Oxford, Miss.

and the world, and his remarkable ability to draw on his knowledge of one to enrich and enliven his discussions of the other.

For their assistance in locating Cohn's manuscript and in securing the necessary copies, I am indebted to Dr. Thomas M. Verich, Director of Archives and Special Collections at the J. D. Williams Library at the University of Mississippi, and to several members of Dr. Verich's staff, including Ms. Naomi Leavell and Ms. Sharron Sarthou. And I am grateful to Ms. Elise Gillespie, a former staff member, who was also very helpful.

I wish to thank Mr. Robert L. Lansberry, the executor of the Cohn estate, and Mr. Leon J. Millner and Mr. Henry Posner, who gave their permission to publish the manuscript. Mr. Cohn's nephew, Mr. Louis Lavine, was kind enough to provide me with copies of some of his mother's correspondence with his uncle. Ms. Betty W. Carter shared with me her recollections of Mr. Cohn.

I particularly appreciate the work of the editorial staff at Louisiana State University Press and the diligent and cheerful work of Ms. Jane Taylor, who copyedited the manuscript.

Professor David R. Goldfield of the University of North Carolina–Charlotte provided many helpful comments and suggestions.

Finally, as always, I am heavily indebted to my wife, Lyra, who did much of the initial editing of the manuscript and proofread a number of subsequent versions as well.

The Mississippi Delta and the World

Introduction

This is not an autobiography except in the limited sense that everything one does is inevitably autobiographical for, as Walt Whitman put it, "A man's personality strikes through his flannels."

The present book is primarily an evocation of persons and places. It is an effort sometimes to see the persons through the places in which they lived, and sometimes to see the places through the eyes of those who lived in them, including myself. I have therefore imposed no autobiographical sequence upon these narrative reflections but have been content, as it were, to talk, to reflect, and to recollect as men may do while sitting on the gallery of a southern house in the cool o' the evening.

Since, however, I am describing the physical and spiritual terrain of my youth, I am inescapably evoking the suns and moons and rains that went into my own shaping; the men and women, friends and neighbors, who fruitfully touched my young life and filled me with an abiding affection for the place where I was born and raised; the great river that deeply entered into my being; the cotton culture that claimed us for its children; and the ancient tragedy, not of our making, through which every one of us, white and Negro, endured—no matter what his pretensions—in an estate half-slave and half-free.

This, too, is how it was in some respects in the little world of my youth, before it had acquired radio, television, "hi-fi," picture magazines, self-service stores, bubble gum, ulcers, paper napkins, nylon stockings, precooked frozen french fried potatoes, falsies, zippers, tranquilizing pills, "picture window" houses, drum majorettes, baby-sitters, "dinettes," do-it-yourself tools, quick-mix beaten biscuit dough, electric can openers, and similar manifestations of our neo-Byzantine civilization that make it one with the nation in its abundance of gift-wrapped blessings.

1

Growing Up in Greenville

Blacks who grew up alongside but apart from Cohn in the turn-of-the-century Delta might have disputed his opening assertion that the Delta constituted "a good place for a growing boy." As the following chapter reveals, however, Cohn was considerably more secure in the bosom of parental love than in the larger physical and racial environment, which he admits "weighed heavily" on him, causing him to feel "a doom on the land where I was born and raised."

The Mississippi Delta, in the opening years of the century, was a good place for a growing boy. The simplicities, serenities, and optimism of the nineteenth century still lingered among us. I had the amenities, such as they were, of our little town of Greenville (population about 6,000) and reveled in the life of the countryside. The Mississippi River was my playground—the levee that contained it, the fields, the forests, the creeks. I came to know in some degree the ways beyond marvel of birds and beasts and growing things. I was stained ineradicably with the autumn's and summer's juices.

The nose, primitive, with the unforgetting memory of the primitive, stored its reminiscences forever fresh against the ravages of time: the fragrance, faint and far, of clover after rain; the aromatic pungency of woodsmoke; the soft scent of rambler roses running red fire along white picket fences; the rich fatness of black-eyed peas simmering with bacon in a black iron pot; the washed-baby smell of new-turned plantation loam; banked honeysuckle impregnating with perfume the warm, star-entangled summer night, drifting blue upon a sea of blue. Food became flesh; calcium bone; tissue muscle; the young body an arrow eager to the bow.

In the town, as in all towns since men began to live in ordered societies, there dwelt lust, hate, greed, bigotry, and envy. But there also dwelt love, generosity, and fairness. Daily we repeated the long experience of the race. Whatever had "happened" from dawn to dawn in Baghdad on the Tigris, happened to us in Greenville on the Mississippi.

The Delta's (and Greenville's) early citizens were unique among pioneers. Here were no lean Yankees marching with rifle, family, and meager possessions across the Western plains. No refugees from the Germany of forty-eight. No

Irish of the famine years, empty handed and eager, searching for a new home in a new world. The men who came to the Delta were the embodiment of a seeming contradiction—pioneers with means. They were the sons of wealthy and moderately wealthy planters of Virginia, Kentucky, and the Carolinas, come to a virgin land to open new cotton plantations. Traveling like princely patriarchs of the Orient, they brought with them their slaves and their household goods. They also brought numerous volumes of the classics, Greek and Latin textbooks, and tutors for their children. They left an ineradicable mark upon the community.

And so it was that the town's greatest blessing for me was this. If most of my townsmen were not of the Attic breed, there was among them the saving remnant—a meaningful group of mellow, informed, perceptive men and women. From them, in many ways, I drew my essential life; a life anchored in a happy household.

My young, newly married parents had come to Greenville shortly after The War from a village lying in a twilight zone between Germany and Poland. The town overwhelmingly Christian in creed, my Jewish parents were welcomed by their new neighbors with dignity and warmth. They were one with them throughout their lives in sickness and death and hard times and rejoicings, and they lie now in the soil of the Delta where there lie also those who were young when they were young together in the young community.

(I am sometimes surprised by what one might call the tautology of the newspaper obituary column. Thus, for example, "William Llangollen Lewis died last night . . . leaving $142,000,000. He came here a penniless immigrant." Why say "penniless"? Did any rich European leave his castles, wines, mistresses, and other amenities to emigrate to Wyoming and live there on jerked beef while fighting Indians? Everyone who came here came to improve his economic or social condition or because he was run out of town where he lived. Everyone, that is, except Negroes. They alone, among our people, were satisfied with their homeplace and saw no reason to leave.)

Members of the tiny Jewish group of Greenville, they [*Cohn's parents*] repeated the experience of pioneers: others had gone up into the land of Canaan before them and, finding the land good, had bade them come. They had been preceded to Greenville by some of my mother's relatives who had made a place for themselves in the business and farming areas of the community, and my father had worked awhile for them. After acquiring English, he became a traveling salesman and later a merchant. His labors provided for the needs of his wife, two daughters, and three sons; his task was made the easier because there was little pressure upon anyone to emulate our few "highflyers." But more important to me—how important I was to understand only in retrospect—we were familiarly secure. The harmony between my parents made for the tranquillity of the household.

I believed therefore as an article of faith that all fathers and mothers endured in a relationship of harmony and mutual respect; that parents loved and sheltered their children while children loved and respected their parents. Even now when someone tells me that he hated his father or mother, I find it unnatural and hard to believe.

As a small Sunday school boy I had no understanding of most of the Ten Commandments. They appeared merely addenda to the catalog of "don'ts" with which little boys are often assailed. But I seemed instinctively to understand the injunction "Honor thy father and mother" and gave it spontaneous obedience. How could it be otherwise? You loved your parents. They loved you. Besides, they were not only parents but "older people." You respected them because—well, because they were older. You did not sit before older people sat or "sass" them. You did not think out these things. They were part of you, and, you were sure, they were part of all boys everywhere.

My father was a big, genial, life-loving, laughter-loving man, marked by the gentleness so often characteristic of big males. Impeccably dressed, warm, friendly, a lover of good food, cigars, and the noble game of poker that he played with zest, it was perhaps inevitable in the atmosphere of the town that he should be brevetted "Colonel" by many of his fellow townsmen. He wore white linens in summer, and a broad-brimmed Panama hat, and carried a walking stick—I was proud to go with him to a baseball game between Greenville and another team of the Cotton States League. I missed him when he left home on business trips, and I never tired of being with him when we were at home together. Neither he nor my mother ever "demanded" anything of me or asked me for an accounting of my behavior, and since this was equivalent to putting me upon my honor and treating me as a responsible adult, I responded to the best of my ability, as boys usually do in such cases.

We embraced one another in the European fashion upon meeting and departing, and we were at peace together all the days of our lives. I was the fortunate son whose father had admitted him early to the warm companionship of his tender spirit.

My mother, cast in a less heroic mold than my father, was the exemplar of the old-fashioned woman who was preoccupied with her household. She was inexperienced in the affairs of the "world," but I soon found her judgments about it sounder than those of many who pretended to know it. Thus I early learned to value the conclusions of so-called impractical people, and to be dubious of the conclusions of the practical concerning things that are not the subject of measuring devices.

An indefinable sadness marked my mother's eyes and was part of her spirit, yet she was given to laughter and to a humor that found expression in drolleries illuminative of the seriocomic situations of life. From childhood until I left my parental roof, I had found it comforting to talk lengthily with this sad, wise, humorous mother of mine, loving her as a son and adoring her as a friend, not least because she sometimes permitted me to glimpse her secret sorrows.

The earth of the Delta in which I lived is a violent earth. Its fields are fecund to the touch of the plow. They seem to cry out for fulfillment of life under the blazing suns of summer. Heat then stands upon the Delta during long days and nights. It stings the flesh. It opens cracks in the fields. It drains men's minds and wearies their bodies. A clear sky suddenly blackens with cloud, rolls with thunder, crackles with lightning, and tumultuous rains flood the steaming earth. Then they are gone. Now the trees shine richly green, the dust-gray mules gleam black, the ditches gurgle with water. Soon the soil is dry again, white clouds float high in the sky, jaybirds shriek from thorn trees, buzzards circle loftily against the blue, and men once more walk the endless cotton rows of the Delta.

Against this landscape, variable, heat-tortured, shifting; amid swamps dark and mysterious and lost; in the presence of the mighty river rolling onward to the Mexican Gulf; under sudden suns and swarming stars; never far from the Negro speech and the Negro singing; within America and yet withdrawn from it, whites and Negroes, in the strangest mass relationship of men on this continent, painfully tried to work out their singular destiny together.

So outnumbered were the whites by Negroes that on the streets of little towns on Saturdays, where country people had come to do their tradin', you might have to look hard to find a white face.

In Coahoma County there were 3,000 Negroes for every 1,000 whites.

In Humphreys County there were 5,000 Negroes for every 1,000 whites.

In Tunica County there were 7,000 Negroes for every 1,000 whites.

There the Negro was a problem to the white man, and the white man was a problem to the Negro. The question was the more acute because Negroes hugely outnumbered whites. More than seven out of every ten persons in the Delta were Negroes. In some sections of the area, nine out of ten persons were Negroes. But Negroes accounted for only one out of ten persons in the nation.

Race, religion, or color prejudices tend to rise in relation to the numbers of the so-called despised minority. And as war—not peace—is the normal state of mankind, so prejudice rather than love is the normal state of mind of most men. This melancholy theorem is somberly illuminated by Pascal's figure who is made to say to another: "I shall have to kill you, little brother, because you come from the other side of the river. But if you did not come from the other side of the river, I shall not have to kill you."

The Delta whites were racially of a piece. More than 99 percent of them were native-born of English, Scottish, Welsh, or Irish ancestry, or they were mixtures of these stocks. Together with their brethren elsewhere in the South, they constituted the largest racially homogeneous bloc of whites in the United States.

Here were nearly all of the elements of tribalism, including a fierce insistence upon the maintenance of taboos held inflexible. Nor is this all.

Wherever European kinsmen of these men had gone as conquerors and colonizers, they had set up a color bar. The Dutch colonial in Java might marry a native girl, rear a Eurasian family, and retire to the Netherlands to live with them in honor. But the Englishman, Scotsman, Irishman, Welshman not only did not marry colored women of the colonies but generally had no free social relations with the colored population. And if we look to Latin American countries— Brazil, say—we shall see that the color bar is not a device of Latin peoples. It is a device of the groups I have mentioned, and Delta whites almost to a man were of the same racial stock.

Both whites and Negroes of the Delta, through a tragedy not of their making, were prisoners of their environment. Since many a Delta plantation contained more Negroes than lived in Vermont, and one county had more Negroes than lived in eight western states, the white Deltan had never been a free man in the sense that the Vermonter or the Westerner had always been a free man. The Deltan's whole society—its laws, customs, manners, and institutions—and how he bore himself in innumerable ways were conditioned by the presence of the Negro. Nor was the Negro a free man, since his society was conditioned by the presence of the white man.

A society that had no counterpart outside the Deep South, it was kept going by the use of intuitive and exquisite tact on the part of both whites and Negroes. It was governed less by the written law than by unwritable codes, an intricate ritual of manners, and a constant adjustment among members of both races. All this was a drain upon the spirit and a sapping of the energies of everyone in the area. It was quiet there. But it was the quiet of a storm center.

Secure within my own household, the environment in which I lived often weighed heavily upon me. I felt there was a doom on the land where I was born and raised. The moccasin coiled by the stagnant pond. The buzzard defiled the white of summer clouds. The mosquito sang a song of chills and fever. The turtle lifted from the slime. Beyond the town, beyond the levee, beyond the willows, the river ran heavy and muddy and slow: timeless, ceaseless, waiting.

The sun was too hot for too long, the rains too heavy, the soil too passionate for fruition, the vegetation too dense, the honeysuckle too sweet, the fields too flat, the horizon—mocking the limited eye—too wide. The dog howled, the ax rang afar off, the lamp smoked, the ripe persimmon fell with silent plop to the forest floor. In the thorn tree a butcher bird impaled a wren.

Members of two races lived out their lives on parallel lines, to meet but in infinity, each with a wound in his heart and a torment in his mind. They savored salt and the moon and tasted delight and felt bitterness in the constricted throat, heard the cry of the newborn child and made way for the pale guest; passing pilgrims, they met in the dreadful marches of the desert and, giving no sign, went on. Living, their ways were separate. Dying, they became a common but not commingled dust. Of these things each spoke only to his own kind.

Theirs was the fatal flaw. They were a little lesser than the angels. But there had been withheld from them the divine calculus by which they might bridge the gulf between themselves and the angels.

2

The Idea of the Soldier

Here, Cohn reflects on the all-pervasive influence of the Civil War on the society in which he grew up. His observations reflect as well his awareness of his Jewish heritage and the concerns of one who had lived through two world wars and the Korean conflict only to spend the last few years of his life worrying about another war that promised to be far more terrible still.

The sun rising blood-red, the air sweet after a stifling night, the new morning tender upon the landscape, I could see across the street from our Washington Avenue house, on the courthouse lawn, the monument to the Confederate soldier. White in the risen dawn, he stood tall, youthful, leaning slightly on his rifle, a bird singing from his marble cap.

He had come, I heard as a small boy, from a faraway place called Italy. It was a strange land. Many of its men were "artists"; probably because they were foreigners and knew no better. Their work, folks said, was not entirely unbecoming even manly men. But it had no appeal for our Delta men. They aspired to become cotton planters or cotton merchants.

The Italians, however, who settled among us, quickly became Americanized. Abandoning the follies of their homeland and adopting the wisdom of ours, they became cobblers, peddlers, merchants, keepers of restaurants. No one of them, clinging to the outmoded ways of the old country, was an artist. Some of them, on the contrary, rose even to the eminence of cotton farming, among them the former barber, Mike Tamburo.

He came often to our house to shave my father during his last illness. Small, dark, belly drum-tight with pasta, the accent of Sicily garlic-pungent upon his English, Mike, brought to Father's bedside not only the tools of his trade but also a gentle manner, dimpling smiles, and a gushing stream of commentary upon the town's events of the day. These were medicaments soothing beyond any known to science.

Mike came to talk knowingly of middle busters, pedigreed cottonseed, cover crops. But the Mediterranean so strongly marked him that if one could hold him close to one's ear one might hear the murmurings of that hyacinthine sea.

A much condensed version of this chapter appears as "The Idea of the Soldier," *Saturday Review of Literature* XXXV (February 9, 1952), 8–10, 24.

Despite the stigma of the artists, there were redeeming features about Italy. A few local Italians peddled bananas from mule-drawn wagons, the great golden stems fatly recumbent upon straw beds. Swarthy men, one wore earrings pirate fashion, the sword-and-cutlass effect heightened by the red handkerchief at the throat. We boys believed they got the fruit from banana plantations in Italy, and we envied Italian boys who could stuff themselves to bursting with bananas as we stuffed ourselves with dewberries that grew wild on the protection levee at the edge of town on the farthest rim of the known universe. From Italy, too, came not only the organ grinders who sometimes appeared on our school grounds but also, we thought, their cunningly dressed monkeys that, cap in hand, ran about among the crowd collecting nickels between bursts of music. (My own favorite—the clanging of it still sounds in my ears—was "The Anvil Chorus" from *Il Trovatore*.) And somehow, in time, the bananas, the organ grinders, the monkeys outweighed in my mind the unfortunate tendency of Italians to become artists.

After the Confederate soldier, in a huge crate, had arrived at the Yazoo and Mississippi Valley depot from New Orleans whence he had come by ship from Italy, Crockett brought him to the courthouse lawn. A tall, reddish skinned, well-liked, prosperous Negro, Crockett did all the heavy draying in the town; he was the only Greenvillian who could move such ponderous objects as gin boilers, having for this purpose logging wagons with wide wheels drawn by six-mule teams. And when the soldier finally stood upon his pedestal, he was covered with cotton sheeting to await the day of his unveiling.

I vaguely remember the crowds, among which a small barefoot boy trod nimbly to keep grown-ups from stepping on his "stone bruises"—the occupational disease of barefoot Delta boys in school-free, delirious summer; the minister's invocation during a period of interminable immobility when I stood stark still lest God strike me dead for "disobedience"; the martial music and wild yelling as Professor Dixon's band played Dixie ("away, away, away down South in Dixie"); the orator saying something about "gallant men in gray"; and, unaccountably, elderly men and women acting like little girls as they openly cried or blew their noses into handkerchiefs.

Places of honor were reserved for Confederate veterans—venerable, bearded men who, except for their medals, resembled the Moses of the *Illustrated Sunday School Lessons*. They were captains, majors, colonels. There were no privates in the Confederate army. Certainly there were none from Mississippi, the second state to secede from the Union and home of Jefferson Davis. If a man was good enough to fight for the Confederacy, he was good enough to be an officer.

Yet, as I later learned with disillusionment, in east Mississippi—far from the Delta—there was, by an unexplainable vagary of behavior, a former private named John Allen.

About twenty years after The War had ended, he was suddenly called upon to make a speech in his hometown explaining how the South had been defeated. He found himself on a platform surrounded by former Confederate officers, and said: "Ladies and gentlemen, as I look about me I see on my right Major ———, Captain ———, and Colonel ———, and on my left General ———, Lieutenant ———, and Colonel ———, all, ladies and gentlemen, high-ranking rear ranks. Now, ladies and gentlemen, I was asked to account for the Confederacy's failure in the late conflict, but I will be brief. I will ask you to look at these officers, and at me, and then draw your own conclusions."

The speech instantly made him well known, and he ran for Congress. The people of his district, whether admiring his eccentricity or from love of novelty, sent him eight times to the House of Representatives, and he became nationally famous as "Private" John Allen.

Although memories of the unveiling ceremonies are dim in my mind, I vividly recall the pop. On the courthouse lawn there were rows of washtubs, each containing dozens of bottles of pop, the sun glinting blue-white off the surrounding ice, touching to greater glory the glory of their colored contents. There were the violently red strawberry, most prized of all, and the dun brown sass-prilla, least prized; pink peach, purple grape, pale yellowish lemon, each with the name of the flavor stamped on the crown for the benefit of grown-up people who had no other means of identification. These treasures, ungraded although comparable to those amassed by the Black Pirate of the Spanish Main, were "free" for the taking, the word "free," in conjunction with pop, sounding with circus-parade music upon the ears of a little boy.

My companions and I drank and drank and belched and belched, with a fine sense of well-being. Sometimes, nearly sated, we took the smallest nips from a bottle. Then we shook it to "make more foam" and drank the foam, or we took swallows from one another's bottles for the rare delight of enjoying two flavors at once.

By late afternoon nearly everyone had gone. The tubs stood filled with the water of melted ice and empty bottles. Here and there on the lawn the clover, the dandelions, the daisies were crushed where men and women had walked. Noise gave way to silence, movement to stillness.

I felt sorry for the Confederate soldier because all had gone and left him alone. I wanted to tell him that I would come to see him tomorrow. But the sudden silence frightened me. I ran swiftly home. I wanted to make sure that my mama and papa were there—Mama sweet-smelling in her freshly laundered gingham dress and Papa spotless in white linen clothes with the masculine aroma of tobacco faintly upon him.

Growing into youth, I became rather a companion of the Confederate soldier for, living across the street from the courthouse, I saw him during my comings and goings. Occasionally I looked closely at him upon his pedestal, marveling that hammer and chisel in the hand of a man would reproduce in stone with photographic fidelity a soldier and his trappings. The monument seemed to me a superb work of art. But when I was grown and saw that artistically it was but a poor thing, it did not strike me as ridiculous. It had a pathetic dignity. It had sprung from the hearts of the people of the community, and if their aesthetic perceptions were untutored, their native simplicity had saved them from committing the pompous absurdities so marked in many of our grandiose public monuments.

Almost on the eve of the first world war, when a high school student, I had sat on our gallery reading Norman Angell's *The Great Illusion*. It "proved" that since modern wars were profitless, wars would cease, and lifting my eyes sometimes from the book to the monument across the way, the soldier seemed clothed with an especial pathos. He belonged to an old, unhappy, far-off era, whose kind would never again recur.

Individually men comfort themselves with the vain but warming illusion that the disasters which afflict others cannot come to them; an illusion saving and sedative seeing that they walk tightropes all their lives. Men are collectively subject to the same illusion: the catastrophes of other times cannot occur in their times. I therefore felt a certain security, and even a touch of smugness, feeling certain that ours was a period in which men, at last civilized, had forever abandoned war. All this seemed to be confirmed by the spiritual that Negro prisoners often sang in the jail behind the courthouse, their stirring voices reaching me as I sat on our gallery:

> I'm gwine a lay down my burdens
> Down by the riverside,
> An' study war no mo.

The heroes of my early youth were nearly all Confederate soldiers, perhaps because soldiers were the only heroes of the South of that day. This was a result of the order of values that The War ordained in the South, and so it was that, with the exception of Thomas Jefferson, soldiers pre-empted our hall of fame.

Foremost among my own heroes was Stonewall Jackson, grave and bearded in the steel-engraved portrait of him that hung in my schoolroom, along with a reproduction of Rosa Bonheur's *The Horse Fair*. I was stirred by the cavalier dash and the dangerous grace of Jeb Stuart. But it was Jackson who deeply moved me. In his terrible loneliness as a field general, this Old Testament warrior knelt to an Old Testament god of battles and prayed before fighting. ("And the Lord said unto Joshua, Fear not, neither be thou dismayed: take all the people of war with thee, and arise, go up to Ai.") Then he rode into battle, often sucking a lemon. Jackson—oh, the unutterable woe of it—accidentally shot by his own men at Chancellorsville as he rode ahead for personal reconnaissance. His last words tore at my young heart: "Pass the infantry to the front.

Tell A. P. Hill to prepare for action. Let us cross over the river and rest in the shade of the trees."

I had no memories of the Civil War (or, as we scrupulously called it, The War between the States), even at second hand from my parents, who had arrived in the Delta only after its end. There were few marks of it in the vicinity. Yet it was often vivid to me, and sometimes it lay oppressively upon my heart.

We continued to dwell in darkness. Fifty years after The War's close, who could say precisely what had caused it? Yet for all our blindness here, we were almost arrogant in the certainties of "science." The telephone linked our little community with the world. A few of our citizens, with the assurance of madmen, predicted the day would come when cotton would be picked by machine. But for all this, we knew little of individual human behavior. And we knew almost nothing of mass human behavior in its most destructively aberrant form: war.

Had The War resulted from conflicting interests of the industrial North and the agricultural South? Had the nation's destiny hung upon the legalisms of strict or broad interpretation of the Constitution? Had the struggle been precipitated beyond hope of rational settlement by Boston fanatics on the one hand and Charleston fanatics on the other?

Or did one have to go to Leo Tolstoy for murky light on the question? When an apple falls from the tree, he asked, why does it fall? Because winds have weakened it upon the twig? A worm is at its heart? Or the boy under the tree wants to eat it? But Tolstoy, for all his inquiring, knew how many doors were shut against the inquiring mind. He sadly observed that there are questions "put only in order that they may remain forever questions." We could look into the eye of Aldebaran. But we were eyeless in Geza.

Yet, for all the questions unanswered and perhaps unanswerable, I felt one certainty. My neighbors who had known The War had had an agonizing trial. It was not the conflict itself, whatever the horrors. It was the imperative of a choice of loyalties between section and nation and sometimes between father and son or brother and brother. But the Bible-reading men, as the scriptures bear witness, knew that theirs was not the first civil war: "And the children of Israel wept before the Lord and asked counsel saying, Shall I go up to battle against the children of Benjamin my brother? And the Lord said, Go up against him. Go up against thy brother."

Sometimes, seeing a Confederate veteran, I wondered what storms had blown about his youthful head and, wondering, fell into debate with myself. What would you have done, I asked myself, had you been a young man in 1861 at Centenary College in Shreveport, Louisiana, and you had read on the bulletin board: "War has been declared. Classes are suspended. May God preserve the right."

I thought I knew what I should have done. I'd have gone with my classmates, the tribal compulsion strong upon me, the heady certainties of youth singing high and clear in my mind, the dear, familiar faces warming me with their presence.

But the discussion was not ended. A man is many things. He is more starred than the heavens. He peers with more eyes than the housefly with its thousand-faceted eye. Multiple voices speak within him, sometimes faint and far, like music heard at the end of a long street; sometimes loud and near, like the storm that roars overhead. His ears hear above the tone scale. There is no leaf trembling upon a tree that does not tremble also upon his spirit.

It was not alone I, then, who debated but also the myriad man that I am (and you are). I was man, a man of the South. As such I had been ineradicably stained with an essence not quite like any other upon our American soil that, integral, contains so many essences. I was also a Jew, one stained with still another essence.

What wars had not my ancestors known? Thirty centuries ago, for example, Hebrews and Philistines had cracked one another's skulls in their interminable struggles. Eventually the Philistines vanished into the shades of antiquity. But a thousand years later my kinsmen faced the Roman legions at Jerusalem. A saint—one who was no friend to them—reluctantly found them admirable, not for their peaceful virtues, but for their warrior qualities. "Was not the Jewish nation," wrote St. John Chrysostom, "seen to arise and arm against the Romans . . . and create for the Caesar of that time very serious difficulties? Such was their great energy and valor."

Long after St. John Chrysostom—in a world of which he never dreamed—I heard Confederate veterans discuss another war. No one of them talked bitterly about it. But bitterness sometimes crept into the talk of their womenfolk. For it was they—more than their men—who had suffered most grievously the humiliations and hardships of enemy invasion and occupations. It was the women—bearers and bringers-up of children, bakers of bread, growers of flowers, makers of window curtains—whose role as conservators of hearth and home had been violently outraged. Not theirs even, the warm camaraderie of the campfire or the dark passion of battle. They stood, as women always stand in wartime, waiting before the well of time, the bucket rusting on the rusting chain.

Surveying the long perspective of history—its halls mournful with wraiths of poets never born—war appeared to me malevolently childish. It seemed unworthy of men who could arrive at the stupendous conclusion that two and two make four. And so feeling, although the soldier is a commonplace spectacle, it is one to which I have never become entirely accustomed. The musket-bearing mammal, with a cylindrical steel limb superimposed upon arms of flesh and blood, strikes me as unnatural. Whence this unspeakable deformation of bright youth?

The soldier had come newly minted into the world from the womb. The miracle of his birth was twofold. It was not only that two had summoned another out of the void—one equipped perhaps to be greater than they—but they had also fashioned one unidentical with any other who had ever lived. Centuries ago rabbis had asked, "When you destroy a life, what do you destroy?" And they had answered, "One solitary man was brought forth at the time of Creation in order to establish God's greatness, for when a human being uses one die to stamp many coins, they all come out alike, but God stamped all men with the die of Adam, yet each is different. Therefore every man has the right to say, For my sake the world was created. . . . It was done also to teach that whoever destroys a single life is as guilty as though he had destroyed the entire world, and whoever rescues a single life earns as much merit as though he had rescued the world."

One day a youth becomes a soldier. He is married to his rifle. Every day, with the rising of the sun and the setting of the sun, the silver bugle witness to its coming up and its going down, he is reminded of his marriage. Still in our world, he is no longer completely of it, for now he belongs to a jealous order that sets him apart from us.

At his birth, another infant boy was born in another land, and upon a day, a rifle is put in his hands. The soldiers in many ways are more alike than those they defend, and this is the truer as rank rises. Then one morning, by inexplicable circumlocutions in time and space, the farm boy–soldier from Bavaria and the farm boy–soldier from Minnesota destroy one another on a Belgian field where they become dust with the Roman soldiers, so like them, who died there two thousand years ago.

I thought much about war whenever I visited Natchez, a town that had an especial fascination for me. There was about it a warming melancholy, a touch of genteel madness, a diffuse impression of whilom greatness, a note of remembrance growing ever more vague until the past and the present, the real and the unreal, what had never been and what would never be, become one.

Chekhov would have been at home in Natchez houses, through whose heavy draperies twilight perpetually seeped. He would have understood the thin biographies of their tenants' lives; the bread and wine of their pride upon which they supped; the suspension of their wills; the silken cords of memory, steel strong, that attached them to their old silver and great-grandmother's slippers that she wore as a girl to a Paris ball; their talk that was like the spinning and fluttering of autumn leaves to fall upon a river that would never reach the sea.

He would have comprehended what lay in the eyes of the town, down looking and sorrowful as the eyes of a pietà. He would have understood these men and women whose lives were passed under the drowsy-sweet spell of tomorrow and tomorrow. For Natchez, one of the richest and most urbane American towns of the 1840s, was the frozen embodiment of a dream shattered long ago at Appomattox, even if its chamber of commerce did call it "the place where the Old South meets the New." The place, so to say, where any spring afternoon along the vine-entangled Woodville road, bright with the flashings of red-winged black-birds, one might meet the president of the Natchez Coca-Cola Bottling Works taking Mr. and Mrs. Jefferson Davis for a ride in his new car.

(The urbanity and high civilization of early Natchez is symbolized perhaps by its preachers. "About eight years ago," reads a contemporary diary, "Creek Indians seized and took away a large lot of whiskey belonging to Parson Blackburn. . . . He was one of the most eminent Presbyterian clergymen in the West, and was largely engaged in the whiskey business, and came near involving the country in war with the Indians on account of the seizure."

In the 1840s, the diary continues: "The best whiskey brought to Natchez was brought, twice a year, in a flat-boat, by the Rev. Moses Trader, of Ohio, an eminent Methodist, who did a large business in this line for years, and preached at Natchez . . . with great unction. He was a most excellent man, though he enjoyed his bitters, his midday toddy and his nightcap, saying that he was not afraid of his own whiskey, but 'a little skeery about any other.'")

In Natchez I felt with pain the destruction of the Alexandrian library, the burnings by Turks of Greek sculptures of the Parthenon to make limestone. These are crimes against the race. They are also crimes against me. By so much is my inheritance diminished. By so much is my being violated, for he who lays rough hands on Phidias lays rough hands on me.

We Jews knew these things. Others also knew them. But ours was the sorrowful knowledge of contemporaries. Why, then, did no one come to me and say, "Brother, companion with me on this transient journey, let us first partake of bitter herbs and unleavened bread as your people are wont to partake of them in commemoration of your ancestors going out from the land of Egypt, and then counsel together how we may remove the curse of war from men." But no one came. No one asked.

This is how it was, I remembered, when Sancho Panza talked long to his donkey in the forest. "And," said Cervantes, in a moving evocation of human loneliness, "the donkey did not answer."

3

A Walk Down Washington Avenue

Cohn's recollection of his journey down Washington Avenue leads him to reflect on many aspects of the human condition. The reader will note the many diverse ethnic groups and nationalities Cohn encounters on his sentimental journey. Though decidedly in the minority overall, immigrants of all sorts made their way to the Delta, giving its outwardly provincial society and culture a definite cosmopolitan hue.

In our little town, all of us walking the same paths, we were bound in a relationship of enforced intimacy. One was sure to pass those whom one loved or despised. But nearly everyone said he liked living in Greenville because you knew everyone you met, while in New York you could live there forever and hardly know a soul.

Such talk made me feel the lonelier. I felt that not only did I fail to know anyone in town but I could not ever see the face of a fellow plain. When I met one on the street, his face was written and overwritten with hen scratchings of things about him known to me, suggested by others, perceived, imagined. Waves and counterwaves of association and suggestion flooded my mind as we approached one another. I fell into subconscious revery and reflection about my fellow. The more familiar his face, the more blurred his image.

I had seen the same people daily for a long time. But I could not swear that I truly knew them. I could say that I knew their water and mineral content, their cubic displacement in space, and even how a crown composed of the lavender flowers of the chinaberry tree might become each one. Yet that was all, for they were like the sea. And the sound of the sea varies with the velocity of the wind, and the color of the sea changes with the color of the sky, and the face of the sea is now plain and now obscured by sea smoke. I knew in my heart that if one morning, as I trailed my fingers in the fire-opal waters of the great Australian barrier reef, leviathan should slowly swim through them, he would neither be more alien to me, nor less familiar, than neighbors I had known all my life.

Life stirred early in Greenville. During most of the year, dawn came with the singing of birds, the acrobatics of squirrels, the hoppings of toads, the barkings of dogs, the crowings of roosters. Thus was the new day proclaimed long before it was announced by the six o'clock whistle of the Leavenworth Lumber Mill.

Out in Newtown, where a large part of our Negro population lived, breakfast came early for those who walked long distances to work, and in many a backyard a fire blazed under an iron pot as washladies prepared for the day's task.

Before the first intimations of daylight, butchers and bakers came to work, to be followed at intervals by keepers of eating places with their Negro cooks and waiters; merchants of dry goods and groceries, their clerks often awaiting them on the sidewalk outside locked doors; and, last of all, the sun now high, lawyers, bankers, cotton buyers, pool room operators, barbers.

All day they pursued their separate tasks, a community in the sweat of their faces, competitive but strongly bound in the commonwealth of toil. Then, as the rising sun had gathered them, the setting sun dispersed them; each to his separate cell. The signal for their in-gathering and out-going was derived from the revolution of one planet around another; fiction become faith. By tacit convention, we were permitted to doubt God or hoodwink the law. But we were not permitted to question any of the fictions by which we lived.

The spectacle of the daily in-gathering and out-going on Washington Avenue, this combination of the transient and the permanent, this interplay of the forces of the centripetal and the centrifugal, always affected me. But sometimes the same spectacle, enacted upon a more compact stage than our main street, has affected me with an especial poignance.

The liner sails, the train runs, the bus moves, their passengers one in the solemn communion of time and space. The vehicle arrives at its destination. The faces of your fellows, strange, alien, even faintly hostile a moment ago, suddenly become dear to you. Then the communion you have shared with them impels you to touch them and say, "I'll see you again." But shyness plucks at your sleeve. Besides, you yourself do not know where you are going. And as you remain silent and hesitant, the star explodes and its fragments dissolve in the firmament.

All this, I suppose, because I felt myself so often a stranger here, and I wanted so much not to be a stranger. But every man, I suspect, has occasionally felt himself a stranger walking directionless the alien roads of an alien earth, and this was sometimes my mood when I walked down Washington Avenue, our principal street, at sunup, going the long way across town from my house to the Mobile and Ohio depot. There I'd catch a train to go fishing either in the nearby Bogue Phalia or in the more remote Quiver River.

The deserted streets of a living town lie in a twilight zone between being and not being; a region where death has not entered, but living is suspended. There fantasy stands perpendicular to reason, and the errant mind moves along secret paths known only to itself.

The enchantment of night still upon Washington Avenue, its stores closed, their owners asleep at home, I felt it odd that men should spend their lives in the airless prison cubicles that lined the street instead of sitting under trees, walking by the river, or—their earthly tenure of fellowship short—engaging in amiable discussions with their souls. But far from doing this, they spent their lives handing out dry goods (as my father), groceries, hardware, drugs. Others gave medical or legal counsel, repaired shoes, trimmed hair, or fried ham and eggs.

All of them—by an apparently well-understood convention—received for their goods or services bits of metal or paper to which they attached a high value even though they seemed less useful than the salves or horse collars they exchanged for them. Sometimes paper or metal was lacking. Then men resorted to a curious course. They inscribed the details of the exchange in a large book as an act of faith. (What is faith?) It was all seemingly done by faultless pantomime, each man knowing well every movement of the stylized ritual, so old it was and so familiar.

Whenever I walked down Washington Avenue, I passed the Olympia Cafe, Sam Goodman's (dry goods), Hirsch's Butcher Shop, the Greenville Dry Goods Company (my father's firm), Greenley's (men's furnishings), the Kandy Kitchen (ice cream parlor), Carter's Stationery Store (the only Negro-run business on the street), Stoll's (dry goods), Finlay's Drug Store . . .

Inside the fly-specked windows of the dry goods stores, amid overalls, shoes, clothing, clocks, millinery, lay sheets of flypaper black with insects, a few struggling for release from their sticky prison, and roaches dead along lines of white insect powder at the windows' edges. Each proprietor or one of his more artistically gifted clerks "trimmed" the windows. Some of the more fiercely aesthetic festooned their displays with loops and whorls of colored crepe paper, a form of decoration popular among us. (The *Democrat,* reporting dinner parties, constantly said, "The green and blue motif was carried out in Dennison crepe paper.") The loops and whorls hung there faded and forlorn throughout the hot summer until fall came. Then a merchant could comfortably enter what had been the fiery oven of his window display.

Once, on a winter's night, I stood in a Washington Avenue store huddling close to its glowing stove. Suddenly a young Negro and a girl came in through the door to be seemingly propelled by the wind blowing outside. Thinly dressed, wet, shivering, the couple came to the stove, almost embracing its fiery iron as water streamed from the man's broken shoes. After a while he said to the clerk near him, "White Folks, I wants to see a pair o' shoes, please suh." But moving to the place where shoes were kept, he saw a guitar suspended from the ceiling. Then he stood transfixed, his eyes shining as though, in the words of the Negro song, he had "a mouthful o' moon, a pocketful o' stars." "Boss man," he asked, "does you reckon I could pick that guit-tar a little?" The clerk, in no way surprised, handed it to him.

The couple sat on a packing case, and the man picked the guitar, the girl leaning affectionately toward him as he softly sang, unmindful of those listening. After so long, he asked, "Cap'n, how much it is?" "Five dollars," said the clerk. The musician brought a handful of silver coins from his pocket. (In the Delta, when a man's money is in this form, he is identified either as a preacher carrying the offerings of the faithful or a dice shooter. But this man was plainly not even a pulpit hand, let alone a deacon or pastor.) He carefully counted and recounted the nickels, dimes, quarters, putting like coins into little stacks. Then he said, "Cap'n, I ain't got but fo' six-bits. Does you reckon you could let the two-bits be betwixt us?" The clerk replied, "Okay" and scooped up $4.75 in small change.

The musician lovingly tucked the guitar beneath his thin coat and then motioned to his girl to follow him, and the couple went out into the blowing rain, a thin trail of water from the man's broken shoes marking his path to the door. On that night a poet walked among us.

At one point along Washington Avenue I detected the acrid scent of ammonia in the air and heard noises coming from the nearby ice plant. There two-hundred-pound blocks of ice were being prepared for shipment. Packed in sawdust, the early morning "accommodation freight" would drop them into eager hands at forlorn little stations along the way. Racing against time and heat, melting ice spattering dusty roads with drops of water, the blocks would be taken in buggies, wagons, and Fords into the countryside for the comfort of the fever-ridden and the heat-tortured; for making ice cream, lemonade, toddies; or for general purposes of refrigeration in zinc-lined, sawdust-insulated, wooden ice boxes. Manufactured ice ranked high among our blessings. It ranked with mosquito netting (imported from Nottingham, England) and the quinine that softened the rigors of the disease that affected nearly all of us—the malaria we called "chills and fever."

(What Giovanni Verga wrote of his native Sicily might have applied to us: "And truly the malaria gets into you with the bread you eat, or if you open your mouth to speak as you walk, suffocating in the dust and sun of the roads, and you feel your knees give way beneath you, or you sink discouraged on your saddle as your mule ambles along with head down. . . . The malaria seizes the inhabitants [of the village] in the depopulated streets and nails them in front of the doors of their houses . . . and there they tremble with fever under their brown cloaks, with all the bed blankets over their shoulders.")

Seated at the counter of the Olympia Cafe, near the Yazoo and Mississippi Valley depot, were several overalled railroad men eating breakfast. They talked little. The enveloping shell of the night from which they had just broken still lay upon them in fragments. The only time-obsessed men among us, even though they seemed to move their trains between fits of abstraction, they glanced occasionally at their turnip-sized watches or stared unseeingly at a garish poster that had been hung above the coffee urn by the Olympia's proprietor. He had come among us from a Greek village. Framed by cans of Clabber Girl Baking Powder, the poster depicted a desperate naval battle. One Greek warship was sinking four Turkish cruisers, their rails crowded with sailors jumping into the shell-churned waters.

The immigrant to our shores is often more heavily burdened than the native born. In his rucksack he may carry, in addition to the impedimenta all men bear, the burden of prejudices and hatreds of his homeland. So it was with Socrates Spiro, the Olympia's owner, who was on his way to acquiring American citizenship. Through the poster, he reminded himself of the Greek-Turkish wars and gave himself renewed assurance that his forebears were no less valiant than their enemies.

Let Socrates enjoy his harmless triumph. It is needful for him. Besides, one knows, in this amiable American air the lion that was a Turk and the lamb that was a Greek will go together to a doubleheader. Let Socrates be comforted by this evidence of his patriotic pride, this turning to the homeland that gave him birth. There is a canker at his heart that he can never remove. It lies at the hearts of all immigrants, and it would lie at your heart if you should emigrate tomorrow to the Amazon.

Motoring one day past the cemetery, where branches of weeping willows fall in cascades of pale green light, Socrates said to me, "It's funny. I like Greenville. I love America. But I won't sleep good in that graveyard. My children will. When they die, they'll go back to the earth they came from because they were born right here."

Adjoining the Olympia was Hirsch's Butcher Shop. There Butsie Hirsch was prying the lid off a big container of Armour Star brand pork sausage while his brother Herbert stood over a carcass of beef, spinning the wheel by which men exist on earth: from flesh to grass to flesh to grass. Short, plump, olive-skinned with small, twinkling brown eyes, his curly hair gave him the incongruous appearance of a faun come, not from a sea-girt Aegean isle, but from Heidelberg, and *gemütlich* for all that his butcher's apron concealed cloven hooves.

Farther down the street, half hidden by overalls that hung before the entrance to his store, stood gnomelike Old Man Stoll. Midwife to the street's daily birth, winter and summer, before sun or birds, he opened his little store at five in the morning. Now he looked up and down the emptiness of Washington Avenue as he had looked for a lifetime of mornings, muteness in the cloudiness of his eyes, traces of the East upon his wizened, Mongoloid-suggestive face, his upper lip wearing a thin, scraggly mustache, in his mouth a half-smoked, unlighted cigarette.

Upon what Carpathian night of iron cold, in what rude mountain hut— snow blowing outside, featherbed warm inside, room black—had swimming sperm met descending ovum and created this gnome who stood now remote in time and space from the spot where he had been born? By what miracle had he got to this alien Mississippi pavement, doll-sized in the perspective of the massive nearby levee: this American citizen who had been born a subject of Alexander II, the Little Father, Czar of All the Russians?

Thistledown floats on the wind as it lists. But great storms of tempestuous conflict had had to rage before Old Man Stoll, thistledown light, should become airborne. What thinker-terrorists had slain the Little Father and begun an abortive uprising that brought terroristic countermeasures compelling many of Old Man Stoll's kind—unknowing innocents—to face flight, Siberia, or death?

How had he, in any event, escaped the twenty-five-years' military service that Imperial Russia demanded of its Jewish males? It is true that he was physically puny. But is it not also true that war is like a cider press? If you throw big apples into it and little apples—firm, round ones and soft, misshapen ones—do they not all emerge cider?

I longed to put these questions to Old Man Stoll. But I merely said, "Good morning" to him; he said, "Good morning" to me; and I went on.

Compact of mysteries, he belonged to a numerous company among us, the brotherhood of the obscure—the anonymous living who, dying, immediately become the anonymous dead. Its members do not stain even faintly with their personalities the parchment scroll of their environment, but seem to swing suspended in a cocoon from which the bright butterfly never emerges. One sees them daily, yet they make but a faint impression upon the retina of the mind's eye. It is as though they walked always beneath leaves of trees, no shadow striding before them. When they are gone it is as if they had never been. Dwellers on the margins of the town's consciousness, one struggles to remember how they looked, the clothes they wore, the things they said, some mannerism of speech or gesture.

Most obscure of all were our night watchmen. When the day's work was done, most men went home to their families. But some men then left their shacks and families to vanish in the night as guardians against fire and theft of the town's treasures of cotton, lumber, coal, groceries. They were old men in whom the pulse of life beat faintly. We could have forgiven them if they had been merely wretchedly poor. As such they might even have enabled us to fatten our hump of self-love as we sent them our old clothes at Christmas and baskets of groceries. But we could not forgive them that they were no longer productive. Yet we did not kill them or let them die, as men have often done in such a case. We were too civilized to be brutal. Our religious faith cried out against it. Our laws and our humane feelings forbade it.

We did not, therefore, do in the old men. We merely hid them from sun and sight. In darkness we wrung from them their last ounce of strength. Lest they fall asleep and expose our treasures to loss, we ordained that through the night they should punch time clocks so that we might know how faithful they had been to the trust we reposed in them. We made watchdogs of men. We exposed them to the winds and the rains and the cold while we slept snug and warm. They entered into the statistics of employment ("prosperity") and we, I supposed, because of our goodness, into the grace of God.

Yet it seemed strange that, zealous for our property, we permitted poor men to watch over it for, by the nature of things, a rich man would make a better watchman than a poor man. Who has a stronger sense of property than a man of property? Who is more jealous of property's prerogatives than a propertied man? The rich man, therefore, might be expected to be more diligent in guarding property than a poor man, one who was a watchman because he had never acquired any property whether out of indifference to it, a lack of animal cunning, or a small sense of acquisition. But no well-to-do men in town seemed to want the job of night watchman. Hence it was greedily monopolized by poor old men.

If watchmen were the most obscure of our brotherhood of the obscure, all were alike in this: they were shy, withdrawn, self-effacing, gently polite. Crushed perhaps by an inward sense of failure, or inadequacy, or victims of fate—the child-yearning woman never married, the aspirant singer mute, the adventurer condemned to the cage of the salesman's rounds—they dwelt in an impenetrable world of their own.

In the *Democrat*'s account of the funeral of a member of this group, there was no list of pallbearers and honorary pallbearers such as starred an account of the burial of a prominent citizen. Nor was there any eulogy beyond the conventional "Mr. Clearwater led a noble Christian life." The heart of the matter lay in the bleak public record of definitive departure from the community: "Reverend Cyrus Eastlake of the First Baptist Church conducted the services. Interment was at Wayside."

The closed stores along our principal street, filled with mute drama, had a funereal aspect because their merchandise covered with heavy cotton duck resembled shrouded corpses. (The duck was used to prevent dust from settling on the goods when the porter swept the floor. But when an obscure genius invented a sweeping compound composed of sawdust-impregnated oil to absorb the dust, the covers vanished.) Here within constricting walls, men spent most of their lives competing for money, a commodity scarce among us.

We expressed conflicting opinions about money. There was, for example, the old English rhyme: "God made bees and bees made honey, / God made man and men made money." But, as we interpreted it, money was something you had to have—"No money, no honey." Speechless, "money talks." Some of us believed that "every man has his price." But few would say this of ladies.

None of us yearned for poverty, but we often heatedly maintained its advantages over the disadvantages of wealth. Poor men slept soundly. But the cheating rich tossed conscience tortured on their beds. Take the matter of health. We said we wouldn't trade places with Jawn D. Rockefeller. He could buy anything he wanted, but all he could digest was milk and crackers. Yet we could eat cast-iron stoves. Therefore . . .

(Even if Samuel Johnson had come among us and boomed, "You never find people laboring to convince you that a man may live very happily upon a plentiful fortune," we would have mulishly maintained our position.)

"The best things in life are free," we held. But these things were in smaller demand among us than those that cost money: a trip to Memphis or a visit to a "new" girl in a house on Blanton Street. As for a rich man attaining heaven, we all knew that it was easier for a camel. . . . Yet some of our best church members, risking heaven, chased the dollar with bloodhound persistence.

Negroes were less concerned with money than whites, an attitude that whites deplored as backward. But they were not bored, as whites so often were. Nor were the wellsprings of their joy poisoned at the source by forebodings of the morrow.

We had one unshakable faith: our faith in life insurance. We would do almost anything to "meet the premium"—go without a new shotgun or give up poker. But Negroes—their faith perhaps in a providence who provides for his children—did not share our fears of the future. Sometimes one of us, peering through the bars of the cage of his forebodings, would wryly say, "If I ever come back to this earth after I'm dead, I just want to be a nigger on Saturday night."[1]

Our preachers, white and Negro, tirelessly denounced the evils among us of tomcattin', pollyfoxin', cardplaying, dancing. They sternly castigated the sin of fornication: "Cursed be the fornicator, an abomination to the Lord. . . . And the Lord shall smite him in the knees, and in the legs, with a sore botch . . . with the emerods, and with the scab of Egypt." And even if the sinner escaped punishment on earth, he was sure to burn eternally in hell.

Yet our preachers, quick to quote the scriptures concerning the sins I have mentioned, were curiously blind to the text that the love of money is the root of all evil. Many white and Negro landowners cruelly exploited Negro labor. A passage from James applied precisely to them. But its flames scourged no one from any of our pulpits: "Go to now, ye rich men, weep and howl for your miseries that shall come upon you. . . . Your gold and silver is cankered; and the rust of them shall be a witness against you, and shall eat your flesh as it were fire. . . . Behold, the hire of laborers who have reaped down your fields, which is of you kept back by fraud, crieth: and the cries of them which have reaped are entered into the ears of the Lord of Sabbath."

The defrauded laborer was more likely to find his champion in the courthouse than in the church. On the rare occasion when a Negro sued a white landowner for robbing him, the all-white jury almost compulsively found for the Negro. Jurymen knew that when a Negro had been driven to the extremity of suing a white man, the right was on his side.

But we still regarded some money as "tainted." Thus, mouse-poor Baptist

---

1. This is a version of a common folk saying among southerners of both races. Faulkner used another version in *The Reivers* when he had Ned McCaslin tell Colonel Linscomb, "If you could just be a nigger one Saturday night, you wouldn't never want to be a white man again as long as you live." William Faulkner, *The Reivers* (New York, 1962), 291.

churches might refuse gifts from John D. Rockefeller, billionaire Baptist layman, because they felt he had acquired it by unethical methods. (In our simplicity, we had not yet learned to do the trick that would later distinguish so much of our progressive culture: that is, to keep the outside of the cup shining clean while leaving the inside immaculately filthy.)

In short, we held contradictory attitudes about money, and we might have become hopelessly confused had we thought about them overlong or tried to reconcile them. Wisely, we did not do so. Many a man, we said, has gone crazy from thinking too much.

Nonetheless, one thing was clear on Washington Avenue: there money was more than a medium of exchange. It was often a species of transubstantiation by which a man's work, worry, and sometimes the sacrifice of his health became his son's college education or his daughter's dowry: fruits of the intricate alchemy of sweat. We all believed that "business is business." Yet for the little tradesmen—the majority of those among us—business was often effected with a quiet desperation. Sometimes it became a heavy pressure on the chest, sometimes a diuretic stimulating the bladder whose sensitivity to emotional disturbances caused the ancients to denominate it the locus of the soul.

What dumb agonies have I not witnessed along this quiet street. Ike Friedman's customer hesitates. It seems unlikely that he will buy the suit of clothes. How can Ike tell him that he is nearly broke; that he has borrowed all he could from friends and relatives; that—may he never again experience such shame—he had sneaked up to Memphis to pawn the diamond engagement ring he had given to his wife, Ruth, forty years ago? How can Ike tell the customer that he must, he simply must, buy the suit? For next week, unless he raises some money, one of his creditors, patience exhausted, will throw him into bankruptcy. How can Ike, abandoning "manliness" and giving way to the emotions that rack him, tell the customer, a stranger, that he had always prided himself on paying his bills promptly and the disgrace of bankruptcy would kill him? How can he say to him, "If you and forty more like you buy a suit from me, 'I'll be saved from disgrace.'"

Ike stifles the wide voices of his heart and says nothing of this. He talks persuasively of the suit's features: its sturdy fabric, fashionable cut, modest price. Then the light drains from his eyes and bile stands in his mouth as the customer says, "Well, I'll think it over and let you know." The suit limp now in his hands, Ike abstractedly hangs it upon a rack and looks at his watch, but he does not see what time it is. He walks out into the little yard behind his store. There he opens his pants and lets loose a torrent of urine. It falls upon a furry caterpillar crawling toward the chinaberry tree that stands amid a wasteland of crumbling paper cartons and fading rags.

If I have witnessed agonies along Washington Avenue—what street on earth is not at some time a via dolorosa for some of its tenants?—I have also seen contentment shining there. It often shone most glowingly in the faces of our smallest tradesmen. They were little successful by the crude indices we used for measuring success: wealth, prestige, "influence." Yet they achieved contentment for themselves as they raised their families, sent their sons to college, married their daughters to "nice boys."

Nor were they strangers to ecstasy. They conducted lifelong love affairs with their businesses, devoted long hours to them, and frequently returned to them for intervals of reaffirmation of love on holidays and Sundays. Such moments were dear to the adoring lovers. For them, streets deserted, doors locked, a man could be alone with his mistress, see her plain, shamelessly fondle her without fear of interruption.

These men were kings when they gave orders to the salesman from the wholesale house: "I'll take 12 blues, 36 pinks, 10 blacks. No, Jim, you'd better make that 18 blacks." They were lords of the manor distributing largesse when they granted credit to neighborhood customers. They were men of substance when the wholesale house gave them credit. And they were Jawn D. himself when they wrote checks in payments of their bills, reading and rereading with satisfaction, "Pay to the order of——," followed by a signature the bank honored.

They were true proprietors; members of a proud race that was beginning to vanish when I was a boy. They owned their businesses. They also ran them. Thus they were masters of themselves and of their houses, however modest. In a country whose cult is competence, they were not highly competent. In a land where riches are the measure of success, they were not rich. But they had innocence. They were wise because they were tamed. In life, they paid their bills. At death, their books were balanced.

Only yesterday they and all their fellows along Washington Avenue had been boys. They had done what I had done; what we all had done. They had flown kites on the embankment of the levee, twine playing out swiftly as their homemade vehicles, bound with flourpaste, soared high and ever higher into airy lanes where wild geese moved on silken wings; robbed birds' nests in cottonwood trees whose branches swayed in the breeze to the summer-sleepy music of whispering leaves; stained their hands mahogany with the juicy hulls of green pecans; indulged in brief, furious spasms of wrasslin' with one another as they walked homeward from school along the narrowing corridor of the dying afternoon; looked shyly, calf-eyed, upon some girl more lovely than ever Helen was, flowering into womanhood beneath her middy blouse.

Now they did business—away to the dewberry patch, no more, no more— in a Ferris wheel. It turned and turned until, the allotted period up, the man in the red, grease-spotted coat blew a whistle. Then it halted, the topmost chairs swinging empty for a moment after their occupants had gone.

My path to the M&O railroad depot led me close to the Greek temple of the First National Bank. Its entrance was guarded by a black metal lion I had sometimes ridden as a child; the exotic steed of a stationary "flyin' jinny." (Our local term, evocative of childhood's squealing delight, seems to me more fitting than the pretentious "carrousel.") Our lion was the beast one often sees before public buildings: fierce, crouched, alert, febrile tail coiled and forepaws advanced for the spring. Such animals are professional animals who take themselves with the dreary seriousness that is characteristic of their kind whether man or beast.

The bank's lion, standing in its valley mild, had about it the boisterousness of a puppy, its leonine countenance softened by a fat, cherubic smile. In the *dolce far niente* atmosphere of our town, not even an iron animal could have sustained a humorless fierceness and our lion did not try to do so. I felt certain indeed—especially in summer—that although the bank trusted its guardian beast, it would have deserted its post if anyone had asked it to step around to the Kandy Kitchen for a Coke.

The bank's walls were hung with huge photographs of old-time Mississippi River steamboats. Riding low in the water, cotton bales stacked to their Texas decks, they were an evocation of the vanished dynasty of river captains, and they were also a reminder that, although the captains and their craft were gone, the bank, its customers, the whole community, still drew their livelihood from cotton.

Inside the teller's cages were small stacks of gleaming five-, ten-, and twenty-dollar gold coins. Few wanted gold coins. They were in demand only as Christmas or school graduation gifts or for making into lockets. It was otherwise with silver coins. We used them more often than paper currency. When a man had, say, ten silver dollars, reassuringly heavy in his pocket, he had "more" money than when he possessed a flimsy, unreal ten-dollar bill. In the name of such reassurance, many employers paid their employees in silver dollars or fifty-cent coins.

The First National was our most imposing business structure. It was more splendid even than the newly erected Weinberg Building for all its four stories and novel elevator in which children rode for sake of the adventure. My elders said an imposing bank building gave people confidence in the institution's solidity. But I found it difficult to believe that we were affected with an immigrant mentality, as when the poor of Europe coming here preferred ships with four stacks because, they believed, the more numerous the stacks the more seaworthy the ship. Whereupon ship owners rigged old tubs with false stacks and packed them with immigrants.

It seemed to me, such is money's spell among men, they find it meet to deal with it in the replica of a temple rather than in a workaday structure. So strong indeed is money's spell that (as you can see every day in Texas) few men are more obsequious than a millionaire in the presence of a multimillionaire. We had no millionaires among us, but in the bank one could witness demonstrations of money's magic.

Its volume of business and profits was lower than that of some of our cotton merchants—the town's lordliest tradesmen—whose shabby offices were nearby on Poplar Street. A few of them wore voices as big as sombreros, but the bank's precincts sharply affected them. There they talked less loudly than was their wont and muted their gestures in this place where the mass of money was perpetually sung.

The granite columns, the ornate iron grilles at the windows, the high-ceilinged banking room of palatial dimensions, the open mouth of the great vault yawning black against its gleaming steel face with time-clock eyes: all these proclaimed this to be no pedestrian mart of trade. Here a churchly quietude prevailed. Here men communed in hushed tones to the occasional tinny music of silver coins ringing upon marble counters. Sometimes they left this building to face ruin. Sometimes they went exultant with renewed hope.

Here a mystery was celebrated: the darkling mystery of money. (During the Age of Faith, one recalled, Baltic merchants signed their ledgers, "Jesus Maria, amen.") Alone among man's possessions, money is touched with the pitiless indifference of the gods. In great accretions it has often stood above race, religion, family, country. It is of the nature of the case that it should tend to consort only with its own kind and compulsively seek its own increase. Among us, as elsewhere, the well-to-do generally married the well-to-do. Who has not seen marriages that are the expression of the desire of men and women to keep dwindling trust estates within their families?

The temple of the First National—as others of other faiths—had its holy of holies. The devotee reached it through the offices of a guardian priest bearing a key of which he was sole custodian. He applied it to the face of a block of steel, a tiny door swung open, and the priest retrieved a black tin box from eternal darkness. Then he handed it to the devotee, who, holding it as though it were the Ark of the Covenant, retired with it to a secret room. What he did there, what relics the box held, what rites he performed, no man knew. One assumed, since this was a place of money, that the note had to do with it. But such is the awesome role of money among us, one does not ask another about it, as none except a rude interloper would ask a Zulu, who counts his wealth in cattle, how many beasts he owns.

Visiting the bank, I was struck by the momentary complacency of depositors who stood before the teller's window. There was often a faint air of self-satisfaction about them, a pale irradiation of triumph. They had wrested a little money from the flinty rock, sometimes with bleeding fingers. The proof of their success lay snug in their hands. Yet as they passed their money through the teller's wicket, conflict stood in their faces. Happy to look at their wealth, they were fleetingly unhappy to see its dear identity lost in the common fund where the teller casually mingled it with other men's money. Then the well-remembered glory suddenly seemed to go out of it, as a herring's scales, of a silver more argent than silver, fade when the fish is removed from the water.

I thought this a matter of some moment. The income of the rich—especially that derived from investments—is often impersonal and touched with anonymity. It is wrought by distant men toiling for distant corporations. For all that such income is rooted in careful calculation, it is affected with insubstantiality—sweet waters gushing from a spring without visible source. But the wages of laborers, the salaries of clerks, the revenues of small tradesmen, the savings of housewives from their allowances—nickel upon nickel, dime upon dime—are fiercely personal. These are wrought in their bowels, often with pain.

Occasionally on Saturday mornings I stood in the bank and watched townsmen moving toward the tellers' cages. Some deposited money. But the majority withdrew it, for Saturday was payday, the day when "the ghost walks." On the next Monday much of the withdrawn money would return to the bank. It would come from grocery stores and dry goods stores and doctors and dentists and preachers and whores and barbers and loan sharks and gamblers and sellers of hot tamales, for men have many wants and urgently seek their satisfaction.

The lordly and the lowly, the rich and the poor, whites and Negroes were equal in the teller's eyes. Members of the races could not jointly worship God. But they could jointly glorify the god of money. Here there was no segregation of the races, and Negroes, by the accident of timing, sometimes took precedence over whites. Here, too, if one woman was not as "good" as another, judgments of social or ethical status were for the moment suspended, while "tainted money," washed, as it were, in the blood of the lamb, became immaculate and was one with the widow's mite and the contents of the child's piggy bank.

One Saturday there stood in the teller's line a small man with doe-brown eyes and weather-beaten face beneath thick, unruly, steel-gray hair, holding his passbook in gnarled fingers whose nails were broken and blackened. (His fingers resembled horseradish roots that Mr. Schwab, the Walnut Street grocer, kept in a pail of water.) I had long known Mr. Wilder. But I did not know where he came from; neither did anyone else. He had simply appeared in town long ago; appeared out of nowhere as suddenly upon an October morning migrant bird choristers greeted me from the snowball bush outside my window. (How delicious to lie there warm, secure, and half asleep, wooed by airy music in the first faint chill of autumn.)

Part Gypsy, part leprechaun, Mr. Wilder was a tinsmith who, moving to his tasks in a heavy covered wagon drawn by a huge, sleepy, white mare, seemed a figure out of Thomas Hardy, denizen of Egdon Heath, companion to shadows and furze and scudding moon. He lived with Martha, a strapping, big-breasted, broad-hipped, good-humored mulatto woman, and their brood of windy children in a shack near the levee. Tall, strong, long-limbed, her noble proportions when she reached to hang washing on the clothesline made her reminiscent of the Winged Victory of Samothrace. Capable, cleanly about her person and her shack, a lover of flowers that she cultivated with some success, this woman living beyond the pale of society seemed the incarnation of an old-fashioned term that has gone out of the language—helpmeet.

Sometimes when our gutters leaked, I was sent to fetch Mr. Wilder, and this I did with such grace as I could summon. For, skillful with shears and solder and wise in the ways of the medium in which he worked, he was no vulgar journeyman who could be hired at will, but a temperamental craftsman responsive more to respect shown for his craft than to money reward for his labor. He was also— the fire smoldering but never bursting into flame—something of an artist. He had created and filled his shack with tin ducks, tin fighting cocks, a tin logging wagon drawn by tin oxen, and a tin portrait of Abraham Lincoln.

I used to approach his abode near the levee through a tiger-bright jungle screen of cane to find him sitting sometimes in a rocking chair covered with turkey-red carpet, the suntan of his face dark against the whiteness of his nude torso, Bible in hand, steel-rimmed spectacles upon his nose, corncob pipe in mouth. He sat there reading in the gathering dusk of summer as his mate fried fatback and hominy for supper and his copper-colored brood swirled around him with liquid grace— a pagan-puritan surrounded by fauns.

Near Mr. Wilder in the teller's line stood Mr. H. Finkelstein, owner of a little dry goods store. Unable to write English, the bank permitted him to sign checks drawn upon it in the mysterious hen scratchings of Yiddish; a signature that it took upon faith, for neither Mr. A. B. Nance, the cashier, who wore a Mark Twain mustache, nor Mr. Bayle Shelby, the teller, was at home in the language. Slight of figure, bewhiskered, dark-eyed, slope-shouldered, black alpaca-coated, Mr. Finkelstein seemed not to be standing there at all but swimming without motion in a portable pool of patience that he took everywhere with him.

He wore time like a prayer shawl and so made me ashamed of my callow beliefs that time is of the essence of the contract, or is money, or has to do with saving nine stitches. I was, however, always glad to see him. He not only spoke English with a foreign accent that smote deliciously upon the ear in a town where foreign accents were seldom heard, but he also sometimes gave to a word or a phrase a freshness reminiscent of the luminous morning time of the Elizabethans.

He did not know we had become frightened of our language and fearful of rhetoric, that we were afraid to let the language sing or let it soar and had abandoned our rich heritage for the pidgin English of the ten-word telegram. He did not know that we were forbidden to pour the sauce of the adjective even upon the dry bones of yesterday's chicken. Nor did he know that we had arbitrarily assigned words certain places in the tongue as prison wardens assign cells to convicts.

Mr. Finkelstein knew nothing of all this. Undeterred, therefore, by rules that bound me with chains, he would sometimes give wings to a word, inspiredly accent it, or place it in a novel context. Then, for the first time, one would become aware of its grace, how various it was, or filled with beauty.

The First National was a repository both of its customers' money and their faith. There men left money: the substance of their businesses, the underpinning of their material lives, the security of their old age. But none felt that if he handed his money over to Mr. Wade Hampton Negus, the bank's president, he might lose a penny, and no one did. Tall, slender, silver-haired, gravely courteous, punctiliously dressed, he embodied personal integrity and to me conveyed more of an impression of the bank's solidity than its structure.

Many of his fellows thought of him as aloof from mankind, perhaps because he was no backslapper. But once, at least, this morally punctilious man technically violated the law in the name of kindness. For when my brother Joel was long sick and overdrew his account in the bank, Mr. Negus saw that his checks were paid, and when his wife telephoned to him in distress, the banker said, "Now there, Miss Clare, don't you worry about that."

Leaving Washington Avenue to go into Walnut Street, I had to pass Ehlbert's Harness Shop. Before it stood a great papier-mâché horse, the animal marking the nature of Mr. Ehlbert's occupation following the practice of eighteenth-century England. Full seven feet tall, it had large, noble, agate eyes, a magnificent mane, and a powerful body, but now it is one with the Trojan horse of legend. It was dealt a mortal blow from an unexpected source. How could this superb beast know that an obscure mechanic named Henry Ford would sneak up on it from an obscure workshop in faraway Michigan and do it to death?

Nearby was Wetherbee's Hardware Store. It had been a place of enchantment for the little boys of the neighborhood. Its dim interior was soothing to the eyes after the stare of the summer sun, its cool cement floor caressing to bare feet come from hot pavement. Here stood racks of rifles and shotguns in all their clean beauty, and I yearned for them although not yet permitted firearms. But I got BB shot for my Daisy air rifle. In this treasure house there was a bin filled with them from which a clerk, accustomed to riches, casually took them in a metal scoop. How round and smooth and tingling to the touch they were—a whole nickel's worth of them—in my sweaty, smudgy hand. Then I went out and stalked sparrows in rose bushes; stalked them as though they were tigers, heart throbbing, body sweating, eyes glued to the gunsight, the world narrowed to the tiny circumference of my quest.

My first shotgun, from Wetherbee's, was given me as a present, a stimulating reminder of approaching manhood. Still close to the frontier in spirit, forests still girding us round, game abundant, the shotgun (and rifle) among us had ritualistic intimations as well as utilitarian uses. My gun was certainly the most beautiful of its kind ever made, with its pale walnut stock and single barrel of mirror-bright bluish steel, a wonder of the gunmaker's art that sold for only $4.95. I bought black powder shells for it. Smokeless shells, besides being hopelessly expensive, were dull. When fired, they made only a wisp of smoke. But black powder shells, after the pleasing "boom" of their explosion, emitted a dense cloud that increased my hunter's pride.

Going along, upon a smooth-worn bench in front of Hardin's Cafe (For Colored Only), I saw Wash Jackson, an ancient Negro and a man whom I had known since early childhood, warming himself in the sun. In his youth he had married a girl much fairer of skin than he, and the couple had three children all of whom were fair-skinned. In Mississippi, as in India, as among all the colored peoples of the world, a high premium is put upon fair skin. But Wash's wife put upon it an extreme premium. While the couple's children were small, she left with them one day for an unknown destination, saying in the neighborhood that she wasn't going to disgrace herself and her children by continuing to live with a black man.

Soon afterward Wash entered the household of Mr. Will Henderson, owner of Deep Snow plantation, where he became butler and won the enduring affection of his employer. One day Mr. Will died, and when the will was read in Lawyer Campbell's office, Wash found that his old boss man had left him $1,000, the house he lived in, and twenty acres of land. He was now affluent.

Some months later a letter came for Wash, and unable to read, he asked Miss Mary, his boss lady, to read it for him. It was from his former wife. She said they children missed they Poppa so bad they cried theyself to sleep every night, and she was pore hongry to lay eyes on her dear husband. Did he send some money to come up yonder on the train, they'd soon be there. "I closes this letter but not my love," she concluded.

Wash asked, "Miss Mary, will you be here in a minute?" Told she would be there, Wash went out and returned with a postcard which, at his request, she first "backed" (addressed) to his wife. Then he said, "Miss Mary, please ma'am, write something for me," and he dictated a single sentence of four words. It read: "I ain't fade none."

[*Readers familiar with the rules of caste and color in Brazil will note that Wash's experience seems to bear out the Brazilian adage, "Money whitens."*][2]

There sat Wash, spotlessly clean, sunning his old bones. His family had been long lost to him. His white folks were dead. Most of his colored contemporaries were gone. He regarded younger Negroes—the older generation decrying the younger—as "the triflin'est folks ever I seen in my bawn days." Wash sat there looking up and down the street, looking for death to come on his white horse and take him away to the embracing arms of Sweet Jesus. Would he come from the East or the West, the South or the North? In the daytime or in the nighttime? It did not matter. Wash was ready. The pale rider would be welcome whenever he came.

2. Carl F. Degler, *Neither Black Nor White* (New York, 1971), 105.

Separated from Negroes in death as we were separated from them in life, we did not think of death as they did. Theirs was a greater serenity in the acceptance of death, while we, no matter how often it happened, still said unbelievingly to one another, "Why, I saw him only yesterday!"

Yet as "white" death differed somewhat from "Negro" death among us, so all death in the sensual South was, in a manner, unlike death in the Gothic North. Seeing Wash waiting to die recalled to me with painful sharpness of detail the spring morning when my young, widowed sister died, her weeping children at her bedside. I could scarcely hear her agonized breathings above the flood of birdsong that beat against the windows of her hospital room. Outside, the loins of the soil seemed to tremble in their shadowing forth of life; blossoming trees skipped down the street like pink-frocked girls dancing homeward from school; bushes burst with their budding; perfume rose in the air; and the rising sun poured torrents of light upon the little town caught in the great crescent of the wide river.

Then one could say with the Mogul emperor who had caused to be inscribed in stone at the entrance to his magnificent Delhi palace: "Here, here, is paradise on earth." On such a bridegroom morning who could believe in death? It was an outlandish anachronism, the practical joke of a boorish god. Besides, one felt, my sister would soon leave the hospital with her children. We would all breakfast together, and since the joke had done no harm, we would laugh about it.

Death among us was, from another point of view, unlike death in the city. There it is shrouded in anonymity. A private affair, it affects principally the dead man's family and his friends—an enclave within enclaves, as Oriental boxes are "nested" one within the other. Many a city apartment house held more people than our town, and as their tenants were unconscious of one another in their daily lives; so they were unconscious of one another when death came among them.

But since we were few under the pitiless dome of heaven and we huddled together for warmth against the chilling winds of cosmos, death was often a public affair, especially if it was that of a vigorous man in his prime (our tribe in its struggle for existence). It then seemed a blow to the collective strength of our tribe—the drowning of the man next to you on the levee as you furiously fought together to keep the flooding river out of the town.

When death came, neighbors took over the house of the dead. Women cared for the children, prepared meals, arranged flowers, set out empty milk bottles, answered the telephone. Men comforted the bereaved in the awkwardly affectionate way of males at such a moment; stood between them and the undertaker; shouldered the coffin upon its graveward journey.

Death, moreover, often bent the parallel lines of race so that for a split second they touched. Negro friends, sober faced and sometimes grief stricken, came with flowers gathered from their premises, offered to help around the house, comforted the mourners. Their women had a capacity—exceeding that of white women—for consoling a whimpering child who had lost a parent.

They seemed to me to possess this faculty natively—whether, themselves loving children, they had a way with them, or, their lives hard and premature death no stranger to them, they had often to discharge this office. Or it may have been, their faith strong, they had no doubt that the dead had ascended into heaven and were able to instill some of their serenity into children. (We whites also had religious faith. But it was corroded by doubts and reservations.) Whatever the reasons, I had often seen a gray-haired, capacious-bosomed Negro woman who looked the universal mother gather a white child to her and by some magical transfusion of loving warmth so comfort it that tears fled, a wan smile came, and it began again to find the path to the dream world from which it had been snatched.

We had no true social-political democracy. But death has its own democracy and the commonwealth of misery its citizens. Here there is neither caste, class, nor color. Many a white person among us visited his sick Negro friend, provided medical services for him, and if he died attended his funeral.

Negroes were pleased when whites came to their funerals. They felt—as whites did—that a large attendance at a funeral was a matter of family prestige, an attestation to the good works of the dead man, the final accolade the community could bestow upon him. When our cook's mother died, Julia said to me with somber pride, "There was as many white folks as colored at the funeral."

Whites, too, were pleased when Negroes attended their funerals. You never saw one at the burial of a "mean" white man. Hence their presence meant that the dead man had been kind and decent.

Ours was a life-loving community. Yet a few of our appurtenances that pertained to the dead were more splendid than those used by the living. Occasionally, when I was a little boy, I stared wonderingly at one of them. Before the house of a neighbor there stood two great black silken horses hitched to a shining black vehicle whose rear door standing open revealed parallel bars of radiant silver. No carriage in town could match its sumptuousness.

So, too, it was with respect to graveyards. Many of our Delta towns were almost unrelievedly ugly. They were horrendous with their rusty tin roofs, crazy shacks, patches of weeds, rutted streets, the sun blazing on a treeless area that yesterday had been shady forest. But the graveyards of these towns were trim. They had trees, shade, lawns, flowers, bird music, pebbled walks, and ordered avenues of the dead. Maintained with a care that was not lavished upon places of the living, they were often the only areas of loveliness amid planes of depressing ugliness.

As death among us was sometimes a tribal affront, a weakening of the group in its collective struggle with the fates, so, somewhat similarly, was the departure from town of a young man to make his fortune elsewhere. The affront became the greater if he greatly succeeded. For then it became clear that the talents which had enriched another community might have enriched his own, while his departure was, in a sense, vaguely disloyal, since the tribe had nurtured him, given him his preliminary training, set him upon his path. But it nonetheless vicariously shared his triumphs, warmly welcomed him on visits to his old home, and tribesmen boasted to their neighbors that they had given a distinguished man to Metropolis.

Yet, even as they embraced the homecoming exile, mute, accusing queries stood in their eyes: "Why did you leave us?" they asked. "Why did you fail us, we who needed you?"

Farther along the street from Hardin's Cafe, near the firehouse where the big horses were aired in the soft morning and the forgotten cemetery where lay the victims of an ancient yellow fever epidemic, stood the brothels of Central Avenue. There our idlers said Satan had his abode. Satan was evil, as God was good. But I found, amazedly, that he was like God in this: he, too, was everywhere.

("Now concerning the things whereof ye wrote unto me: it is good for a man not to touch a woman. Nevertheless, to avoid fornication, let every man have his own wife, and let every woman have her own husband. . . . I would that all men were even as I myself. But every man hath his proper gift of God, one after this manner, and another after that. I say therefore to the unmarried and widows, it is good for them to abide even as I. But if they cannot contain, let them marry; for it is better to marry than to burn.")

In these houses, it appeared, men lost their souls and were condemned to hellfire everlasting, while on earth they slowly rotted from loathsome diseases contracted in them. Yet—such is Satan's power—they continued to visit them. Nice ladies, walking on Washington Avenue, sometimes pulled their long skirts close about them when they passed a woman outrageously resplendent in blue ostrich-plumed hat, blue velvet high-top shoes, and a blue velvet dress, a diamond-encrusted chatelaine watch pendant from the shoulder. But men furtively smiled to her as she made her stately way down the street, the air for a moment heavily redolent of ylang-ylang or heliotrope.

("The lips of a strange woman drop honey, And her mouth is smoother than oil: but in the end she is bitter as wormwood, Sharp as a two-edged sword. . . . Rejoice in the wife of thy youth. As a loving hand and a pleasant doe, Let her breasts satisfy thee at all times, And be thou ravished always with her love.")

The houses where these women lived looked, however, just like those occupied by so many nice people: simple wooden structures with morning glories clambering over their galleries and in their sunbaked, grassless yards, great sunflowers whose heads bent beneath an insupportable burden of gold. Sometimes in spring or summer one saw their occupants, kimono-clad, lying in hammocks or sitting in rocking chairs, talking, laughing, as other women, no visible stigmata upon them. Occasionally some of them sat upon their doorsteps dry-ing their shampooed hair in the sun, eyes closed against the light, their long tresses and languid postures suggesting the Rhine maidens of whom I had read. I stared at them wondering what bittersweet poison lay in their chalices; how would fare the lost traveler come to these alien isles.

Across the street from the Mobile and Ohio depot was Al's Cafe. Negro-owned, Negro-run, whites sat at one of its counters. Negroes sat at a counter opposite them. The groups were vaguely separated by a paper barrier of Kel-logg's Toasted Corn Flakes, a barrier that was stronger than steel.

Outside, rays of light that had left Aldebaran a hundred thousand years ago were lost in the counter rays emitted by Al's electric sign. It repeated over and over with infuriating repetition: EAT.

Elroy, a small black boy with a great head that dwarfed his frame, served me breakfast. Once he had whispered to me, "When the leaves o' the trees gets to flutterin' too bad on the boughs, that's the time for niggers to go and hide." But now he said, "Don't ever be vexed in yo mind, Mistuh Dave. Jes pray to the good lawd to grant you the circumcised heart, an' if you prays to him in humility he will grant what you wants in grace."

Breakfast over, I went across the street, entered the train, and made myself comfortable after sweeping cinders from my red plush settee. From the car win-dow I could see Negroes stirring about their shacks. There were men in overalls fixin' to go to work; children playing; women sweeping their porches; other women, kitchen knives in hand, carrying baskets, bound for the levee to dig wild greens for salads. The red ball of the rising sun narrowly missed the tall incin-erator of the lumber mill. Then, as though it were an acrobat who had de-signedly first missed the swinging trapeze to heighten the suspense of his act, it mounted sure and free to float away over the river to the misty, willow-green shores of Arkansas.

Dan Agnes, the Negro train porter, saluted me with a warm, wide, gold-toothed smile and a hearty "Good mawnin', suh." He had a certain unique fame in town because he had learned to speak German while working for Mr. B. B. Goldman, proprietor of Goldman's Saloon. When Dan had married Julia, our cook, mother baked a huge cake for the wedding reception held in Julia's little house that stood in the rear of our own.

The bell of the locomotive clanged. The dinky train chugged past the sawmill, the whine of its saws in my ears as they ripped through the stout hearts of oak logs, the pungent sweetish aroma of green lumber in my nostrils, and in my mind the words of the haunting Negro song:

> Ain't but the one train on the track,
> Gwine straight to heaven,
> An' it ain't comin' back.

4

Change and No Change

In this chapter Cohn touches on a theme familiar to students of the South—the juxta-position of continuity and change. In the course of his lifetime Cohn observed changes he had never dreamed possible—whites doing common labor, accepting tips, and settling af-fairs of honor and the heart with litigation rather than gunfire. For all such evidence of changes in social mores, however, the Delta remained throughout Cohn's life a politically obsessed and fiercely Democratic region. In this chapter Cohn also discusses the Delta's po-litical relationship with the remainder of the state and offers his analysis of the almost mys-tifying visceral appeal of arch-demagogue Theodore G. Bilbo. Cohn's emphasis on the depth and intensity of the commitment of Delta whites to the Democratic party suggests that change in this area was next to impossible. Yet, four years after Cohn's death, in 1960, Delta whites deserted the Democratic party in droves, and their behavior in subsequent presidential elections indicated that they had become as orthodox in their Republicanism as they once had been in their commitment to the Democrats.

I was an infant when Horatio Alger died, his Phil-the-Fiddler "philosophy" strong in the land. It was a cynical philosophy for a people not only virile but given allegedly to the concept of marriage-for-love-only, since it taught that the easiest road to success was marriage with the boss's daughter. As nearly every other American boy, I read Alger. His rags-to-riches success story would long remain staple fare of the people, but although many continued to win prizes in the great American lottery, it would, as time passed, carry less conviction for fewer people until, its hold gone, the country would see the spectacle of skep-tics in shiny Cadillacs, the successful who doubted their own success.

I was a college freshman when the first world war began in 1914 and mankind entered upon that long agony whose duration and outcome no one can foretell. I was about to leave college when the Bolsheviks triumphed in Czarist Russia and tidal waves of their revolution began to break upon the shores of distant lands. (The while Karl Marx, Sigmund Freud, Albert Einstein—each in his way—were shaking the foundations of man's material and immaterial world.) I was a young businessman in New Orleans upon that Black Friday of October, 1929, when panic struck the New York Stock Exchange and the Great De-pression was at hand. America would begin to move upon untrodden ways, and the American Dream would begin to lose some of its luster. At this time, too, some of my college classmates who, following Alger's creed, had married the boss's daughter found themselves saddled with the boss.

The Delta, a quiet backwater of the brawling world, dreaming, unaware, unhurried, reluctantly and slowly changed with the changing world. This is how it was there—in some respects—when I was young.

My early years at the turn of the century were spent in a society that, for all of its complexities of caste, class, and two-race system, still retained in many of its aspects an almost pastoral simplicity. It was a society bucolic by comparison with the present, when caste and class are in a state of transition, the two-race system is undergoing many modifications, and the Delta, along with the rest of the nation and the world, has entered into the Age of Anxiety.

Yet as the century grew older the airborne virus of change came to the Delta, remote though we were from the infected change areas of the country. Thus it was that, with incredulous eyes, I first saw white men doing common labor on the public roads. As an inhibition of caste and a hangover from the days of slavery long vanished, white men did not do manual labor; the exceptions, and they were few among us, were "low-down white folks" variously denominated, by white and Negroes, as "po' white trash," "rednecks," "peckerwoods." There were "nigger jobs"—heavy work of all kinds, unskilled labor, agriculture. The classification, however, was by no means accurate because many of our most skilled artisans were Negroes and some were contractors.

There were also "white men's jobs"—white-collar occupations, skills, superintendencies. Theoretically, in any event, the white man worked in the shade and the Negro in the sun. The daily language of white men confirmed what was nearly always the fact and the mark of the division of labor. "I've been working like a nigger," a white man would say. Or, "I got out there and sweated like a nigger." But here, unbelievably, were white men doing common labor; this was a sharp break with the past. It was also the death of the cherished myth that only Negroes and mules could work in the hot sun, while before long there would be not only white men and white women working in the cotton fields of the Delta, but all over the South there would be more whites than Negroes in the fields. It did not matter that in the Delta the summer sun was so hot that it had been the Delta plantation custom—seeing that a mule is valuable—to take him out of harness at midday and "shade" him for a while.

Soon I would see white men, employed by Delta municipalities, collecting garbage in Negro neighborhoods and, more impossibly, white waitresses in restaurants. The process was already under way by which whites would preempt the monopoly that Negroes had long had as barbers, field hands, waiters, bellhops, while both in the towns and in the country whites and Negroes would work alongside one another without friction or sense of novelty.

One witnessed also marked changes of attitudes. If a man were grossly slandered or libeled by another, the community of my early youth would have visited its contempt upon him if he had resorted to law for redress of his grievance. Law courts, in our theology, properly dealt only with such crass things as torts or breaches of contract, not with delicate matters of personal honor. Hence, a man's honor involved, it was the sense of the community that if he sought redress he should do so by taking it out on the hide of the man who had "insulted" him. But the time would come when libel suits would be heard in the Circuit Court of Washington County, and money damages would soothe the wounded honor of a man.

In the graver matter of the adultery of a wife, the same theology prevailed. The cuckolded husband could not, except upon pain of incurring the community's scorn, sue his wife's lover for "alienation of affections," that curious action at law which seems to give a man property rights in his wife's person. He was honor bound at least to horsewhip the lover—the more publicly the better—or preferably, in the grand matter, to shoot him. If he did so, the "unwritten law" saved him from punishment, while at the same time he ran little physical risk. It was not precisely cricket, but no stigma attached to a husband who shot the lover in the back. So it was that from time to time the temptation—even the compulsion—to murder being great under the circumstances, one man shot another.

Sometimes, however, the shoe was on the other foot, a small foot in silken stockings. Then the outraged wife shot her "tomcattin'" husband, often using a tiny, becomingly ladylike pistol sold by Sears and Roebuck under the trade name of "Miss Junior." It is part of our folklore that the husband (or wife) is the "last to find out." Yet the wife often "found out" through her Best Friend. "Now, Sarah Jane, I hate to tell you this, but everybody is saying that . . ." And it was legendary that the hand that rocked the cradle never missed the mark when it pulled the trigger of a pistol.

Occasionally, in pedagogical mood, the wife might shoot her husband's "lady friend" to "teach her a lesson." (A certain refinement, however great the provocation to its abandonment, kept us from using the explicit word "mistress." We always had on hand a large stock of euphemisms appropriate for varying occasions.) Still another variation on the theme occurred when, to spare a lady's delicate feelings, her father or brother undertook the messy job of killing a footloose husband.

Killings occurring because, as Negroes put it, "a man was kickin' in another man's stall," were not without incidental benefits to the community. A lurid respite from the daily routine, they gave everybody something morbidly fascinating to gabble about— "Now let me tell you what I heard" confirmed the righteous in their rectitude and offered fresh texts for stale preachers. They nearly always, moreover, helped the surviving wife. Sometimes, when her husband shot her lover, she became reattached to a man who had gone to so much trouble for her and who had so dramatically demonstrated his love for her. Then she effected reconciliation with him, and they lived happily ever afterward.

But if her husband—lacking the finer instincts of a gentleman—still disdained her despite her willingness to forgive and forget, she was nonetheless in good case. For since he had paid her the extravagant compliment of killing a man over her affections, she became instantly desirable in the eyes of other men—a female "playboy of the Western world"—and almost invariably married a richer or handsomer husband than the one she had before.

There was, however, a loose conventionality that governed our unconventional crimes of passion. Once the aggrieved husband's revenge took a sinister form that horrified the community. "He hadn't oughter done it thataway," complained a stickler for the proprieties.

In this instance the erring wife, whenever her mate was out of town, received her lover in her house. The husband, after so long a time, learned of it. He thereupon sent for his faithful Negro servant, gave him a shotgun, told him he was leaving town, and instructed him to sit on his back porch from "first dark" until daylight and shoot any intruder who might appear. "I want you to guard the Missus while I'm away," he said.

On the same evening, when a man attempted to enter the house by the back door, the Negro, faithful to his white boss man's orders, killed him. Then the husband, with tender solicitude for his wife's good name, gave it out that the man had mistakenly entered his house while drunk and had been mistakenly shot for a burglar. A year later he quietly divorced her.

The time would come, however, when cuckolded husbands and outraged wives would withhold their fire, as libeled men would resort to the pedestrian law. Cold winters apart, we were one with Vermont.

Less dramatically, but almost as significantly, change came in another quarter. When I was a boy in the Delta, no one would have offered a tip to a white man or woman as a gratuity for a service, while the man who offered the tip, unless he were obviously a Yankee who knew no better, would have been rejected with scorn. Tips went only to Negroes. For the acceptance of a gratuity, by Delta reckoning, put one unmistakably in the servant class and on a footing, therefore, with Negroes, who were the area's sole servants. Yet eventually the pattern of the clutching hand and shining coin would appear in the Delta as elsewhere in the community's changing attitudes.

Social and political change frequently occur together. But in my youth and young manhood, we remained politically unchanged and apparently unchangeable. White men, with rare exceptions, were Democrats. Such eyelet embroidery variations as Hoovercrats, Democrats-for-Wilkie, Dixiecrats, Trumancrats, and Democrats-for-Eisenhower lay in the distant future. Voting the straight Democratic ticket, we bred straight in those days. Our one concession to hybrids was mules, and since the status of hybrids was low, it was common for a politician to heap scorn upon another by saying, "There he stands like a mule, without pride of ancestry or hope of posterity." We were, in short, Simon-pure, hog-and-hominy Democrats, who regarded any deviation from the orthodox doctrine as at least a venial sin. Many a child grew up in a household where there hung an enlarged photograph of William Jennings Bryan (the Great Commoner, the Boy Orator of the Platte) so that he or she, until adolescence, believed that Bryan was a member of the family.

Yet we were not completely inflexible. Once, when a Greenville girl, through some unaccountable whimsy of love, married a Republican while visiting in the North and compounded the crime by bringing him home to live, the community nonetheless graciously forgave her in time and so, with some difficulty, did her family. But it remained bad form to mention the misalliance in polite circles. It is characteristic of those born in the Deep South that they carry with them a catalog of Things Not To Be Mentioned.

I had two classmates, Mickey and Ernest Waldauer, whose father, a respected citizen and cotton planter, was a Republican, and I regretted that this bar sinister should light upon the family, seeing that in all other respects they were such nice people. One could even forgive them that as a reward for his Republican perfidy father Waldauer had been appointed local postmaster, where he handled Democrats' mail. It was not that Republicans ate mice—as we boys believed true of the community's Chinese—but they were queer fish just the same.

If it was scandalous of a Deltan to be a Republican, the reasons lay in the past. The people remembered the Republican government of bayonets that went by the cruelly ironic name of "Reconstruction," while the conquering Republican North seemed never to have heard of the sage admonition given by Talleyrand to Napoleon. "Sire," he said, "you can do everything with bayonets except sit on them." The South (and the Delta) also remembered the rewards that Reconstruction heaped upon Negroes by appointing them to public office, where the late slaves became masters of their late masters. And since the region feared Negro domination above all, a citizen who lent his name to Republicanism won less than its ardent approval.

So, too, Reconstruction was regarded as a rivet in the South's neck because it seemed an effort of industry-minded Republicans to monopolize national power at the expense of agrarian Democrats. As for the charter of freedmen's freedom—the Fourteenth Amendment to the Constitution—this was widely construed by southerners to be no true charter at all but written primarily more to serve corporate privilege than the civil rights of the freedmen.

Men took their politics with a fierce, Balkan intensity, as did the Greeks whom I later heard arguing passionately all night over tiny cups of syrupy coffee in their everyman's forum of Athens—the Place de la Constitution. Southerners—as the Greeks—are a politics-obsessed people, while the one-party sys-

tem and the rise of factions caused elections to turn upon personalities rather
than issues and often assume the bitterness of a family quarrel with its peculiar
cruelty, for in no other quarrel are men so familiar with the tender spots of their
adversaries. Our people, besides, were given more to emotion than reason; violence fermented beneath the calm surface of events; and I never heard the word
"objectivity" mentioned in a political context.

It is a concept, if I may digress briefly, for which I have little enthusiasm;
proof that I am not—thank God—always objective. Thus I was infuriated when,
long ago, I heard Americans being "objective" about Stalin's slaughter of kulaks and the deliberate starvation of unnumbered Russian peasants as part of
his plan for building the Soviet paradise of workers and peasants. "It is sometimes
necessary," they said, taking a cocktail, "to sacrifice the few for the many; the
present for the future." They were "liberals." "Conservatives" were equally objective about Hitler, Mussolini, Tojo. Hitler, they said, was the victim of the Versailles Treaty. He had to do what he did. Mussolini, I was told, made the trains
run on time. Tojo would restore order to disorderly China and Manchuria. All
this would make for better business. The while we grew fat as Gadarean swine
upon acorns, grapefruit-size, that dropped from heavy-laden corporation trees.

Men's so-called objectivity, it seems to me, is often a bogus judiciousness that
permits them to approve of the otherwise unapprovable, a poisonous flowering
of smugness and fancied security, a passing of cool judgments by those far from
the fires of conflict. Such men, frost in their testicles, could fructify only ice-
bergs. Yet their objectivity vanishes the moment their dear objective heads are
imperiled, as when Hitler, Mussolini, Tojo at last threatened them in their
sound-proof burrows and as the Soviets presently threaten them.

This is not to decry true objectivity, the indispensable faculty of seeing things
as they are and thus the way to that tough-mindedness from which we as a
people have always shied. It is to express contempt for that phony, drugstore science judiciousness which may easily degenerate into nihilism or into a form of
finishing-school, fragile-teacup gentility whereby passionate belief and passionate statement erupting from belief are made taboo. If I am sometimes less than
objective, I not only make no apology but pray that this blight may never descend upon me. My obduracy is perhaps strengthened because I am in good
company, and among it is that rather stubborn, unobjective figure called the Lord
God Jehovah.

In the Delta, objectivity unknown and passion often running high during
elections, there was an occasional shooting, as when a partisan, failing to see the
light, light was let into him through a bullet hole drilled by another partisan, or
as upon one occasion, when a Bilbo hater named his dog "Bilbo" and was
promptly shot by an admirer of that statesman who, although traduced in this
way, had been "elected to the highest office within the people's gift."

I remember this hotly controversial figure, who kept Mississippi in political turmoil for many years, as a gnomic little man who seemed to have been re-moved from the pickling vat when its process had been but half completed so that he looked partially raw and partially cured. In his loosely knotted necktie he wore a trademark in the form of a diamond horseshoe stickpin, and on his forehead there was a scar that had come to him in the course of his wild slanders against others. Not one to be impressed by subtleties of opposition, he had been hit over the head with a pistol by a political enemy whom he had described from the platform in typically Bibloesque language as a "cross between a hyena and a mongrel . . . begotten in a nigger graveyard at night, suckled by a sow, and ed-ucated by a fool."

Since, however, he had no monopoly of superheated talk, he was often an-swered in hydrophobic epithets that matched his own or even, in the case of the rare master, excelled his. But their sole effect, so far as I could see, was to cause those who used them to secrete an excess of adrenaline in their anger. Bilbo was secured against them in a hide of battleship armor. So vicious indeed were the epithets employed by him and against him that it seemed to be almost exquisite evasion when Fred Sullens, editor of the Jackson *Daily News,* called Bilbo a "self-accused bribe taker, a self-confessed grafter, a foul-tongued slanderer, an un-mitigated liar and contemptible crook."

Then, having paid his respects to Bilbo, Sullens visited his wrath upon the electorate. Bilbo would not have been elected, he went on, "if a majority of the voters, fooled, deluded, blinded, lost to all reason, had not said . . . they would rather wallow in filth than to walk clean ground." But this calamity having come to Mississippi, the editor suggested substituting a "carrion crow" for the eagle on the state's capitol with a "puking buzzard."

This somewhat unrestrained language of politics is, however, by no means unique to Mississippi. It is in an old American tradition and a century ago was common to Britain before the enactment of her strict libel laws. Thus in 1835, when Benjamin Disraeli fired the wrath of Daniel O'Connell, who was Irish leader in the House of Commons, he let fly at Disraeli in this manner:

> At Taunton this miscreant had the audacity to call me an incendiary! . . . Then he calls me a traitor. My answer to that is, he is a liar. He is a liar in action and words. His life is a living lie. He is a disgrace to his species. What state of society must be that could tolerate such a creature. . . . He is the most degraded of his species and kind; and England is degraded in tolerating a miscreant of his abom-inable, foul, and atrocious nature. . . . He possesses just the qualities of the im-penitent thief on the Cross, whose name, I verily believe, must have been Disraeli. For aught I know the present Disraeli is descended from him and, with the im-pression that he is, I now forgive the heir-at-law of the blasphemous thief who died upon the Cross.

Disraeli, writing to the *Times,* called O'Connell "a systematic liar and beg-garly cheat, a swindler and a poltroon. . . . He has committed every crime that does not require courage." Then, transcending our relatively tranquil Mississippi ways, he challenged O'Connell to a duel, and when his antagonist refused because he had just killed a man, challenged O'Connell's son, who had Disraeli bound over to keep the peace under a surety bond.

We had, therefore, distinguished precedent for our incendiary political language, while nothing could stop the political progress of Bilbo more than momentarily—neither pistol whippings, the opposition of "nice people," nor obscene epithets. State senator, he twice became governor of Mississippi, and was contesting the right to take his seat for a second term in the United States Senate when he died. An idol of the people, he rallied platform audiences by leading them in singing that sturdy old hymn "Bringing in the Sheaves," and he aroused them to wild applause with such words as these:

> Friends, fellow citizens, brothers and sisters—hallelujah. My opponent—yes, this opponent of mine who has the dastardly, dewlapped, brazen, sneering, insulting and sinful effrontery to ask you for your votes without telling you . . . what he is a-going to do with them if he gets them—this opponent of mine says he don't need a platform. . . . He asks, my dear brethren and sisters, that you vote for him because he is standing by the President (F. D. Roosevelt). . . . I shall be the Senator and servant of all the people. . . . The appeal and petition of the humblest citizen, yes, whether he comes from the black prairie lands of the east or the alluvial lands of the fertile delta; . . . yea he will be heard by my heart and my feet shall be swift . . . your Senator whose thoughts will not wander from the humble, God-fearing cabins of Vinegar Bend, . . . your champion who will not lay his head upon his pillow at night before he has asked His Maker for more strength to do more for you on the morrow. . . . Brethren and sisters, I pledge . . .

William Alexander Percy, whose scorn for Bilbo was such that he would not mention his name in his *Lanterns on the Levee* although discussing him at some length, there reveals one reason why so many people were for Bilbo: "Glib and shameless [he was], with that sort of cunning common to criminals that passes for intelligence. The people loved him. They loved him not because they were deceived in him, but because they understood him thoroughly; they said of him proudly, 'He's a slick little bastard.' He was one of them and he had risen from obscurity to the fame of glittering infamy—it was as if they themselves had crashed the headlines."

The people did proudly say of Bilbo that "he's a slick little bastard." Theirs was a profound pride that was not without overtones of pathos. Their pride was profound, it seems to me, because it was deep-rooted in vicariousness. It was the pride of a people enduring in the wasteland of ignorance, poverty, near hopelessness, and orgiastic religionism, who saw one of their own kind—an Untouchable—come to sit upon terms of equality with Brahmins. A United States senator, he could talk man to man with the president of the United States or the king of England, command newspaper headlines throughout the country, appear on newsreels, and be featured in publications of national circulation.

They themselves, white Anglo-Saxons whose ancestors had fought perhaps at Cowpens and Shiloh, had long been regarded with contempt by the Quality of Mississippi, whose charity toward them was less than it was for Negroes. 'Way back in 1836, for example, Colonel Thomas S. Dabney migrated from his ancestral tidewater estate, Elmington, in Gloucester County, Virginia, to a tract of land in Hinds County, Mississippi, forty miles east of Vicksburg. There he owned a cotton plantation of four thousand acres worked by slaves.

When he first came to the neighborhood, its small farmers included Colonel Dabney in their rustic social gatherings. But their relations soon became strained. One day the Colonel brought twenty of his slaves to a house-raising. This was generous of him and neighborly. Yet since he kept his hands gloved while directing the work of his slaves, his beneficiaries were less grateful for his kindness than offended by the undemocratic manner of its rendering. They were furthermore offended when, anxious to return the favor, Dabney made no call upon them for assistance. They felt that the rich might patronize the poor in the caste-class society of the Old Dominion. But in new, poor Mississippi, such patronage strongly implied that an alien stratification was beginning.

"Every social class," says Marcel Proust, "has its own pathology."

Here in Mississippi were tens of thousands of poor white men, some of the "lesser breed" under the Stars and Stripes. And here was Bilbo. He was their own kith and kin. Like them, he was no stranger to forlorn shacks in lonely clearings; to women broken in youth by deprivation, toil, and constant childbearing; to hookworm, pellagra, and malaria; to a diet of sowbelly, cornmeal, molasses; to chills and fever and baptizings in springtime creeks, a hard-eyed God looking sternly on from a pale sky. He and they had sprung from the same womb. They had been hammered upon the same anvil. But—hosanna to the Lord, who had raised up a stout champion among them—he had escaped their fate because he was slick. So the people took pride in Bilbo.

Pride, one learns early, is sinful. More important perhaps, it "goes before a downfall." Look what happened to the proud Lucifer when cast from heaven's ramparts; "from dawn till dewy eve he fell." All this we granted. Yet the Delta was filled with people poor, proud, prolific. Sometimes we spoke approvingly of a family that was "too poor to paint and too proud to whitewash." And we were extremely careful—pride outwardly manifest—of "appearances."

Perhaps pride is silly; so are many manifestations of self-esteem. Yet a becoming pride is essential to most of us. Destroy a man's pride and you destroy the man. Elementally human males pride themselves upon their stallion virility. Hence everywhere it is a hurtful taunt to call a man a eunuch.

Pride is essential to most men because it is of the essence of self-respect. It lies not only in what one is or does but perhaps even more in what one may be permitted to do or become. For, as Nietzsche acutely points out, "Our self-respect depends upon our ability to make reprisals in both good and evil things." The new state of Israel bears pathetic illustration of the truth of this remark. There a man will sometimes deliberately stand in the middle of the road and defy motorists to run over him. Savagely repressed, as his ancestors had been before him in the land of his birth, he displays his newfound freedom and self-respect by making an aberrant reprisal against the society of which he is a part.

The inability to make reprisals, for good and evil, often accounts for otherwise unaccountable individual and mass explosions. When men find little in themselves or in their environment that makes for self-respect, or when self-respect is denied them by their "betters," they take a fiercely vicarious pride in their exceptional brothers who rise to fame, whether (among Negroes) as prize-fighters, blues singers, operatic stars, dancers, or (among whites) as senators, governors, millionaires. Thousands of the poorest, most submerged, white Mississippians took pride in Bilbo upon these terms.

There were other factors in the Bilbo success story. Men have always been beguiled by the personal for the obvious reason that a cause is an obstruction, and until it has become personified in a man, it is not likely to move their imaginations or stir their hearts. And nowhere are men more beguiled by personalities than we, for the paradoxical reason perhaps that, while we all dote upon having "personality" and buy personality pies, bras, and bread to that end, few of us dare have a personality. Hence we find vicarious gratification in the political leader who has a personality. It is, therefore, hurtful to an aspirant politician that he should be "colorless" while, even if a political genius, his chances would not be good as against a colorful opponent.

[*Cohn's observation about the affinity of voters for a politician with a "personality" notwithstanding, Mississippi's direct white primary made the Democratic primary the only election that mattered. Hence, it consistently attracted a large number of candidates who saw flamboyance as a key to distinguishing themselves from a host of other competitors for the same office.*][1]

Bilbo knew this as well as the next man and carefully cultivated his personality, adding bit by bit to his actor repertoire until he was a successful ham actor upon all public occasions. He had also the politically valuable gift of a streak of coarseness, a quality in public men which, whether or not we admit it, is esteemed by many of us. Thus it was that when President Truman wrote a furious letter to Paul Hume, a music critic of the Washington *Post*, castigating him for his unfavorable review of Margaret Truman's singing and saying that he would kick the critic in his whatnots, nice people shuddered at what they took to be language unbecoming to the president. But the legendary man on the street

1. For a discussion of the impact of the white primary on southern politics, see J. Morgan Kousser, *The Shaping of Southern Politics: Suffrage Restriction and the Establishment of the One-Party South, 1880–1910* (New Haven, 1974).

approved. It was not only that he, as the president, would have given unshirted hell to anybody who criticized his daughter, but that Mr. Truman used the vigorous language he himself liked.

Bilbo made the people laugh and, more valuable to him, made them laugh at someone. He was as entertaining as a medicine show; he was a diversion preceding the nostrum. He brought color and variety into the colorless, monotonous, flat lives of his audiences. He excoriated the Quality of Mississippi, a group they had no reason to love. He was, furthermore, as slick as a greased pig. But slickness is admired by many of us throughout the nation. "Well, I'll give him credit," we say of a dishonest businessman or politician. "He got away with it." Besides all this, he was—on the platform at least—violent, emotional, Negro-hating, pious. These factors appealed to his followers. Uninterested in attempting to reconcile the irreconcilable, they were themselves violent, emotional, Negro-hating, pious, and so at one with their champion. Then, to top it all, they were poor and ignorant, conditions that Bilbo—upon a stack of Bibles—swore to improve.

Here—lest we grow smugly disdainful of Bilbo and his followers—let me say this. As James Madison points out in the famous tenth paper of *The Federalist,* the manner in which men look at society depends upon their place in it. (In a grandiose recognition of this fact of life, we have latterly been spending billions to improve the condition of the poor overseas.) The rich look at society in one way; the poor in another. The chase is not the same to the hound and the fox.

Again, if you will permit me a digression, the rich also look at individuals in a certain way that has kept me from ever having a warm friendship with a man or woman of great wealth. I think of them in terms of Virginia Woolf's remarks about foreigners in England. A percipient foreigner, she said, could come to England, make friends there, and within a relatively short time gain a keen understanding of the country. But, she continued, he could never be cozy with his English friends as they are with one another.

The fault may be mine, but I, similarly, have never been able to be cozy with the massively wealthy, for their wealth has worked changes in them and wrought transformations in their character that inhibit a feeling of shared experience and a shared point of view between us. We are in the same world but upon quite different terms, a condition deterrent to warm friendship.

Mississippi was our poorest state (as it still is); Bilbo's followers were the poorest of the poor. They seldom had "meat vittles" and not too much "spoon vittles." Added to this compelling bond, Bilbo solidified his following by appealing to, or fomenting, their dislike of another group—Negroes. But far from being novel, this is an ancient, time-dishonored way of solidifying one group against another. It has respectable origins. No sooner had early Christianity triumphed over its persecutors, than its leaders solidified the group—originally banded together in the name of love—by causing them to hate and persecute non-Christians. It did not matter that "this medicine, love, which cures all sorrow," had been prescribed by Christ and long before him by Gautama Buddha. So, too, in our times, Russian Communist leaders sought to create solidarity among workers and peasants by causing them to hate the middle classes (bourgeoisie) and well-to-do peasants (kulaks), while Hitler fired the fanaticism of his followers by inciting them to hate and kill Jews.

Here is Bilbo on the platform in 1946, as described by Hodding Carter in his *Where Main Street Meets the River:*

> He was speaking in Leland, eight miles from Greenville, . . . to a crowd which overflowed into the soft . . . night. For an hour he had spat a frightful effluvium. . . . Negroes he had put in their place by recalling that the fathers of today's black men and women, who had the temerity to seek the vote, had only yesterday eaten nigger steak for breakfast back in Africa. . . . He paid his respects to me, promising a skinning party when he came to Greenville, which he never did, and explained that no "red-blooded Southerners . . . would accept a Poolizter-blitzer prize given by a bunch of nigger-loving Yankeefied communists for editorials advocating the mongrelization of the race."

Carter continues:

> All this was Grade-A-vote-getting technique in Mississippi. But in Leland he blundered. He complained satirically that folks had been saying lately that The Man Bilbo . . . was anti-Semitic. . . . A little Yankee girl reporter had come to him just the other day in Washington and asked whether such reports were true.
> "I said, 'Little lady, why of course that ain't true,'" Bilbo told his rapt audience.
> "'Why,' I said, 'I'm for every damned Jew from Jesus Christ on down.'"

The next day the nation's newspapers reported that Bilbo was for "every damned Jew from Jesus Christ downward."

Then, writes Carter, "I thought we had him over a barrel for while a majority of Bilbo's supporters didn't much mind what he said about Jews or niggers or Catholics or Dagoes . . . they were God-fearing folk who didn't like a man getting sassy with the Lord."

But Bilbo won. He explained that he was for every good Jew from Jesus Christ down. He wrote offended Protestant clergymen saying that he had always loved Jesus and that Carter was a lying Communist. Thereupon, Carter concludes, "Accepting the distinction between a damned Jew and a good Jew, his pious supporters marched as Christian soldiers to the polls and voted for The Man Bilbo, who had reverently included among his good Jews the Son of Man."

The Delta, land of large plantations, relative prosperity, and a population majority of Negroes, who were the backbone of its economic life, was long opposed to Bilbo. Most of its white people regarded him as a rabble-rousing, thieving, Negro-hating politician. But when he ran for the United States Senate in

1946—the election of which Carter wrote—large numbers of Deltans voted for him, planter and redneck standing together for the first time in decades. This was because many of the area's economic upper class were opposed to Washington's "socialism" and alleged threats to their way of life.

[*Coming in the wake of the 1944* Smith v. Allwright *decision striking down the white primary, the 1946 election reflected the exacerbation of racial tensions that led to the Dixiecrat revolt in 1948. Cohn goes on to describe the rise of a strident anti–New Deal conservatism that fed into the Dixiecrat revolt and the birth (in the Delta at Indianola) of the White Citizens Council in 1955.*]

Probably because of moral blind spots of my own, I retain a fairly amiable attitude toward many of men's frailties, including, of course, my frailties. I am less amiable, however, toward phony virtue and Sunday-clothes hypocrisy. Consequently, when well-to-do Deltans, up to their long-unaccustomed ears in fish-tailed Cadillacs—a display that at other times they might have called "nigger rich"—cussed Franklin D. Roosevelt for his "socialism"—an un-American doctrine carried on by Joseph Stalin's Washington deputy, Harry S. Truman—I found it a little hard to bear.

Roosevelt (the federal government), through loans and handouts, had rescued them from bankruptcy in the early 1930s when, as they granted, they lacked even the proverbial pot to cook in. The government had lent money to their banks, railroads, and other businesses; federal funds had gone to the building of the community's roads and other services. Above all, it had supported the price of cotton (and cottonseed) at artificially high levels. There was scarcely a man in the area who had not received a federal handout or benefited in one way or another from handouts received by others. But once the Delta had been restored to prosperity, many of its leading citizens sat in their new houses amid their paid-up furniture and denounced Roosevelt as though he were the Antichrist.

"Socialism" about to overwhelm the country and fuse Mississippi into one with Tadjikistan, I suggested to passionately democratic Deltans that they could make Washington County a Paul Revere to warn the sleeping nation that the redcoats were coming. I would, I said, draw a memorial to Congress asking Washington to withdraw its hated subsidies and handouts. It could firmly state that Washington Countians were still rugged Americans who spurned money tainted with the foul odor of a repulsive foreign doctrine. Such a memorial, I continued, would express not only their own attitudes, but, since it would be widely published in newspapers and proclaimed on the radio, it would be a warning to the nation. Yet, for some strange reason, no one wanted the memorial drawn.

[*Years later the process whose beginnings Cohn describes would be summarized by Walker Percy: "Planters who were going broke on ten cent cotton voted for Roosevelt, took federal money, got rich, lived to hate Kennedy and Johnson and vote for Goldwater—while still taking federal money."*][2]

2. Walker Percy, "Mississippi: The Fallen Paradise," *Harper's,* CCXXX (April, 1965), 169–70.

At Bilbo's death, his (contested) second term in the Senate hardly begun, it was thought by many Mississippians and by many more elsewhere that he would surely be succeeded by Representative John Rankin. He, too, was Negro hating, Jew hating, hydrophobically demagogic, and hammily emotional. Yet the aftermath was quite different.

During the campaign he could nowhere get more than a handful of people to listen to his ravings in an oratorical slaughterhouse of his own creation. In Greenville, to a small audience augmented by courthouse loafers, he spent half of his time denouncing Hodding Carter, the anti-Rankin editor of the local newspaper, and the other half denouncing Jews. When the returns were in, Rankin ran fifth in a field of six. Carter then sent him a present. It was a copy of Hitler's *Mein Kampf,* required reading for the student of hatred.

John C. Stennis, the elected senator, was at the opposite pole from Bilbo or Rankin. A former circuit court judge, quiet, dignified, free of Eliza-crossing-the-ice theatricals or appeals to hate, he easily led the field.

What were the sources of this phenomenon? I made a local inquiry into them after the election and emerged with at least some tentative conclusions that illuminate behavior at the polls.

Bilbo had a large following for the reasons that I have stated. But he had no social program. Primarily he stood for nothing and believed in nothing, except himself. An amoral opportunist, he ranted against Negroes because that was the surest way to election. Then, gaining the Senate, he introduced a bill providing for the deportation of American Negroes to Liberia. The bill, as he knew it would be, was permanently tabled. This, however, satisfied the amenities of the occasion. His methods were akin to those who sell "sour stomach" remedies of high alcoholic content to Prohibitionists. They are not selling forbidden whiskey whose consumption might compromise the consumer's hopes of heaven. But sufferers could enjoy constant mild jags while treating their "sour stomach," the great virtue of the remedy being that, although it allayed the symptoms of the disease, it never affected a cure. This miraculous medicine in hand, the victim could go on happily fighting his disease for a lifetime, piety and alcohol pulsing harmoniously in his blood.

In a somewhat similar manner, the demagogic politician could gain continuing favor by proposing to do what he knew could not be done—such as repealing the Fifteenth Amendment to the Constitution or deporting Negroes to Liberia—and remain serene in the knowledge that he would never have to make good on a promise that could not be fulfilled, while the promise itself was convincing evidence of his zeal for the commonwealth.

So it was that Bilbo introduced his deportation bill. Then he forgot about it, as did his followers. Successful hating is a full-time career, and his supporters had other things to do, such as, for example, scratching for a living.

Why, then, did the public that embraced Bilbo reject Rankin, who seemed so like him? Bilbo, however much he may have been a liar, a fraud, a grafter, and demagogue, was not, I believe—and so most Mississippians seemed to believe—a convinced fanatic. He was merely, by comparison, a relatively innocuous, slick opportunist, gifted with the valuable gifts of the buffoon.

But John Rankin was grim, tight lipped, humorless—characteristics of the fanatic. He was, I believe—and so most Mississippians seemed to believe—a blown-in-the-bottle fanatic. When he raved against Negroes and Jews, he meant it. This was not opportunism. It was fanaticism. The people could embrace a buffoon. But they could not stomach a reptilian-cold fanatic. And so they would not send John Rankin to the Senate.

Still close to the frontier and the elections without issues, it was more useful to the political candidate that he be endowed with picturesque and colorful speech that included a wide range of homespun invective and barnyard humor than with the solid, but often drab, equipment of statesmanship. The emotional kindling point of many of the people was low. Their rate of illiteracy was high. Their state was the poorest of the states so that even the honest politician could not have fulfilled his promises to improve their lot appreciably. All this made them the easy prey of charlatans.

One of the most flamboyant and passionately discussed political figures of my youth was James K. Vardaman, our governor and later United States senator, whose final years were passed within the shadows of insanity. A tall, dark, handsome man (unlike the gnomish Bilbo, who was first his champion and then his successor) with raven locks, flowing Buffalo Bill fashion over his collar, he often wore white flannel suits to accent his exoticism. He published a personal political organ called *The Issue,* and I read it with wondering fascination because its language of brutal vituperation and unbridled hatred of Negroes was unlike anything that was in our high school library.

Vardaman appeared a demigod when he strode before his audiences of Negro-hating, overall-clad whites, and they made a demigod of him as he promised to lift them into a heaven of their own by degrading the already degraded Negroes. In all this there was an immense pathos. At bottom the pro-Vardaman whites (as later the pro-Bilbo whites) did not, I believe, natively hate Negroes simply because they were Negroes. Here once again was the bitter and melancholy struggle of the poor against the poor, of poor whites against poor Negroes in an environment that had provided little for most of them and promised less so that the hungry fought the hungrier over already gnawed bones.

Thousands of our white people—to say nothing of Negroes—were degradedly poor, many of them feebly moving within the shadows of fever and hunger, dragging the shackles of disease. Perhaps Mississippi was too poor to do much about it. But at nearby Stoneville, three miles from Greenville, the federal government maintained a splendidly equipped cotton experiment station where expert agronomists searched for better strains of seed and a greater yield of cotton.

Our Agricultural and Mechanical College taught students how to grow and care for high-producing breeds of cows, pigs, chickens, thoroughbreds. In the United States of that day, we did much to improve our livestock, poultry, and field crops. But men and women were permitted to languish and languishing become perhaps the scrub stock of the next generation.

Under the circumstances of their environment and the fenced boundaries of their hope, the Negro hatred of Vardaman's white supporters was in reality an explosion of wrath at their misery, as today the Orient is exploding in the wrath of its long pent-up misery. They were perhaps grateful to Vardaman in their frustration, because he gave them an outlet for it in hating Negroes. The wretched malevolently urinated, as it were, upon the dispossessed, enjoying, as one of their few pleasures, the sharp pleasure of emotional evacuation.

Even the hot Mississippi sun did not always breed overwrought politicians whose merest words were a compromise between eloquence and epilepsy. Sometimes voters were faced with a choice between colorless mediocrities or, as occasionally happened, another face of mediocrity—between scoundrels who were merely smallbore. Then we plumped for the mediocrity who was a "nice feller" or for the scoundrel who confessed his skullduggeries with disarming frankness. The latter was frequently successful with the Robin Hood theme, especially when he varied it by saying that he stole from the rich to help the poor—including himself. "Yessuh, ole Bill Cutsone sure is a case," folks would say admiringly of such a pirate from the Spanish Main of Catfish Creek; the word "ole," in Deep South usage, denoting affection. Occasionally men would say—more judiciously perhaps but as affectionately—"Well, he's a sonofabitch and a good man too."

Elections among us of state and national officers were more than a manifestation of democracy. Before the coming of good roads, cars, radio, television, they were a temporary anodyne against the boredom of isolated towns and the routine of farms. The evil effects of boredom upon men are incalculable. No one knows—or can know—how many domestic quarrels, fornications, adulteries, mayhems, and even lynchings have proceeded from this source. I believe that much of the Delta violence of my youth had its roots in boredom while, as Dreiser noted in his *A Traveler at Forty,* "Denied the more varied outlets of a more interesting world, humanity falls back almost exclusively on sex."

Political campaigns, therefore, came as welcome diversion, and because of our rural economy, they came in late summer. Then crops had been laid by. Heat had laid its interdiction upon the land. The communities lay in a state of suspended animation, awaiting the coming of fall, the transient feverishness of cotton-picking time, and the brief, annual flurry of high business activity.

Candidates, like boll weevils in an excessively rainy season, appeared in great numbers out of nowhere. Each in tow of a local supporter, dripping goodwill and sweat . . . his hand shooting out automatically to grasp any hand within reach, called upon voters. (Woe to him, the uppity one, who missed a single citizen.) Departing after a brief chat, he left a card bearing his name, occasionally his photograph, and nearly always this legend: "Joe Brown will appreciate your vote and if elected will serve the people without fear or favor."

This pledge of our fair and fairless candidates was inherently the stronger because not one of them, it appeared, was moved by such crass motives as seeking office because it would provide them with the novelty of eating regularly or because that office was a source of power and a springboard to fame. Willing perhaps to sacrifice themselves for the commonwealth but not vulgarly zealous for office, they ran because of the overwhelming pressures of their admirers. "At the solicitation of my numerous friends, I hereby announce . . ."

Sometimes the candidate sat in the courthouse square—the local agora—and a rustic Socrates, shooing away horseflies that came from mules at the nearby hitching rack, discoursed informally with shirt-sleeved men about democracy. The more formal discourses came with the campaign barbecues. Democracy now suffered an embarrassment of riches. For the candidates seemed to outnumber the voters, who, attracted by the prospect of oratory, barbecued meat, and the sociability of the occasion, could be reached en masse only in this way before the coming of radio. Circulars and the press had long proclaimed the coming of the great day, and the day having come, stores closed at eleven in the morning to permit all to attend "the speaking" at Greenway Park beyond our city limits. Our streetcar line, in an incomparable burst of energy, had just been extended to reach it.

There, the night before, a Negro skilled in barbecuing, assisted by a few paid and many more unpaid volunteer workers, had labored until dawn. In deep-dug earthen pits they roasted beeves, pigs, and a sheep or two. They sliced and stacked mountains of bread; put soft drinks on ice (no one would risk offending the drys by offering beer); erected rough tables upon which the feast would be spread. At a cautious distance from the barbecue pits that gave off saliva-compelling aromas of roasting meat, watched the houn' dawgs of the vicinity, sad-eyed, patient, licking their chops. Nearer there was a circle of shy, scantily clad Negro children. They gazed in wonder at the Christmas plenty of white folks and awaited the reward that would be theirs before the day was over.

Onto the barbecue grounds poured townsmen and countrymen to fraternize with one another and applaud their chosen candidates—"Who you suppo'tin', Tawm?" Town dwellers greeted rural friends with a hearty "Hi there, Country!"

Many of the men, in a period when it was regarded as sissy to smoke ready-made cigarettes, wore a sack of Bull Durham tobacco attached to a shirt button and skillfully rolled their own. They had brought their ladyfolks to town with them on such locally famous trains as the Peavine, the Riverside, the Bigleben (named for its locomotive engineer, whose long beard flowing in the wind of his cab made him look a machine-age Santa Claus), and the Cleveland Turnaround.

But few came to the speaking. In that Florida-water time when only women of coarse fiber shamelessly admitted the stigma of robust health, ladies of more delicate quality were harmoniously "nervous." It was not, therefore, ladylike to participate in the rough male ways of politics, and country ladies visited with town ladies while their men attended the barbecue.

As Sir Walter Scott, the favorite antebellum novelist of the South, had left it a lingering legacy of castle-turreted romanticism, so the pallid shadows of the southern poet Edgar Allan Poe still rested upon many of our ladies who seemed, whatever they wore, to be all compact of gauze ficus and hyacinth hair and nimbuses of billowing ribbons. They might have been so healthy that they ate like hungry horses—and many did if not always at table—but to avoid the peasant stigma of robust health, they affected to be "ill angels" of Poe's imagination, as that Berenice upon whom disease "fell like the simoon," Ligeia with the crimson spot upon her cheek, or Berenice upon whose bosom lingered the hand of Death.

Ladies absent from political gatherings, our candidates did not drag their families with them when they took to the hustings. This spared us the present rash of "woman's angle" reports in the press about what Wilma, the candidate's wife, wore when he talked at a noonday luncheon in the Hotel Stentorian; what Wilma wore when he talked at late afternoon and presented a gold medal—gift of his admirers—to a messenger boy of eighty whose bones had been turning to chalk for fifty years; and what Wilma wore when he talked in the evening to the annual convention of Potato Chip Manufacturers of the Tri-States. We didn't give a damn about Wilma. Our assumption was that we were voting for the candidate, not for his dear little wife and equally dear little children, making a distinction only when the candidate was running for a local office such as circuit court clerk. Then we might have voted for a man because his wife was impossible and his children improbable, presenting him with office as a booby prize, so to speak, in the game of life.

The nation had not then lost its sense of privacy, that privacy which seems to wither as democracy flourishes and was anciently regarded as an aspect of dignity. It was also an article of faith among us that the family was desirable and was here to stay. Politicians, therefore, did not find it necessary to drag their wives and children to the platform in an almost belligerent display of family continuity and solidarity, a display sometimes so repulsively blatant as seemingly to justify Samuel Butler's surly comment that "more effort has been made to hold together that artificial collection called the human family than any other institution."

A flag-draped rostrum was built for the speakers and local dignitaries to occupy. As many chairs as could be borrowed from the undertaker and Sunday schools were placed before it on the chigger-infested grass. In them sat the early comers. The rest of the people stood and crowded as close as possible to the rostrum to hear in the absence of present-day loudspeakers. The absence, however, was not as great a handicap to the speakers of that time as one might imagine. Many of them had been hog callers in their youth or, playing to the crowd as wholesome, cawn-fed, country boys, boasted of membership in this elect fraternity. Every speaker, regardless of how he achieved his effects, made himself clearly heard on the most distant edges of the gathering as he thunderously discussed the "issues" and gave his opponents "down the country."

The proceedings, as rigid convention required, were opened by a minister who, among other things, asked God to fill the aspirant public servants with zeal and wisdom to serve the commonwealth. One of patient faith, he was undeterred that on former occasions God had been remiss or forgetful to do so. Sometimes the preacher prayed so long that the candidates became fidgety on the platform. For, religion or no, the morning was passing, and it is hard to get a voter's mind on politics when he has it fixed on eating and itches to get in his hands a morsel of barbecued pig rich with rural juices. Hence distraught candidates occasionally set up a silent spiritual counterrevolution and prayed that the Lord stop the preacher's praying.

The audience, no matter how long the preacher sought God's grace, stood with heads bowed. A member of it, the ordeal continuing, had a certain leeway not permitted the candidates on the platform, who stood before the eyes of the pious and impious alike. He could straighten his neck, scratch chigger bites on his legs, shoo away flies or ants, or slap at a mosquito. But the candidates had to stand there with bowed head though they were plagued with ants and flies. For among us, as in so many other places of the nation, we took it that the angle of adoration is equal to the angle of inclination of the neck.

Following the invocation, the master of ceremonies arose. A "distinguished member of the Washington County bar," he introduced the man who would introduce "the next speaker." The next speaker was invariably "one who needs no introduction to this audience." Yet he was always introduced in a nonstop flight of at least ten thousand runaway words, similes fighting for their lives against colliding metaphors, apostrophes suddenly cut down by anticlimaxes appearing from an unexpected direction. Finally, bringing order out of chaos, the verbal battleground cleared of dangling participles, split infinitives, bleeding verbs, and limping adjectives, the speaker rose to his peroration. It was, typically, rather like this:

> Our distinguished guest from the beautiful, majestic hills of Oktibbeha County, where the sun shines and the moon gleams on the fairest land the sun has even shone upon, is a God-fearin', native-born Mississippian who loves his native state, a Redman, a Beaver, an Elk, a Woodsman of the World, a soldier who served his country at Santiago and his county as a justice of the peace, a good church member, a devoted husband and father, a successful hay-and-feed dealer, an outstanding citizen, worthy son of a worthy sire, and loved by all who know him. Ladies and

gentlemen, it is my great privilege and honor—one which I deeply appreciate—
to present to you . . .

Mississippi has had strong men. It has had silent men, but it has had few strong,
silent men. It is a mark of sectional difference that while some New Yorkers may
be born with silver spoons in their mouths, all male Mississippians are born
with silver tongues in their throats. One of them may modestly demur, when
called upon in public "to say a few words," that "I did not come here today to
make a speech." But he will effortlessly make one just the same, words tumbling
upon words like the impetuous raindrops of July. If, then, our candidates often
had little to say, they had a thousand ingenious ways in which to say it.

A stranger to the community often began by expressing his great—sometimes
he made it sound almost lewd—pleasure at being in Greenville "where I have so
many splendid friends" and in Washington County "that has produced some of
the noblest women and finest men in the great state of Mississippi." He had been
born, he confided in shy, autobiographical mood, a po' boy. (If he had had the
sense to choose rich parents at birth, he would have automatically been disqualified for holding office.) His God-fearin' parents, who had raised him to be God-
fearin', had been blessed not with material goods, but with a plentitude of
children. Picking cotton in his youth—"honest labor never did hurt boy or
man"—he had worked his way through that "great school over yonder in
Starkville that has always been a credit to this great state—the Mississippi Agricultural and Mechanical College."

For vaguely esoteric reasons—perhaps because it did not teach useful things
such as how to treat a sick cow—the University of Mississippi was tainted in the
minds of many sturdy yeomen with a touch of the plutocratic. Its highfalutin'
graduates could hardly be expected to be faithful to a public trust reposed in
them by one-mule farmers, many of whom, with a rural distrust of city slick-
ers masquerading as bankers, put their money in mason jars and kept the jars in
bee trees.

Far worse was the fate of the rare candidate who had been so misguided as to
attend a northern university—the fate of Mike Conner, a Yale graduate, who
overcame this youthful indiscretion only with difficulty when he ran for governor. In an extreme form, therefore, we manifested an attitude marked throughout the United States. We were devoted to "education." But were dubious of the
educated.

Young Deltans, then, aspirant to careers in their native state—especially to
political or legal careers—felt that they must attend a Mississippi college. There
they would make "contacts" useful to them throughout life, and because so many
of us spend so much of our lives "contacting" others, one may as well begin early
to master this difficult art, an art overwhelmingly attractive because it "pays."

Since in this context life is a crowded alleyway in which everyone spends his
energies scratching the back of the other fellow and having his back scratched in

turn, there was little point in our going to Harvard, say, or more foolhardily to European universities where so many southerners used to do postgraduate work, including Senator John Sharp Williams of Mississippi. There one would strike up only a useless friendship with men who would never vote in Mississippi or sue a Mississippi railroad for running over a mule.

Obliquely illustrative of the compelling power of "contacts" was my experience at a political rally and fish fry held near Lake Village, Arkansas, across the Mississippi from Greenville. I had chatted pleasantly enough with the governor of Arkansas until His Excellency learned that he was wasting time talking to a man who could not vote in his state. He thereupon dropped me as though I were a wood tick and turned to a Chicot County farmer, a valid voter.

After the candidate—to return to the "speaking"—had recounted a few items of personal history, he forged a glowing apostrophe to the memory of Robert E. Lee—The War still sharply in the minds of many of his listeners—whom he had learned "to revere at my sainted mother's knee." Then he aired his veneration for Jefferson Davis (a native son), "the plumed knight, the peerless leader of the Lost Cause." Once a genius scored a great success by saying that his venerated father, while a soldier boy of the Confederacy, had "held Traveler," Lee's famous horse. As time passed, so many imitators endowed themselves with Traveler-holding ancestors that I finally understood why the South lost The War. Traveler "held" most of the time, Lee rarely moved.

No candidate left the platform without "paying tribute" to the Southern Woman. God, it appeared, the moment he had finished Pike's Peak, lovingly fashioned the Southern Woman of the meringue of snowy summer clouds and nectar from the slender throats of morning glories. One could conclude only that the Northern Woman—since the manner of her creation was not mentioned—was probably thrown together of any old leftovers that God found around the kitchen.

The hyperbolic flourishes of southern chivalry engaged the attention of Mark Twain, who noted this sentence in the New Orleans *Times-Democrat:* "On Saturday, early in the morning, the beauty of the place graced our cabin, and proud of her fair freight the gallant little boat glided up the bayou." This led Twain to remark that the only trouble with southern reporters was women, a trouble painfully evident in this description of the ladies at a New Orleans mule race: "The New Orleans women were always charming, but never so much as at this time of the year, when in their dainty spring costumes they bring with them a breath of balmy freshness and an odor of sanctity unspeakable."

After so long a time, the speaker got down to business. He fearlessly took his stand first on the Bible and then over the bodies of Jefferson, Jackson, Bryan, Robert Burns, and Stoddard of the famous *Lectures.* He was for the Democratic party, a bigger state insane hospital, better schools, and higher prices for cotton. Failing such prices, he stood for a more equitable relationship between the prices of meat (sowbelly) and cotton. Statesmen, economists, and plain folks agreed that a man just couldn't make out on five-cent cotton and ten-cent meat. But I never heard anyone so ill-mannered as to suggest that we might get off our well-anchored bottoms and raise our own meat instead of paying Iowans to do it for us.

In retrospect I shudder at the terrible crises through which we were continually passing. There was always, according to the speakers, a "g-r-r-e-a-t crisis confronting this state." We endured in a hell of our own—though not of our making—since we were never going anywhere along a straight road but, torn by indecision, forever "stood at the crossroads." Under these circumstances, only a certain native robustness kept us from cracking up.

Who kept us trembling on the verge of ruin? What prevented this fair land of ours from becoming an Eden where all that a man had to do was to reach up and pick him some peaches or throw his line into a creek and pull in a mess of goggle-eye perch fit to kill they wanted to get into the skillet so bad?

"Why, my friends," the candidate would tell us, "everybody knows who they are." "They" were the Republicans in Washington, in league with Wall Street and the Devil, who were jointly represented by J. P. Morgan and John D. Rockefeller; the "interests" that drank the blood of the common people; the railroads that were crushing the state in their "octopus grip, every tentacle slimy with corruption"; and speculators, "greedy, selfish, sinister men," who got rich off the sweat of the people by keeping the price of cotton low.

Who could doubt that all these would vanish when the candidate should come into office "as the intelligent electorate of this great state exercises its sovereign right of franchise on November second, I thank you."

Speechmaking continued for hours. Every introducer made a long speech about his statesman-candidate—"a man who . . .". (Other states may have led a wretched existence under the misguided direction of venal, ignorant politicians, but Mississippi flowered—or was always about to flower—under the enlightened leadership of incorruptible statesmen.) Then the candidate arose. If he did not "make the welkin ring," he "uttered a clarion call." One who spoke for only an hour felt that he had wrought a masterpiece of compression. One who spoke for two hours sometimes sat down wondering how he had managed to say so much so briefly.

No man talked a short time or wanted to do so—all remarks were called an "address by the Honorable So-and-So"—for several reasons. We regarded long-windedness in the candidate as the mark of the statesman, just as it was the mark of the good buggy horse. The candidate favored the long talk over the short because his lungs were more attuned to the marathon than to the sprint, while his faith lay more in his powers of concussion than conviction. The political rally, moreover, was a serious as well as a festive occasion because we took politics seriously. The candidate, then, who might make a little, ole, piddlin' talk of only thirty minutes' duration would have been thought to be dealing with us flippantly. Hence the winds of oratory, burdened with rotund periods and heavily freighted with misquoted verse, blew through much of the long day.

Some of our most successful speakers used a language that never was on land or sea. Touched with a bastard King Jamesian eloquence recalling to a Bible-reading audience the majesty and beauty of the Bible, and compounded with a funeral-home sentimentality—faded carnations on a Gates Ajar tombstone—it was almost as useful as colorful invective. One of our governors, for example, often used this effective tearjerker: "I want to live so that when my summons come to cross the Great Divide and enter my Father's house, a house not made with hands, eternal in the heavens, that I shall be able to look upon the long stretching sands of time that flow down across this country and see where my earthly feet have trod, to find footsteps of service to the people of Mississippi. That when I go down to the silent tomb of the dreamless dead, I shall be able to hold in the hollow of my right hand a record of service to my fellow man."

About six o'clock in the afternoon the meeting neared its end. The sun slowly descended into the Mississippi. Crows went sailing by to roosts in nearby woods as mosquitoes began to leave them. Blue woodsmoke curled from chimneys on the farms that surrounded us, evidence that folks were fixin' to cook supper. Sometimes the stately periods of the orator speaking during the late afternoon were blurred as a distant Negro hollered to his laggard homing heifer: "Soo cow! Soo cow! I say cow, soo!" At Greenway Park stood nearly all of our streetcars waiting to take us to town. The motormen chatted as they waited or hunted for four-leaf clovers—there were no conductors because our cars were run on the honor system, each passenger dropping his nickel in a cigar box as he entered—and when silence succeeded the last burst of applause they knew that the speaking was over. Soon we poured out to them, tired but exhilarated. Gongs clanged, and democracy having been served, the cars rattled homeward.

The Delta, however, seldom put a local man into an important office. It was consistently outvoted by the hill section of Mississippi, and there was a long-standing antipathy between the areas. Hill folks regarded Deltans as sinful, show-off " 'ristercrats," the catalog of their vices long. They had hogged the rich bottomlands of the state, where they lived in "painted houses" and drank "package cawfee" as did the wicked rich elsewhere. Some of them sent their children to school up North as though Mississippi schools were not good enough for anybody, while others, communicants of the Episcopal church, were uncomfortably close to Popishness. Fine-feathered folk whose farmers called themselves "planters" and wore Sunday clothes 'most anytime, they disdained honest manual labor as beneath the dignity of white people, and their area teemed with Negroes who were unwelcome in the hills.

Worse still, Negroes not only were an essential part of the Delta's economy but also shared to some extent the blessings of its fat lands. The while God-fearin', Bible-readin', church-goin' white hillmen, whose pappies or grand-pappies had fit the Yankees, were condemned to till scrawny, upside-down acres. There nothing but a little ole rabbit mule could crawl up the steep turnrows, and it was said that you had to tie a stone to the tail of a big-headed razorback hog so that he could keep his balance while hunting scaleybarks on the slanting hills. It wa'nt right!

Deltans, on the other hand, looked askance at hill people because they had small, diversified, subsistence farms, instead of big plantations. Hillmen grew little cotton but produced instead such unromantic things as sweet potatoes, sorghum molasses, chickens, and other items unbecoming gentleman tillers of the soil. (It scarcely mattered to the Delta that it led a prince or pauper existence or that the hill agriculture was more rational and stable than its own.) The Delta, moreover, for a variety of reasons social and economic, preferred Negroes on the land to whites; for one thing, they had the inestimable virtue of being far more docile than hill whites and less likely to resort to the pistol in the event of a quarrel. The Delta was therefore pleased that when the river threatened the levee it frightened back into the hills some who had come from that section, people who, among other shortcomings, toiled with their women alongside them in the fields. Yet a few hill folks clung to the Delta—they were later to arrive in considerable numbers—and occasionally one saw how sharply different from the natives were their attitudes toward Negroes.

My friend Bob Wing was once a member of a Washington County jury trying a Negro for a minor criminal offense. The defendant, who had a good reputation in the community, had achieved the eminence of becoming a "jump-steady," that is, one who "jumps steady" when the straw boss hollers "jump!" Bob and the other Deltans were for his acquittal. But the one hillman of the group—a bearded patriarch—was set against acquittal. He took off his shoes in the jury room, let down his galluses, settled back in his chair, and defiantly said, "I'm fixin' to stay here a week. I ain't got no reason to hurry home. My wife's pregnant and I done got shet of my milk cows." There was a mistrial.

The Delta had the painted houses and package cawfee. But the good Lord, as colored folks have sagely observed, "scatters out his good things." He had not only blessed hillmen with many children—a beneficence that he strangely withheld from Deltans—but their population was largely white and the Delta's largely Negro. Since, however, Negroes could not vote, hillmen out-voted the Delta. Thus, having a majority in the legislature, they shifted the burden of taxation onto their rich, sinful neighbors of the fertile bottomlands on one of those felicitous occasions when men doing the Lord's work also find that they are doing their own.

[*Cohn's analysis of the Delta-hills schism in Mississippi politics is misleading. Whites in the Delta and other counties benefited mightily from a legislative apportionment scheme that favored black-majority counties where practically no blacks voted. Black-majority counties dominated major committees in the legislature, where such power to govern as existed in Mississippi actually resided. Moreover, a three-fifths vote requirement for approval of all revenue measures helped Delta representatives resist efforts to increase their tax burdens.*][3]

In the long interval between the past of which I have been speaking and the present, great changes have come to Mississippi. Men no longer believe that what was good for grand-pappy is good enough for them. But from this radical revaluation of values they have omitted the Democratic party. For all their cars and painted houses and package cawfee and canned sardines mighty nigh any time a man wants to eat 'em—things as common now in Mississippi as they were once uncommon—the majority of the people remain straight-ticket-voting Democrats.

3. See James C. Cobb, *The Most Southern Place on Earth: The Mississippi Delta and the Roots of Regional Identity* (New York, 1992), 202–203, 211–15.

5

Drunk on Cotton

In 1935, Cohn observed that in the Delta cotton was not just a crop but "a form of mysticism. . . . a religion and a way of life. . . . omnipresent here as a god is omnipresent. . . . omnipotent as a god is omnipotent, giving life and taking life away." Here he elaborates on the "cotton-centric" nature of the Delta's economy and society.[1]

Writing in the New York *Times,* Anne O'Hare McCormick said in 1930, "Cotton is something more than a crop or an industry; it is a dynastic system, with a set of laws and standards always under assault and peculiarly resistant to change. It is map maker, troublemaker, history maker. . . . It was cotton that made the South into a section. . . . On cotton . . . the South built up a social and political economy essentially different from that prevailing in the rest of the country."

Cotton growing in the Mississippi Delta of my youth was all this and more. It was a secular religion, a mystique of the soil, an obsession, a defiance of logic and probability. It remained "peculiarly resistant to change" and went massively upon its way whatever the obstacles before it. This is how it was in Delta cotton fields when I was a boy.

"How's crops?" This phrase, inquiry and salutation, was in our minds or on our lips for much of the year. "Crops" meant only one crop—cotton. It had meant only this crop since the first settlers came to the Delta in the 1840s. And this is what it had meant when Senator Hammond of South Carolina told the Senate just before Sumter: "Cotton is king! You dare not make war upon it!"

Our community was of, by, for cotton. It grew to the outskirts of our little town that was itself the provincial capital of a cotton-intoxicated area. It also grew up to the yard of the planter's house. If he had had his way, it would have been grown to his doorstep. But his ladyfolks, loving lawns, trees, and flowers, kept cotton beyond the gate.

Sitting on the gallery of the planter's house in early spring, one was close to Negro plowmen who jested with the cook as they passed, and one watched birds following them as they sought worms in the upturned earth. The spectacle brought alive dreary homilies that one constantly heard about the early bird, busy bee, industrious ant. But my friend Galley, the hostler, a wise man, held there

---

1. David L. Cohn, *Where I Was Born and Raised* (Cambridge, Mass., 1948), 41.

was no virtue in toil. It was, rather, a penance inflicted on us for our ancestor's sins. "If Ole Adam," said Galley, "hadn't a-got messed up with Miss Eve an' that no-'count snake, ain't nair one o' us would have to hit a lick o' work."

(Years later, I read this passage in Freud: "As a path to happiness," he wrote, "work is not valued very highly by men. They do not run after it as they do after other opportunities for gratification. The great majority work only when forced by necessity, and this natural human aversion to work gives rise to the most difficult social problems.")

Town and country were one in their adoration of cotton and almost complete economic dependence upon it. Wall Street has it that a man must "not fall in love with a stock," that is, permit emotion to affect his judgment. If this is rationality, it is also the death of love. It did not enter into Delta judgments about cotton.

John Henry, the legendary Negro Hercules, was born with a cotton hook in his right hand, and we, children of Greenville, were born with the aroma of cottonseed oil in our nostrils, the sight of cotton in our eyes, and talk about it in our ears. In spring, little Delta towns were drab islands amid green seas of cotton plants; against them in autumn beat white waves of cotton. The waves tumbled foamy upon counters of banks and fell softly before rural churches whose congregations, as the Bible enjoined, tithed.

Our roads were alive in autumn with mule-drawn, cotton-laden wagons creaking toward the gins, a Negro driving and often a companion asleep on the piled whiteness who seemed to go—so he was—Elijah-like upon a gossamer cloud. There were cotton bales at railroad stations and steamboat landings; loose cotton upon the galleries of sharecroppers' cabins; cotton buyers with fragments of the staple—the Star and Garter of their exalted guild—clinging to their clothing; and cotton samples on the counters of banks and tables of cotton merchants and in the hand trucks of the American Express Company.

Mules were everywhere. On Saturdays, our town's big shopping day, buggy and ridin' mules stood at hitchin' racks, their long, velvety-haired ears twitching at unfamiliar urban sounds. We boys sometimes visited mule dealers' barns. There families of sparrows nested and grew fat upon grain, and there light and shadow played a perpetual game of hide-and-go-seek upon the walls.

If you traveled by train through the Delta, mules in the barn lots, made fearful by the locomotive's whistle, galloped in the erratic patterns of panic. If you went by car or buggy, you went down lanes of mules observing strangers with rural curiosity behind pasture fences.

The mule affected our language. "He's stubborn as a mule," we would say. Or, "I been workin' like a mule." If you were "insulted," you might retort: "Well, I just consider the source, like the old lady who was kicked by a mule." Once, when a field hand was tried for manslaughter, his defense was that the deceased had "been kickin' in another man's stall." Verdict: justifiable homicide.

Only men ignorant of mules were foolish enough to say, "He ain't got no more sense than a jug-headed mule." For it was demonstrable that the mule had more sense than any other of our animals and perhaps as much as most of us. The mule, allegedly coarse-grained, ate fastidiously. Yet the horse, allegedly refined, often, so to say, made a hog of itself and foundered on its own oats. The mule, moreover, would not be put upon. You might work men and horses to death. But not the mule. It would work and bear loads only within self-imposed limitations. Thereafter you could beat it or get down on your knees to it in abject beseechment, but it would not stir until the source of its grievance was removed.

Perhaps, however, the mule's essential superiority over men and horses lay in this: A stubborn individualist with an often sardonic sense of humor, it was free of those absurd posturings so common to the human male and the stallion as they flaunt their maleness.

Certainly the mule's contributions to the South exceeded those of most of its politicians, boosters, preachers, bankers, and lawyers. Yet the South has composed no sonnets in its honor or decreed any fete day in its name. Fortunately for the region's honor, however, one southerner at least is aware of the region's shabby neglect of this admirable creature, and William Faulkner wrote in *Sartoris*, "some Homer of the cotton fields should sing the saga of the mule and his place in the South. He it was, more than any other creature or thing, who, steadfast to the land where all else faltered before the hopeless juggernaut of circumstance . . . won the prone South from beneath the iron heel of Reconstruction and taught it pride again through humility, and courage through adversity overcome; who accomplished the well-nigh impossible despite hopeless odds, by sheer and vindictive patience."

As mules entered into our language, so did cotton. Thus a man might say of his health, "I'm fair to middlin'," an allusion to a basic cotton grade—middling.

Sometimes we saw the Bible in cotton terms. There was a legend along Cotton Row in Memphis, where cotton merchants have their offices, that Cain killed Abel because Abel classed Cain's cotton as low middling when it deserved the higher classification of strict low middling.

Men often told the rosary of time with cotton, the remembrance of things past in their eyes as the beads dreamily slipped through their fingers: "I recollect eighteen and ninety-six when we had so much cotton we never did pick it all out." Or, "I recall nineteen and seven. The boll weevil hit us and I didn't make enough cotton on four hundred acres to stuff a mattress."

Among us, cotton was omnipresent. It had a foremost place in our thoughts. Sometimes it entered into community prayer when, in time of destroying rains, men implored the Lord to send his saving sun. It was always present at meetings of local governing bodies and the state legislature. Our representatives swung its white censer in the remote cathedral of Congress. It starred our folklore, was the staple of our talk, the stuff of our dreams, the poesy of many of our songs. It interrupted even the majestic course of the law. For when the cotton was deep in grass and hoe hands fought to save the crop, the regular term of Washington County Circuit Court was postponed. Then defendants, plaintiffs, jurymen, witnesses, and courtroom hangers-on might stay in or around the threatened fields. The law could wait.

Sometimes we tempered justice with cotton. If one field hand was being tried for killing another and the planter and neighbors testified that the defendant was a diligent man who didn't "mess around," the chances were that the jury would free him or give him a light sentence. He was almost sure to be freed if it appeared that the slain man was just a "strange nigger" who had wandered onto the plantation from Lord knows where. You did not imprison a good farmer merely to satisfy the unimaginative law.

Townsmen followed the fortunes of the crop with unwavering interest from planting to picking. They groaned when an unseasonal freeze destroyed the first planting. They were unhappy when too much rain fell. But they were also unhappy when it did not rain enough for the corn needed for the mules that cultivated the fields. (Corn requires more rain than cotton. But since both grew simultaneously, the Lord was hard put to space his rains so that cotton did not get too much moisture and corn got enough.) Sometimes, as all seemed to be going well with the crop, men's composure vanished when a well-known planter casually said at Hallett's Barber Shop that he was troubled by army worms, or an equally well-known planter told L. Pink Smith, publisher of the *Democrat,* that boll weevils were giving his crop "fits." The bad news ran through town. It affected nearly everybody except the young bloods in Dischel's Pool Parlor. Whatever the impending calamity, they coolly adjusted their armbands and calmly chalked their cues in preparation for a difficult shot, the usually noisy onlookers silent, as protocol demanded, at this critical moment.

As the crop grew, the *Democrat* reported that "John Wilks, a negro farmer of near Wayside, today brought us the season's first cotton bloom." Whereupon old citizens snorted. In their time, they said, before folks got lazy and no 'count with a lot of newfangled ideas, first blooms appeared earlier than nowadays. Thereafter, Greenville awaited Washington's estimate of the size of the forthcoming national crop. It would sharply affect the price of cotton, an element much affected by conditions in Texas, the largest grower. We did not wish Texas any harm. But if its crop was poor and ours was good, I heard few laments for the plight of Texas.

Once, as the time neared for releasing the estimate, I had heard talk confusing to a young boy. Some of my father's friends, it appeared, were buying or selling "futures." One bought cotton from another who had no cotton. One sold cotton he did not have to a man who wanted it. Since this was impossible, I put it down to the craziness of adults, a phenomenon that often troubles children. Yet my assurance was shaken when a friend, in whose big house I played, had to move with his family into a smaller one because, it was said, his Papa had been "ruined by July futures." This made no sense to me, and I turned with relief to Henty's *The Cat of Bubastes.*

The state of cotton during the growing season took precedence of everything else among us. Thus the question of townspeoples' comfort or cotton's progress was spontaneously settled in favor of cotton; that is, if wishing could affect the weather. When, therefore, the sun stood day after day a blazing furnace above our town and the steaming nights were sodden blankets pressing down upon us, we cheerfully endured our acute discomfort. For hot weather, day and night, is good for cotton.

By August the crop was made. Soon the season's first bale appeared and was given a place of honor on the sidewalk of Poplar Street to await its auctioning. There cotton buyers had offices, and the tickers of a "wire house" told us the state of the market in New Orleans and Liverpool. Passing men stopped to look wonderingly at the bale as though they had never before seen one and musingly touched its jute wrapper. Sometimes, as onlookers good-naturedly jeered, one would pull a lock of cotton from the bale and attempt to "class" it—determine its fiber length, whiteness, grade. Then perhaps a professional classer would step up, take the cotton in his sensitive fingers, and class it.

The bale transiently made the group one. It represented their hopes. It was the Golden Fleece they everlastingly sought. It was the symbol that bound them in a certain kind of economic, political, social culture.

After some days on the sidewalk, the bale was auctioned. The seller got several times the going price for cotton while, not less important, he acquired the prestige of grower of the season's first bale.

If it appeared that the crop would be good, the town threw off its summer lethargy. Railroads assembled freight cars. Gins, cottonseed oil mills, and compresses looked to their machinery. Bankers dusted off old promissory notes. Then they made calculations, half actuarial and half dreamful, of the possibilities of payments. Merchants ordered goods from drummers or went on buying trips to St. Louis or New York. Negro household servants anticipated their annual cotton-picking expeditions to the fields. Posters flamed on country barns and town walls announcing the coming of Gentry's Dog and Pony Show. Mr. Harrington, our leading mule dealer, left for Columbia, Tennessee, to buy mules. Cotton buyers, representing foreign and domestic mills, moved into the Hotel Cowan. Reisinger, catcher for our baseball team in the Cotton States League, and Shackleford, our left fielder—a hitter if there ever was one—got jobs in town and prepared to stay until the next ball season began. Soon everybody would eat high off the hog.

Our rich lands, hot sun, abundant rains, knowing labor, and long growing season made for the relatively easy production of large cotton crops. Yet we did not prosper. Men had long argued that the one-crop, high-risk cotton economy was a curse. One might have demonstrated that if a planter should put part of his land in asparagus instead of planting all of it to cotton, he might sharply increase his profits. But asparagus is not cotton. Growing a vegetable might become a poor foreigner newly arrived here. It would not become a cotton planter, while to descend to it would be to descend almost to the status of a tradesman.

(In Spain, landowners haughtily refused the suggestion that they could enrich themselves by devoting their lands and energies to the production of beef cattle. They preferred instead, at whatever sacrifice of money rewards, to grow fighting bulls for the rings of Spain.)

The fatal flaw in the argument of the diversifiers of agriculture was that it was rational. Our planters were moved by many noneconomic considerations, and few errors are so profound as that which regards man as primarily an economic animal. Certainly it is irrational to assume that because men are capable of arriving at rational conclusions, they will necessarily do so. Is human life itself invariably rational?

The Delta owner of extensive lands lived, not on a farm, but on a plantation. He was known, not as a farmer, but as a planter. "Farmer" then connoted among us a cautious, small landowner with a bit of the overalled, goateed hick about him, not unlike the fiddlin', turkey-in-the-straw comedian one sometimes saw upon the Orpheum stage in Memphis.

The word "planter" was rich with other connotations. It was a link with the antebellum past, reminiscent of the dream, if not always the reality, of what had been. It conjured up a certain lordliness of living and a touch of the romantic. (In novels the planter was sometimes a romantic but never the farmer. The planter occasionally died in a duel; the farmer of lockjaw got by stepping on a rusty nail.) It suggested the gentleman sprung of a long line of gentlemen, one who had not vulgarly earned wealth but had inherited it, a man with a flair for command, possessor of a cavalier dash that mocked at the dull virtue of caution and scorned the pedestrian uses of compound interest piling up in a bank. Under these circumstances arguments for diversification were little effective. They left men's hearts untouched.

No occupation, moreover, was so worthy of a gentleman as being a planter of cotton, lordliest of crops. Nothing so pleased men's spirits as growing it. No music was so sweet to their ears as the clatter of cottonseed in the suction pipes of gins. No still life was so dear as jute-wrapped bales on the gin's platform awaiting transfer to railroad station or steamboat landing. No sight was so stirring as the silvery flashings of hoes in the hands of a hundred Negroes getting the cotton out of the grass. No encounter was so warmly pleasant as riding homeward on a horse at first dusk to meet field hands riding the mules to the lot, each politely tipping his cap to the boss man and saying softly, "Good evenin', Mistuh Ed."

No other vocation gave a man such a gracious, spacious way of earning a living, one that almost demanded of him, in a day when the order was elsewhere extinct in the United States, that he should be a *grand seigneur.* These were things of the landed gentry, things that hearkened back to Old England among a group of predominantly English ancestry. They stirred deeply in the souls of men who still called justices of the peace "squires."

These men were descendants of, or successors to, an extraordinary group of men—antebellum planters. They were the most articulate and passionate defenders of the agricultural interest the United States has ever known. There were only a few thousand of them. Yet they achieved the extraordinary feat of creating the image of the Old South that still lingers in men's minds, while imposing their views upon a whole region. This, whether they were right or wrong, they did in the only way possible: dominating the majority of the people by strength of character and force of conviction. This feat seems the more extraordinary to us for the men dominated were neither milksops nor servile but were, on the contrary, proud, touchy frontiersmen with a fierce sense of personal freedom and of being as good as the next man. Yet they not only enthusiastically accepted the leadership of a handful of planters but followed them into the fiery hell of civil war.

While the planter among us was often preoccupied with his affairs, he was rarely absorbed by them. He had brought with him from Virginia and Kentucky a strong sense of personal honor, a liveliness of conversation, a sharp interest in politics, and usually a respect for, if not always a desire to participate in, the life of the mind. He loved gambling, whether at the gaming table or in the cotton fields, and at his best was marked by noblesse oblige. Sometimes this brought him upon evil days because he would not economize by reducing his labor force. How are you going to put on the road old Uncle Tobe and Aunt Sally? Hadn't they worked faithfully for your father for twenty years and equally faithfully for you until old age was upon them? Where could they go in their feebleness? Who would care for them?

[*To Cohn the planter was the ultimate arbiter of good manners in the Delta, and as William Alexander Percy observed, manners were essential to the stability of Delta society.*][2]

Yawps about southern manners still go up. One might commend to petulant critics in the field the words of the Hebrew writer of long ago—Solomon ibn Gabirol. "What is the test of good manners?" he asked. "Being able to bear patiently with bad ones," he replied.

One critic finds it repellent that University of Virginia students greet one another by saying, "Gentlemen," instead of grunting, "Hey." He finds it equally repellent that students and faculty members meeting on the street lift hats to one

2. William Alexander Percy, *Lanterns on the Levee: Recollections of a Planter's Son* (Baton Rouge, 1974), 286, 307.

another. One might assume from such complaints that the amenities would be better served and democracy's frontiers extended if the students should growl and thumb their noses at the faculty, on the assumption that boorishness and republicanism are synonymous.

White and Negro Deltans, however, regarding manners as exercises in good taste and propriety, clung to them. They remembered perhaps the great step upward from the beast that man took when he first brought food to his mouth instead of taking his mouth to the food. And when men discarded the sleeves of their coats for table napkins, they were well on their way to lifting their hats to one another on the street.

Sometimes Delta manners were more picturesque than polished. In one of our towns there was a "widow man" who had brought up two daughters after their mother had died when they were young. When the girls began to have beaux, Papa ruled that they must be out of the house by ten o'clock. He sat up and when the witching hour approached, he uttered a premonitory grunt at the parlor door. But one evening, the swains lingering a bit beyond their allotted time, Papa stood at the door, made a polite bow to the company and said, "Gentlemen, you sons of bitches, it's time to go home." The gentlemen left, but they returned and married the daughters.

Tides of familial and business interests flowing back and forth between townsmen and planters, it was inevitable that the planter's mentality, planter's manners, planter's attitudes should affect townspeople. Values held by elites nearly always filter down and affect the whole society around them. There were differences between townsmen and planters, but the lines were not sharply drawn. Members of both groups, moreover, were largely of the same Anglo-Saxon stock, political party, and Protestant religion. Sharing a common tradition, the perils of the river, and the pains of pioneering, they were bound the closer by intermarriages. It was inescapable, then, that the town should become marked by the planter mentality and the plantation point of view, an outcome made the more certain by the complete absence among us of industrialists and industrialism.

6

It Ain't What I Owes That Worries Me

Shelby Foote described the Delta as a region "where credit is easy and crashes are hard,"
and LeRoy Percy observed that "easy credit has been the curse of this section." In 1930
the percentage of farms that were mortgaged was more than 60 percent higher in the Delta
than elsewhere in the state. In this chapter Cohn takes a lighthearted look at his region's
freewheeling approach to matters of economics and finance. He also describes the easy and
gracious existence enjoyed by whites who occupied the upper strata of the Delta's socio-
economic pyramid.[1]

If our politics was simple but frenzied, our economics was simple but bewil-
dering. Responding to no canons that I could find in the books, without
counterpart in other areas, it would have caused orthodox economists to shudder and might even have deterred Karl Marx, who nowhere in the long, dreary
stretches of *Das Kapital* uncovers anything so satisfying, so congenial, so novel.
Yet homeborn, homegrown, it was as native to the community as gourd dippers.

Our styles, the product of intuition rather than theory, were not planned. We
had no theoreticians among us; no shoeless Adam Smiths lived in the Delta, or
even sockless Jerry Simpsons. We simply evolved an economic way that met our
needs and proceeded happily on our course while the nation stumbled from one
course to another until, calamity upon it, it came to adopt our way nearly
twenty-five years ago.

Aside from its own virtues, the wonder of our system is that it sprang from an
unlikely background. For, you must understand, our people were largely Calvin-
ist. Many of them were given to a primitive religiousness, a Sabbath of unre-
lieved dreariness, an unshakable belief in Original Sin. ("In Adam's fall, we
sinned all.") Ole Satan, they held, walked the earth a-switchin' his tail; sometimes, in favored localities, he switched it around the clock. He it was who lured
the unwary into such devilments as card playing, dancing, and frolicking on Sundays. Occasionally he dragged them almost into the jaws of Hell as they became
victims of "Babylonian harlotry."

A portion of this chapter appeared in modified form as "Lots of Debts, But No Money Worries," *New York Times Magazine,* December 2, 1951, pp. 20, 22.

1. James C. Cobb, *The Most Southern Place on Earth: The Mississippi Delta and the Roots of Regional Identity* (New York, 1992), 310, 132.

This term puzzled me, for the community's harlotry, so far as I could see, was rather on the plain side, was but little gilded, and certainly did no honor to Astarte, the Semitic Venus. Yet primitive preachers constantly denounced our Babylonian harlotry. Crusaders against sin, implacable enemies of the Devil, hellbent from heaven, they described our harlotry in such libidinous detail and with such a wealth of luscious illustration that their congregations, lapping it up, sat bug-eyed, ears straining to catch every word, tongues hanging from their mouths. It was only just that, for delivering hammer blows upon the Devil's thick hide—may he perish in his own flames—these preachers were rewarded with large, enthusiastic, and, not less important, attentive congregations. But nonetheless—such is Ole Satan's deviousness—this was but part of a complex process by which men kept what they wanted of Calvinism and rejected what they did not want.

Thus, it was gospel that man was born into Original Sin. Yet labor—traditionally man's penance for it—was not therefore exalted among us as it was, say, in New England. ("And unto Adam he said, . . . in the sweat of thy face shalt thou earn thy bread.") So, too, business enterprise is a divine calling. Success in it attests to one's salvation and "predestination" to heaven. The Puritans held that the world was run by God's will, that God who "works mysteriously, his wonders to perform." This doctrine encouraged businessmen. There was room in it for the play of chance and competition, while—comfortingly—whatever happened was the will of divinity. Under its impetus there arose the powerful tribe of Puritan businessmen in the Netherlands, England, and New England. From this source also, we assumed, there stemmed the line of the New England poet, Longfellow, which, to our minds, indicated how greatly the wellsprings of American joy had been poisoned at their source: "Let us then be up and doing." We admired the same poet's "Hiawatha" and "The Village Blacksmith," but this line made little appeal to us.

Our people, with a few unhappy exceptions, had a relaxed attitude toward labor. Some, with a touching resignation to the soft airs of the Delta, renounced it completely. As for business enterprise, several young men—bitten by the alien bug of progress—hankered to establish a chamber of commerce. Its purpose was to induce foreign enterprisers to come among us. But most folks were little moved by this ambition. Others made it clear that they wanted no enterprises, for they would "just bring a lot of riffraff to town," "stir things up," and "ruin a nice place to live in."

Certainly work for work's sake had no appeal for us, and if Frederick Law Olmsted had visited us shortly after the turn of the century, he would have found us much as he found southerners when he traveled among them before 1861 and wrote: "The Southerner has no pleasure in labor except with reference to a result. He enjoys life itself. He is content with being. . . . The Northerner enjoys progress in itself. He finds his happiness in doing. Rest, in itself, is irksome and offensive to him. . . . Heaven itself will be dull and stupid to him, if there is no work to be done in it."

Northerners, he concluded, had many virtues lacking in southerners but, he said, they did not have much fun: "The people of the Northern States, as a whole, probably enjoy life less than any other civilized people. Perhaps it would be equally true to add—or than any uncivilized people."

Pleasure loving, we nonetheless clung to a strict Sabbatarianism, and for the majority of us, Sunday went interminably its bleak, joyless way. It did not matter that Calvin had called Sabbatarianism a "Jewish notion" or that James I had compelled ministers to read to congregations from his Book of Sports. There it was said, "For when shall the common people have leave to exercise if not upon the Sundays and Holidays, seeing that people must apply their labour and win their living in all working days."

This is all right as far as it goes, but it does not go far enough. It fails to consider the Devil, the tireless, versatile Devil, against whom good people must always be on guard. In our community, for example, he tempted people to destruction with the newfangled instrument—one of his most diabolical inventions—of motion pictures. Then, after so long when their resistance to evil was lowered, he took the next step toward their ruin. Some folks began to clamor for "Sunday movies," or at least the more godless clamored. Righteous people staved off this peril for a long time, but finally a pagan in high-button tan shoes introduced a bill into the Mississippi legislature to make legal the Sunday movies that were being widely bootlegged. Now one saw where sin leads.

A right-thinking legislator arose to oppose the bill and told a fearsome tale. On the preceding Sunday after church services, he told his colleagues, he was at home when his telephone rang. At the other end was one of his best friends, resident of a neighboring town, who begged him for God's sake to drop whatever he was doing and come to his house right away.

Alarmed and wondering, he drove swiftly to his friend's house to find his pale and shaken wife being treated by a doctor for shock. The most terrible calamity that could overtake a family had come to these fine people. For on that very afternoon, while other young people were at a missionary meeting, their daughter of eighteen, disobeying her parents, had gone to the movies—Sunday movies. And there, right in the movie house, she had been raped. Let every man, therefore . . .

It was an aspect of righteousness to inveigh against man's sinful estate on earth and ordain a cheerless Sabbath; indeed, by so doing a man acquired merit in the eyes of his neighbors and stored up merit for himself Up Yonder. Yet there were limits to the asceticism a people could be made to bear or ought to bear. Thus the ascetic virtues of thrift and hard work—or diligence in one's calling, as early Calvinists put it—might easily be overdone. Benjamin Franklin, employing these virtues as part of the gospel of success, made *Poor*

Richard's Almanack a popular tract in eighteenth-century America. But if he had run for Circuit Court clerk of Washington County on such a platform, he would have gotten nowhere. At bottom, Calvinism or no, our people preferred their way while clinging to some of the old forms, the way of romantic feudalism as against the gospel of success with its repellent attributes of thrift and hard work.

This had one spectacular result. The risks of a one-crop agriculture, plus the indifference to thrift of a pleasure-loving people, caused the Delta to go nearly broke at frequent intervals. Yet it never collapsed. It was sustained by factors that defied analysis, flew in the face of economic theory, and would have driven mad a community given to logic, that bastard child of philosophy never recognized by us.

Our chronic state was this: nearly always everybody owed everybody else. (The prevailing economic mood and wistful ambition of the area was enunciated to me by a Negro friend. "It ain't what I owes that worries me," he said. "It's gittin' to owe.") Hence, by tacit consent, creditors—who were invariably debtors of other creditors—kept their dunning within reason. Even when they repeatedly sent the same bills to the same men—bills that had been gathering moss for years—they maintained the fiction that the debtor had refrained from paying them only because he did not know he owed them. They, therefore, did not press their demands beyond saying, "We call to your attention this past due account that you have doubtless overlooked." Delta eyesight, excellent for wing-shooting or measuring the ingredients of a toddy in a giddily unstable room, was sometimes sadly deficient.

No creditor was so boorish as to sue a debtor. If one had done so, he would not only have faced social ostracism as an offender against a principal article in the category of Things Not Done, but would also have set off what we nowadays call a chain reaction and destroyed himself. Everybody, therefore, owed everybody else until a good cotton crop came along and there was an all-around scaling down of debts. The "clear receipt," however, indicating the erasing of a debt, was a novel document rarely seen, nor did its possession bring the holder any prestige.

Creditors outside the Delta presented a more difficult case to which the community brought to bear its considerable ingenuity in such cases. They sometimes, with a shocking lack of manners and loutish indifference to local customs, sued a local debtor and, the law being the law, got a judgment against him in our courts. But its execution—without which it is an empty thing—faced a high hurdle. The law was not flouted by us. It was merely frustrated.

It could not reasonably be expected of Justice of the Peace O'Bannon or Mr. George B. Alexander, the high sheriff of Washington County, that they should execute a judgment on behalf of some stranger in New York and so straightly affect a fellow townsman, a man whom they had known all their lives, a member perhaps of the same church, or an accomplished wingshot. It was well known, moreover, that everybody up North was just rolling in money. How, then, could a rich northern creditor be injured if he should have to wait a year or two—a short time by Delta reckoning in such a case—for a little ole dab of money to add to his already great pile?

I do not flatly say—for this would be to libel honorable men—that our guardians of the law set themselves deliberately to confound the statutes they were sworn to uphold. The fact is otherwise. As a kindly nature permits a sick man to fall into sleep, so it was that our law officers, in the embarrassing presence of judgment-holding creditors from afar, fell into a state of semi-coma that rendered them impotent to discharge distasteful duties. Semi-coma is a condition common to the Delta in spring and summer—especially when the fish are biting—and a little thing like a judgment can easily escape a man's mind until crisp autumn winds bring wakefulness. The moment, as it happens, coincides with cotton-picking time when, if ever, a Delta debtor might have some money. Then the guardian of the law, solicitous of his duties, mindful of the community's customs, and saving of the debtor's pride, might tactfully sound him out as to the possibility of paying what he owed. In all that pertained to the delicate matter of debts, our people of my day exercised an exquisite politeness.

By virtue of its unorthodox economics, the Delta kept going upon an aberrant course that would have made the heads of Vermonters swim with dizziness; how dizzy, I was able to understand from the perspective of later years. For once, a guest of Sinclair Lewis in his Vermont home, I asked his secretary—a man who had been born and brought up in the nearby village—what the villagers thought of him. Did they regard this restless writer as a red-thatched wild man, an irresponsible artist? I was told villagers thought well of him. They said approvingly, "He pays his debts and keeps his place up." These preeminent criteria of responsibility satisfied, whatever else he was or did was of no concern to the village.

When bad times came to the Delta, people hollered "po'mouf" and swore they would never again throw away their money if they should ever get ahold of any once more. Yet sellers of sackcloth and ashes would have starved among us. For our repentance was fleeting; we went on in bad times much as before, while our resolves melted without a trace in the sunshine of good times.

Things were tough, it was agreed, yet gentlemen continued to get their clothes at Greenley's or Brill's—our most eminent haberdashers—or ordered them custom-made by remote control from a "representative of the Rex Tailoring Company of Chicago, who will be in our store Monday to take your measurements." The more fastidious had their suits made at home by Joe Reilly. He superimposed Savile Row upon Poplar Street but nonetheless, being a proud and proper Irishman, did not hold himself out to be an "English tailor." His suits cost the unbelievable sum of $50.

In summer, when there was little to do, townsmen and planters came to town, played poker together, played the only kind worthy of red-blooded men—table stakes stud, in which you stake all upon your judgment. There were always, night or day, several games in progress, a ceiling fan droning over the players, a Negro close by to bring them a highball and occasionally catch a dollar chip thrown to him by someone who had raked in a good pot. Behind the players stood others watching and waiting to take their places when a participant, tracked down by his wife, had to cash in and go home. Thus the game had continuity if the players varied from time to time.

One of the most faithful of the gaming fraternity was a planter whose son was my high school classmate. I was struck by the manner of his father's rise to riches not only because it was melodramatic but also because, confusingly, it bore no relationship to what our elders, in and out of school, told us. They said that success was the reward of diligence, of savings and hard work. Yet here was success without diligence. What was one to believe?

The planter of whom I speak owed his success initially not to any of the copybook maxims but to a murder and a poker game. Once when he had been a Delta bookkeeper, a Louisiana friend killed a man and decamped. The murderer wrote him that he could have rent-free his plantation near Greenville provided he could borrow enough money to make a crop. The bookkeeper thereupon went to New Orleans to make a loan, but he was unsuccessful and dejectedly got on a boat to return home.

He was traveling in the heyday of Mississippi river gambling and, taking the little money he had in his pocket, got into a poker game. By the time the boat had reached Lake Providence, Louisiana—the last stop before Greenville—he was ahead by about $7,000. But he calculated this was insufficient for his purposes and played on until the vessel arrived at Helena, Arkansas, a day's journey north of Greenville. He now had $10,000 and so, staked for his initial planting venture, eventually became a wealthy planter.

If planters played poker for large stakes, lesser folks played for lesser stakes. One of the inveterate gamesters of this kind was Barney Wachsman, a local merchant whose pretty daughter, Carrie, clerked for my father. He left a legend to the town.

A conservative man who "played 'em close to the chest" in his lifetime, when he died his former card-playing companions sat up with his corpse all night before the burial. In the early hours of the morning, they were horrified to find one of the dead man's arms had become so rigid in an upright position that the coffin could not be closed. They debated what to do, no man daring to push down the lifeless arm. Finally one of the men called the others around him to the corpse. There he led them in chanting, "Barney Wachsman, I got four aces! Barney Wachsman, I got four aces!" The rigid arm immediately fell into place.

In the fall, whatever the state of prices or crops, men hunted deer, wild ducks, quail, sending braces of greenhead mallards or a dozen birds to friends. (Here, I regret to report, technology has dealt a grievous blow to Delta gallantry. For now that game can be kept in freezer lockers, fewer gentlemen send fewer birds to fewer ladies.) Many of our most active men about town made an annual pilgrimage to Hot Springs, Arkansas. Its magical waters were counted upon to volatilize the alcohol in their blood and armor them against another protracted infusion.

Ladies, as usual, bought their seasonal "outfits" at Nelms and Blum's. Dances and parties went their ordered way. Everybody visited and was visited by friends and relatives. "Central" had the time of her life listening in as lady telephoned lady to discuss the party that she was giving for "Mary Lee's vistor." The young married and went to New Orleans on their honeymoon. ("The bride wore a veil of illusion and carried a white satin Bible," reported the alert, omniscient *Democrat*.) They occupied an unaccustomed drawing room, which the curious jumped on the Pullman to inspect as much as to tell their friends good-bye. Behind them the couple left an imposing array of gifts from Binder's or Wallace Arnold's, our leading jewelers, or, more grandly, from the House of Brodnax in Memphis: cut glass bowls, silver bud vases, peacock feather fans, an Edison phonograph with wide, floral-decorated horn. And from a relative, given to the unhappy ways of practicality, there was a Bissell carpet sweeper.

Traveling road shows come to the Grand Opera House were well patronized by country people and townspeople. (Its versatile impresario, Mr. Will Isenberg, also owned the Greenville Ice and Coal Company.) It included William Farnum in "The Squaw Man," Sothern and Marlowe in "Romeo and Juliet," David Warfield in "The Music Master," Lew Dockstader's "Minstrels," and Balfe's "Bohemian Girl." I admired the latter greatly not only for its incomparable aria, "I dreamt that I dwelt in marble halls," but also for its unforgettable scene of the Gypsy encampment twinkling with the lights of innumerable campfires and a great white horse boldly ridden onstage.

After theatre, many of the playgoers—gentlemen wearing claw hammers and ladies in evening toilette with elbow-length white kid gloves—went to Muffulletto's for supper. Mirror-lined, an Old World air about it, our grandest restaurant served food that folks for miles around came to eat. An amiable camaraderie prevailed between its patrons and its proprietors, the Muffulletto brothers—Mr. Cholly, Mr. Sam, and Mr. Paul, who by turns served at the cooking range, the table, and the cash register or yelled to friends. Nearly everybody in the Delta was kinfolks of everybody else—kissin' kin—or was known by name and reputation to one another. Outside, for-hire hacks or privately owned carriages waited to take the company home.

In that far-off day before doctors had become disembodied corporations, a man could have his appendix removed without an embarrassing prior inquiry into the delicate question of his solvency, an inquiry that properly would have been regarded as an unwarrantable invasion of privacy. So, too, chain stores— headless, bloodless, dehumanized—with their unfriendly tactic of cash on the line or no cauliflower had not yet come to town. All of us, therefore, lived almost as well in bad times as in good times. The doctor and dentists waited to be paid, and with them the butcher, baker, ice man, coal man, grocer, dry goods merchant.

There were, it is true, a few things for which one had to have cash; among them, servants. But they were cheap, plentiful, cheerful except during cotton-picking time in the fall. Then, by a convention well understood on both sides, Greenville's cooks largely deserted their kitchens to go to the country and "pick." The work was hard, but it would not last forever, it was a welcome relief from the daily routine, and a good picker might earn as much as $2 a day. In town a cook was paid $3 to $6 a week, her wages supplemented by the universal custom of "totin'," whereby she took home food for her family from the white folks' kitchen.

The cook of that day was hardly plagued with leisure. She usually arrived at the house where she worked around six o'clock in the morning to build a fire in the wood-burning kitchen range and perhaps to make fires in the grates of the rooms where the family slept. She cooked three meals a day, part of the task being the killing, plucking, and dressing of chickens that many people kept in their backyards. In that pre-baby-sitter era, she often watched over children whose parents were out for the evening. And she "maided" her lady when her services were required, as they were often required in the days of tight lacing. Sometimes all the female hands in the house jointly tugged at the lady's corset strings in a contest between unyielding whalebone and the too-solid flesh.

A colored boy mowed the lawn for a quarter, stoked at noon with a pork chop sandwich, hot biscuits, and a jug of cold buttermilk provided by his employer. A washlady did the family laundry for $1.25 a week plus bluing and soap. And—happiest blessing of all perhaps—the best bottled-in-bond whiskey, its age and breeding certified by Uncle Sam's quart, sold for $1.50 a quart. The nation had not yet descended to the sly euphemism of "fifths," a devious method of raising the price of whiskey without coming right out and saying so. This was an important matter in the Delta, where a considerable part of the male population held whiskey in that high esteem which this noblest of alcoholic beverages merits.

Few things are so illustrative of the leisureliness and spaciousness of Delta life in this period as its old-fashioned breakfast. In the days before Americans—including Deltans—had begun to take their food on the run like escaping convicts; before the omnipresence of tin cans, ready-to-serve frozen messes mass-produced by distant, anonymous corporations, and drugstores where men eat standing like horses amid a miscellany of hot-water bottles, packaged candy, and hair dyes; when eggs were a dime a dozen and the Diligent Housewife had not yet become the Domestic Engineer—in that dear, dead time, Deltans sat content-edly down to their old-fashioned breakfasts.

Before considering them at table, let us note this. The observer of American life is saddened by a melancholy phenomenon of our national existence. As the nation has expanded in power and riches to stupendous power and incom-parable wealth, so have the living dimensions of its citizens shrunk. Thus the marital bed of yesterday, as broad as a battlefield, has given way to mean little "twin" beds. For all their rayon trappings, "blonde" wood, and allegedly anes-thetic mattresses of foam rubber, they are but cots fit more for the tossings of convicts than the sound sleep of honest men, indicative of a shabby parsimo-niousness of spirit and unbecoming in a huge continent where it takes the Sunset Limited twenty-four hours to cross the state of Texas.

It is but natural, then, that the once large family of six to sixteen children had been succeeded by its miniscule modern counterpart: Papa, Mama, Sister, Ju-nior. The wispy offspring and their shadowy parents do not eat happily in a proper dining room. They dejectedly pick at their food in dreary corners called "dinettes" or "breakfast nooks." And breakfast—as though the sun has not risen again and the world is young and the Lord has permitted all to gather once more at table—is but a blur between the brushing of teeth and the starting of the car.

On a collapsible table, to be stored away later, paper napkins at each plate, the plates laid upon synthetic mats, there is what nowadays passes for breakfast. It consists of orange juice, a cereal like the wheat straw amid which Ruth gleaned, perhaps a fried egg looking gloomy as a Cyclops' eye upon the plate, toast of fac-tory-made bread popped from a time-clock gadget, coffee brewed in a chemist's retort, and jam ("contains artificial coloring and flavoring") cooked by workmen in a plant adjoining the Worthington Pump Company's factory in Newark, New Jersey. Since there is only enough here to sustain life at a low animal level and nothing for the life of the spirit, with this wretched mess there go a glance at the newspaper headlines, an ear cocked for radio news, a mumbled word or two by the possessors of a tongue that has six hundred thousand words in its vocabu-lary, and a bird-peck kiss by Papa on Mama's forehead as he rushes for car or train.

It was not always like this. Once upon a time, the Delta patriarch, surrounded by his wife, children, relatives, and guests, gathered at a proper table laid with snowy linens in a proper dining room. Then the head of the house—man as well as husband, father as well as procreator—blessed the name of the Lord from whom all blessings flow, and the company fell to heartily.

There were the breads: the well-flavored, largely homemade, saliva-stimulat-ing, aromatic breads, palatable, nourishing, useful for sopping up ham gravy, country butter, cane syrup. They were nearly all hot and of several varieties: bat-ter bread, spoon bread, wheat bread, biscuits, beaten biscuits, Sally Lunn, and lace cakes—batter cakes wafer thin. As they fried in an iron skillet, floury bubbles gathered around their edges to congeal in cooling and leave the cakes fringed with a circle of lace.

By way of meats, there were usually hams and bacon. But no housewife worthy of that lofty title would permit a ham upon her table that was less than two years old and so had begun at least to progress from the rawness of youth to the mellowness of maturity, nor any bacon cut from a hog weighing more than 160 pounds. Sometimes there was fried chicken, golden brown, or steak, often called "chicken steak" because of the way it was prepared. A round steak, cut thin and well beaten with the steak beater, was served with a thick flour gravy. There were platters of fried eggs at either end of the table, while, of course, one could have boiled eggs if one preferred; these were to be eaten from an egg cup with a tiny spoon.

Those who liked them might have, in addition to meats and eggs, broiled salt mackerel, herring, and herring roe. These were great favorites in the Delta and the South; such favorites, indeed, that they provided the humble beginnings of the careers of Washington and Buchanan Duke, founders of the American Tobacco Company. When they returned penniless from The War, they scraped up a few dollars, bought tobacco near Durham, North Carolina, loaded it on a mule-drawn wagon, and made their long way to Albermarle Sound. There they traded tobacco for salt fish, and returning to Durham, they traded the fish for tobacco.

The components of the old-fashioned Delta breakfast varied to some degree with the changing seasons. In summer there were cantaloupes on the table, the deep-fleshed, sweet-smelling muskmelon, cultivated strawberries, and dewberries that grew wild in immense profusion.

After Thanksgiving, when the frost had mellowed the persimmons and touched the muscadines to ripeness for marauding raccoons, when sugar-sweet mist gathered upon hot toddy glasses, and when the hoot owl screamed his anguished query—"I cook for my wife, er, who cooks for you-all"—to an unheeding world, then came the high festival of hog-killing time. It was a festival in which townspeople abundantly participated because nearly all of them had friends or relatives on the plantations whence came the hogs. One might have fresh ham for breakfast; also fried pork sausage piquantly seasoned and served with lye hominy over which was poured rich sausage gravy.

Near at hand were the biscuits. There were large ones, flaky light and touched on top to the faintest ivory by the wood-burning kitchen stove, and tiny, crunchy beaten biscuits born of the marriage of brawn and love of good eating. They tasted especially delicious with crisp bacon and hominy's lesser, but more popular, brother: grits. Pearly white and steaming hot they were. You made a small excavation with your spoon in the mound before you plopped a piece of country butter into it and quickly stirred before the golden stream could pour out into your plate. If you were wise, you surreptitiously slipped down your galluses a notch or two before eating.

This, too, was the time of the setters' and pointers' reward. Fall was the birdhunting season and birds to the Deltan meant only one thing: Bob White quail. Now the hunting dogs that for long months had been but affectionately treated pets, ascended to the summit of the hierarchy of dogdom. Day before yesterday your host had gone hunting—"You know where that thicket is down yonder to the left of the old church?" And this morning there are broiled quail for breakfast: white of meat, as plump as bishops, as tender as the eyes of probationer angels.

The Deltan, who once had a choice of many dishes at his breakfast table, also had several beverages on his table: sweet milk, buttermilk, tea, sometimes cocoa or hot chocolate, and, of course, coffee. Proper coffee, redolent of Araby, it was called "Mocha and Java." Grocers kept the beans, treasures that they were, in large, floral-decorated tin bins. You selected them according to the mixture you liked, roasted them, a little at a time in your kitchen stove, and ground them in a small mill. By way of sweets—counterpoint to the breads—there were several kinds of homemade jams and jellies: damson, wild plum, crabapple, blackberry, strawberry, peach.

The company talked at table cheered by their heartwarming food and, breakfast over, separated to go about their tasks—the children to school, the men to work, the lady of the house to see that all was moving smoothly toward three-o'clock dinner.

While, then, for frequent periods we had little cash money, we did not for this reason draw in our belts as less imaginative communities do in the same case. For all of us, whites and Negroes, lived largely on "credicks." Universal credit, from one point of view, was evidence of our high faith in men's promises. But from another point of view, since it rested principally upon air, it was the economic equivalent of the Indian rope trick—levitation defying gravity.

We had heard, of course, of the word "budget." But we left it where it belonged—in the dictionary. It suggested to us an unbecoming niggardliness and skimpiness—a thin cake baked without a fat abundance of eggs and butter. A budget required, too, a constant counting of pennies and complicated calculations that are a weariness of the mind, as it required also a constant discipline of denial that is a weariness of the flesh.

I could not then know that as the nation grew richer it would, paradoxically, become budget obsessed and that I should one day see a brassiere advertisement reading: FASCINATION WITHOUT EXAGGERATION. BOSOM BEAUTY WITHOUT BUDGET WORRIES. Looking back, a Delta lady of my day may have been concerned about her bosom but certainly not in relationship to a budget.

We managed to live pretty well, whatever the times, by an intuition mounting to the heights of economic genius. For the community had stumbled upon something that the rest of the nation would discover only years later during the great depression of the 1930s: the magic of the freezing of debts. Responding to none of the orthodox canons of economics, and indeed blithely unaware of them, it substituted genial fictions for them and went its easy-going way.

Everybody agreed, when times were tough, that times were tough. But they also agreed that the *next* cotton crop would bring high prices and prosperity. The future was an inexhaustible bank upon which we drew constantly to make up the deficits of the present.

7

Drummers and Peddlers

Cohn's larger-than-life portrait of that "Knight of the Grip" Phil Grimes is decidedly at odds with fellow Mississippian (and childhood Delta resident) Tennessee Williams' recollection of his drunken, womanizing, abusive, and usually absent father — "They're all the same," Williams observed, "shoe salesmen with a bad territory and wives they can't abide." Still, there is no question that the drummer was a legendary figure throughout the Delta and the rest of the small-town South as well. Cohn's description of the Jewish peddler reflects his strong interest in and identification with the origins of the Delta's small but significant Jewish population.[1]

My father was a dry goods merchant—wholesale and retail—who bought merchandise from drummers and sold it to peddlers. Through him I came to know members of these guilds, and occasionally father brought one home to dinner.

I knew one drummer—Phil Grimes—quite well through his repeated appearances at our table. He endeared himself to me at the beginning by giving me a prized Columbia half-dollar for my coin collection, and I was gratified that when I went into "long pants" he never once mouthed those words so repulsive to the self-conscious adolescent: "My, you're getting to be a big boy, a regular little man." He flatteringly treated me, on the contrary, as though I were adult and once—a memorable occasion—took me to see a double-header between Greenville and Vicksburg, I preening myself to be seen in the company of so great a man. It was then natural that I should give him my devotion heightened by a touch of hero worship.

Phil Grimes was a mann'ble [*sic*] man as rural Negroes, themselves natively courteous, say of the courteous. Whenever he took dinner at our house, he went to the kitchen to thank Julia, our cook, and give her a shining silver dollar. He always used new-minted coins as gifts, laughingly saying, "When you give something, give the best." Phil's gallantry and generosity were such that, whenever Julia heard he was coming to dinner, she worried and fretted and said to my mother, "Now, Ole Miss, you know Mr. Phil don't like his steak cooked as much as the Boss, so I'll just fix him some on the side."

---

1. Dotson Rader, *Tennessee: Cry of the Heart* (Garden City, N.Y., 1983), 25.

A Knight of the Grip, he had traveled out of St. Louis into Mississippi and Arkansas for twenty years selling millinery. His line might range from "katy-dids"—straw sailors retailing for thirty-five cents—to superb creations of velvet and ostrich plumes—"just like they're wearing in New York"—that sold for as much as five dollars. As most of his tribe, he liked good food next to fat orders, and when he struck a town where, he said, the meals "weren't fitten for a man of my corporosity," he would track down a good dinner with the relentlessness of the Pinkertons on the trail of bank robbers. However often he came to our house, he was always "reminded" of his first visit to Greenville and how had then fostered a love affair whose ardor never waned: the lifetime love affair of Phil Grimes with his stomach.

A stranger in town hankering for the kind of dinner that eluded him, and his desperation increased by poor pickings before coming to town, he decided upon a novel course. Leaving our small business district, he was soon walking in a sweat-damp, dust-stained suit through some of our residential streets peering into backyards for a sight that did not appear. The heat grew almost unbearable, and his quest seemed hopeless, but he plodded on looking and listening. Finally, will triumphant over weakening flesh, he came to the yard of yards. There, in the shade of a chinaberry tree rested a little flock of fat fryers. Then with the air of one who has just discovered the Pacific, Phil straightened his sloping shoulders, mopped his wet face, adjusted his ready-made tie in the wilted Arrow collar, and walked to the front door of the house.

At his knock a pleasant-faced, graying woman appeared. Phil removed his genu-wine Stetson hat, bowed in a courtly manner, and said: "Madam, I'm not a beggar or bill collector and I certainly am not a boy working his way through college selling magazines, as you can see for yourself. The truth is that I'm a stranger in town and a sick man. A bad case of heartburn is about to kill me. My doctor back home in St. Louis told me I dassent eat anything much except chicken. I like a lot of other things, but most of 'em don't like me. But just now I accidentally passed your lovely home and saw those fryers in your backyard. So I said to myself, Phil Grimes—that's my name, ma'am—I know that the good lady and fine housekeeper that lives here wouldn't let a stranger and a sick man to boot suffer if she could help him. So I want to ask you to do me a big favor that might save my life. Lady, if you'll just have your cook fry me a chicken, I'll be much obliged, and I don't care what it costs."

Sympathetic to a sick stranger, flattered by his words, and glad to be able to talk to a visitor come all the way from St. Louis, the woman said, "Why, you come right on in and sit down and I'll have Lizzie fix you a chicken." As she hastened away to talk to the cook, Phil moaned in a sepulchral voice: "Please, ma'am, don't forget the giblets. The doctor says I have to have giblets to keep up my strength." Hearing this, Phil's hostess immediately brought him a plate of cream cheese and scallions so that he would not faint of hunger before his meal came, and a little later he sat before a platter of golden brown chicken, giblets in rich gravy, hot biscuits, watermelon-rind preserves, and iced tea.

Rested, content at last, and smiling, he sat back after eating and picked his teeth with a gold-mounted quill toothpick that was attached to his watch chain, holding a napkin before his mouth in the manner that politeness required. The lady would not take money for the food. She was sorry for a sick man far from home. She was sure that if her husband had been in St. Louis, Phil's wife would have done for him what she had done for Phil even if it wasn't much, and, besides, fat fryers were two for a quarter in town. And the drummer was so interesting telling her about his family and showing her the snapshots he carried in his wallet. "Now that's Phil, Jr., he's named after me, but I always thank the good Lord for making him look like his mother. There's Earlene, she's named after her mother, and that's the Missus herself, but she's a whole lot prettier than she looks in the picture."

The lady found Phil fascinating as he talked about the doings a few years ago at the St. Louis World Fair. He was such a good man, too. You could see he disapproved of that shameless woman dancer of the Midway called Little Egypt whose carryings-on before godless men had been denounced by her pastor, Reverend Gill. He called hers "the gilded sin of Heliopolis" and preached for two hours on the text: The Hour of Redemption Is Drawing Nigh. There would be no room Up Yonder, he warned, for those who didn't Believe, who hadn't Repented and been Baptized.

Time passed quickly as the stranger talked. It was late afternoon when he warmly thanked his involuntary hostess and walked down Poplar Street, lodge emblems swaying from the heavy gold watch chain taut against his paunch, while he alternately explored tooth cavities he had overlooked in the house and hummed snatches of the still-popular World's Fair song "Meet Me in St. Looey, Ooey."

Filled with fried chicken and good cheer, he was on his way to the Cowan Hotel. There Jenkins, the Negro drayman, had deposited Phil's big sample trunks with their heavy polished brass hardware and bright peppermint stripes that folks noticed as the bags moved slowly down Main Street to and from the Yazoo and Mississippi Valley depot in the creaking wagon drawn by Jenkins' jug-headed, swaybacked mule.

Phil Grimes has long been dead and his tribe vanished from the American earth, but with his going something has gone out of our national life. Phil was a businessman, yet he lent business a note of leisure, gayety, color, almost an air of carnival. Into forlorn little towns of the turn of the century he came as a dazzling tropical bird of passage with his pepper-and-salt, round-cornered suit, his vest often in the popular white-and-red-dot effect with its pockets stuffed with gold-banded cigars that he handed around with patrician abandon. His high-button shoes were tan with razor-sharp points or black patent leather with pearl-gray tops. On his head was a genu-wine Jawn B. [Stetson]. Actor as well as salesman, he cultivated the expansive smile and bone-crushing handshake—you could always tell whether a man was sincere by the way he shook hands—so long that they became almost involuntary reflexes while, like the politician and hotel clerk, he had a fine memory for faces and names.

He was the American troubadour and storyteller as he went from town to town singing slightly naughty songs—"I declare, that Phil Grimes, now ain't he something?"—to the delight of his friends, or, without waiting for an answer, launching into the tale after asking, "Do you know the one about the Chinese laundryman and the lady?" It was he who invented the smoking room or Pullman story; he was the restless American telling tales to beguile his restless way. He was the hero or butt of a thousand fancies about the drummer and the farmer's daughter. It was for the sake of his soul that the Gideons put Bibles in hotel rooms throughout the country. He was a big talker, an incurable optimist, spreader of the gospel of prosperity in a growing nation. Yet he was the only American businessman who ever became a romantic figure in the eyes of ladies and a he-man in the eyes of men.

The drummer might have appeared to be the carefree dude, but he had the strength of a mule, the stomach of a goat, the endurance of a rock. He traveled on slow trains that were a torment to the flesh. Once when Phil was riding the Yellow Dog, the rickety train swaying on an uncertain roadbed made the more uncertain by days of gully-washing rains, Mr. Williamson, the engineer, hollered from the cab of his locomotive to Old Lady Noel. She was walking the muddy road parallel to the railroad track, and the engineer asked her to come and ride to Moorhead where she was bound. "No, thank you, suh," she hollered back. "I ain't got time. I got to get home and fix supper."

Phil (and his kind) made long night trips on the hard, gritty seats of evil-smelling cars dimly lighted by acetylene lamps and poorly heated in winter by dinky coal stoves, but in the morning when he met his customers, he was as jaunty as the interlocutor of a minstrel show. He put up at hotels where he ate greasy, underdone food, drank patent medicines to relieve the heartburn, and often faced bedbugs when he went to sleep, sometimes with another drummer in the same bed. Occasionally he and his fellows played poker all night to avoid the hungry insects that would await them between the sheets or that ominously paraded on the walls while waiting.

From his base in town, using a hired livery-stable buggy, he made the rounds of country stores whatever the weather. He fought clouds of mosquitoes in summer, was sometimes pulled out of the mud in winter by a team of mules, and occasionally took all day to go the few miles from Greenville to Winterville. He suffered such hardships as are unknown to present-day traveling salesmen, but he usually managed to convey the impression that, although he was a businessman, he was primarily a good fellow playing at the serious business of earning a living.

After Phil Grimes had spread his wares upon tables in his sample room–bedroom at the Cowan, he would sally out to visit the trade. In store after store there would be warm greetings: "Hello there, Phil, I haven't seen you in a month of Sundays," and Phil replying, "Well, Jake, if you ain't a sight for sore eyes." Phil would ask about Jake's family—"How's the missus and the kids?"—and Jake would inquire about Phil's family. Sometimes their heads were solemnly close together as the one or the other said his wife was "expecting." Then they would shake hands: "The best of luck."

Greetings exchanged between Phil and the Boss, Phil would greet the clerks who had come up. There was Miss Wilcox, the old maid. She was the star boarder at Mrs. Goode's famous rooming house and, according to local gossip, was a secret paregoric drinker. Invariably, Phil would say, "Miss Irma, I'm still waiting to dance at your wedding." Her coyly embarrassed smile revealed pinkish store teeth as she gigglingly replied. "Aw, Phil Grimes, you just go away."

Ike Greenspan, whose much talked about salary of $90 a month attested to his wizardry as a salesman, came up trailing his tape measure, compliments of Hart, Schaffner, and Marx. There was Old Man Henderson, a Confederate veteran, who kept the store's accounts in his Spencerian handwriting. One of our best posted men, he could tell you the highest and the lowest stages the Mississippi River had reached at Cairo, Illinois, since they began keeping records and the days the stages were reached. There were also Jake's nephew, Abe Miller, a shy greenhorn recently arrived from a Rumanian village and still standing uncertainly between two worlds, and Will Jordan, the Negro porter, who swept the floors, dusted the stock with a heavy turkey-feather duster, and delivered packages.

Phil had a word for all. He asked Miss Irma about her mother. She had been the bedridden victim of a genteel illness for a quarter century and lived with Miss Irma's married sister out in the country. He inquired about Ike Greenspan's Indian runner chickens that were his hobby; tapped his hip pocket and winked meaningly at Old Man Henderson, whose wife, Miss Lutie, had made him sign The Pledge; smilingly said, "You sprechen Deutsch?" to Abe Miller; and handed Will Jordan a fistful of cigars. These were Two Orphans brand that Will liked. They were bound by twos with a paper band, sold for five cents, and were spawned by an anonymous company that could never bring itself around to acknowledging parenthood.

When Miss Irma moved away to measure and ticket yard-goods remnants for the Saturday business, the fun would begin. Then the men gathered around Phil in a tight circle while he told a story that was followed by guffaws of laughter.

In this constantly enacted little provincial comedy, although Phil was seeking business, there was no hint of business. There was time for that later, while manners were manners. You just did not barge in on your friends and start talking trade. But business was eventually done, and these leisurely relationships were profitable to both drummer and merchant. Merchants were loyal to old drummer friends. A newcomer competitor could not then—as he now certainly would—get an order for, say, cheesecloth because he offered it for a tiny fraction less than the price asked by a man who for twenty years had eaten at your table, told you stories, and given you cigars.

Often a drummer—especially an old-timer who had long been with the same firm—saved a customer who might have been forced into bankruptcy by his employer's faraway automaton of a credit man who reckoned in cold figures rather than in warm flesh and blood. The drummer knew at firsthand the circumstances of his customer's existence: whether there had been a crop failure in the vicinity, disastrously low prices for crops, or a flood. He knew whether there had been a serious illness in his family that had depleted his slender resources or if the customer himself had long been sick and unable to attend to business. Knowing the integrity of his customer, he would recommend leniency to his firm or even the extension of more credit and so save him from bankruptcy.

On summer nights, willow rocking chairs were placed on the sidewalk before the hotel, under the cottonwoods whose fruit drifted white and silent in the moonlight. Then a small group of townsmen would gather around Phil as he told the Latest Ones he had heard in St. Louis. One of his constant devotees was Sam Manelli, the number-one man at Hallett's Barber Shop. People said you couldn't find a better barber shop in Memphis—shaves fifteen cents, haircuts twenty-five cents, shines five cents, suits pressed while you wait, twenty-five cents.

Sam was nearly always present on such occasions. He was generally free to walk downtown in search of entertainment for the paradoxical reason that he and his big, good-natured wife were devoted to one another. From their love sprang a constantly increasing group of Manellis, and when one was coming along—devotion become fruition—Sam's wife saw no reason why he should hang around the house and urged him to go out and enjoy himself. Full of warm Sicilian mirth, for weeks after Phil's visit, he repeated the drummer's stories in quaint English to his customers as they, bemused by his recital, sat in his chair while he absentmindedly stropped his razor and talked on and on.

Among others faithful in attendance upon these drummer's evenings were Bill Mulligan, a silent, withdrawn little man, who was the star third baseman of the Star Hoo-Hoos in our amateur baseball league; Walter Dinkins, a widower, who crazily prophesied that cotton would one day be picked by machine; Will Nash, a lumber dealer, who stayed away from home as much as possible because his wife fancied herself Mary, Queen of Scots; and Ed Cruger, our town miser, out for free entertainment. Once, to the delight of us all, he got his come-uppance. A woman, described as being no better than she ought to be, messed him up, and he had to pay her the staggering sum of $500 to keep her mouth shut. At the edge of the group stood a little knot of shy adolescent boys. They looked wonderingly at the great man from St. Louis, dreaming of the day when they might become drummers and see the gilded world.

For local newspaper editors, the well-known drummer was news:

> Phil Grimes, the popular Knight of the Grip, is here again calling on his trade. Phil looks sassier and fatter than ever, and his friends, who are legion, are giving him a royal welcome to the Biggest Little Town in Mississippi.
>
> Harry Rosenberg, proprietor of the Golden Eagle Store, bought a big bill of the new picture hats that Phil says are all the rage in New York, and when Harry gets them in by rush express, they will be advertised in this paper.
>
> When we talked to Phil the other morning, he said that this is the fastest-growing little town in Mississippi with the friendliest people and never-say-die spirit. He says you couldn't duplicate the regular fifty-cent dinner at the Porter House for less than $1.50 in St. Louis. But knowing Mrs. Porter's homecooking like we do, we don't believe you could duplicate it up yonder for any price.
>
> Phil will be out at Baird Park tomorrow rooting for us when our boys play the Silver City Tigers, and they'll be wearing the new uniforms that just came in from A. G. Spalding, each one carrying on its back the name of the organization that donated it. Professor Hardy's band will be there, and the stores will close at one o'clock to give everybody a chance to be there and root for our guys, who are going in to win.

If the drummer was an appealing combination of business, news, and salty masculine friendship for men, he was a romantic figure in the eyes of women. Many a Delta girl, on a broiling summer's day, dressed in her best linen lawn shirtwaist, Panama-cloth skirt, and high white-button shoes and futilely sheltering herself from the sun under a changeable silk parasol while Java rice powder ran down her face, would wait at the depot to see the drummers get off the train. When it ground to a stop, fatigued cylinders wheezing, the drummers emerged, mopping their faces and beating dust out of their clothes. Then the girls would huddle together at some distance from them, hardly daring to look directly at the knights adventurers, too ladylike to address them, and too womanly to avoid furtive glances at them.

There would ensue an animated tableau: the girls under their multicolored parasols looking like massed poppies, sunlight gleaming on their silvered chatelaine mesh bags; the drummers giving their baggage checks to draymen and their handbags to hack drivers; little boys admiring the locomotive; and Charley Shepherd picking up the mailbags as he had done for many years. Soon the train pulled out for Vicksburg, and the station platform was deserted. Then the girls walked to the Kandy Kitchen to have ice cream sodas and giggle over their adventure.

The unhappy truth about the drummer, however, is that he was less romantic than he appeared to be to the girls. He was more interested in food than in love, more beguiled by second helpings than "romance." His one vice was all-night poker sessions. His fatal weakness, derived from his incurable optimism, was that he drew to inside straights. At heart he was essentially a sentimental family man. He wrote long letters to his wife from lonely hotel rooms, sent them cane syrup and hams given him by his rural customers, and was forever showing snapshots of his family to his friends. But, aware of his reputation as a gay dog, he could quickly become for an audience the man-about-town, the traveler familiar with the dazzling pleasures and glittering sins of St. Louis, Chicago, and even remote New York.

Phil Grimes has gone. His place has been taken by the so-called scientifically trained salesman who moves with card-indexed data about his customers and a smattering of "psychology" to bend them to his will. Traveling swiftly in a car over good roads, he stays briefly in each town along the route. He knows little of his customers' private lives and cares less. He is perhaps more efficient than Phil Grimes was. But he himself is merely a cog in a huge, cold, impersonal corporate machine set in motion by men he will never know and kept in motion by forces he will never comprehend. He is one with the automatic vending machine, the self-service store, the vast, dehumanized fabric of business, and as such he is representative of that remorseless progression by which a once puppy-friendly people tend more and more in their business relations to approach the state of automata.

There is now no one to ask, "Say Jake, did you hear the one about the ten men and the girl on the sleeper leaving Denver?" No one to hand out richly gold-banded cigars; to inquire of Miss Wilcox about her mother and with a wink promise Old Man Henderson a drink of forbidden whiskey; to prowl the streets of little towns looking for flocks of fat fryers; to be at once a storyteller, political analyst, economic expert, a romantic figure to women, a snappy dresser, and a hero to men, yet soundly conservative about all the things that count.

The fast train, the airplane, the automobile, and the long-distance telephone have killed the drummer who visited Greenville when it was a tiny town dreaming by the Mississippi River. His successor is the traveling efficiency expert. We are richer than we were in the days of Phil Grimes. But we are also poorer, and there are moments when we seem to know it.

The trader is contemporaneous with civilized man. The will to trade is almost unbreakable. A true international and a form of communication that often continues to function when others fail, trade remains essentially unchanged in its objectives throughout the millennia, as does the trader's nature. Thirty centuries before Christ, Mesopotamian merchants traded to distant lands for silver, spices, and "fair-skinned slaves," while Solomon's ships brought ivory, apes, and peacocks from Tarshish. Centuries later, "King" Derby of Salem, Massachusetts, sent his clippers on trading voyages to China. Antiquity broods over trading. The Mona Lisa of Pater's famous essay not only is as "old as the rocks among which she sits" but also has "trafficked for strange webs with Eastern merchants."

The guild of traders is ancient and enduring. The drummer was of it and the lowly peddler. For more than two centuries peddlers moved across the face of America, moving as the frontier moved, following into whatever backwaters the restless people who were their customers. Throughout most of the nation, the man with the pack on his back was a Yankee. In the Delta of my youth, there were a few Italian peddlers who traded from mule-drawn wagons gaily caparisoned in the Sicilian fashion, but the Delta's first peddlers were Jews.

This Jewish peddler was unprepared either by his environment or philosophy for frontier life in America. Usually he came from an eastern European village where time had stood still for centuries, where the bulbous domes of churches proclaimed the East that looked to Byzantium, and there was more than a touch of the Oriental. Here the Jew, an ancient dweller, earned a scant living as artisan or petty tradesman. Steeped in Hebraic lore but innocent of Western culture, he clung to the faith of his fathers and dreamed of returning to Jerusalem ("If I forget thee, O Jerusalem"), its temple destroyed nineteen hundred years ago, the holy city itself a provincial capital of its Turkish masters.

Jerusalem, a mirage, haunted him and evaded him. Then America, the compassionate, all-embracing mother, beckoned. They came to her in their thousands and their tens of thousands: the dispossessed, the skimped of experience, the heavy laden, the hunted and the harassed, the bereft of hope, those who had walked among shadows with eyes downcast and shoulders bent. America took them to her bosom. She made them whole in her image. In time they looked straight ahead, and their shoulders bent no more.

A few Jews drifted to the Delta, particles of the great immigrant stream flowing across the Atlantic. After a while they brought over a fellow townsman, and some of these became peddlers.

A "greenhorn" worked for a friend or relative until he had acquired some knowledge of English, the customs of the country, and a little money for a peddler's stake. Peddling was a good business for such a man. There was a need for him. He could raise the tiny capital required. No large experience was required and a man could learn as he earned. Peddling, moreover, enabled a man to earn a living in a severe school while perfecting his knowledge of the language and customs of the country.

It demanded stoic endurance of its practitioners, the capacity to suffer cruel hardships, and the willingness to suffer them for small money rewards. The Delta peddler plied his trade in an area largely crude. The roads were mule-belly deep in mud during winter and stifling with dust in summer. Aside from the sketchy railroads, men traveled on horseback, on buggies, or on the rivers. The peddler's work, moreover, took him away from the roads. Towns and hamlets were the province of local merchants who would have driven him away. Lowliest of businessmen, his were the lowliest of customers: Negroes and poor whites who lived in cabins encompassed by forests slowly yielding to fire and ax.

The heavy rains of the region made swamps of the lowlands and often sent streams out of their banks to convert miles of countryside into a lake. Then the peddler might be long immured in the cabin where he had sought shelter. From the swamps mosquitoes rose to torture him by day and by night. Malaria stalked him with chills and fever. Yellow fever struck at intervals until after the turn of the century. The peddler ate what he could get when he could get it. There were few doctors or hospitals, and calomel was the prescribed remedy for a host of ills.

Violence flared in the pioneer community. Tempers and trigger fingers were touchy. The homicide rate soared. A Circuit Court judge of Bolivar County (our county adjoined it) in the heart of the Delta told a grand jury that homicides committed there during the preceding year exceeded those committed in the whole United Kingdom. This was an interesting statistic, and it was accepted as such. But it did nothing to flatten the curve of shootings and stabbings.

Into this region the peddler, a timid stranger in a strange land, earned his living. Tommy Ruben, whom I long knew, was of their number. A small, slender man, with small, shapely hands and feet, silken brown hair, and quizzical, shortsighted eyes behind gold-rimmed eyeglasses, he looked rather the dreamy Talmudic scholar of his native Lithuania than the businessman however humble, fit more for theological hairsplittings than for the rigors of peddling. He was a kind man. And rural Negroes, who are quick to read the white man's character, saw that he was kind and affectionately called him "Jew Mistuh Tommy."

He was a walking store. This small man carried upon his back a pack—oilcloth-wrapped and rope-bound—that weighed upward of a hundred pounds. Inside was a varied merchandise: needles; thread; buttons; calicoes; ginghams; dress trimmings; cotton stockings for women and children; coarse cotton socks for men; combs, including the fine-tooth kind that Negroes called "can't-you-don't-you" combs; scissors; hand mirrors; harmonicas; Jew's harps; men's garters; armbands; Hoyt's ten-cent cologne. Tommy's customer was where he found him; his place of business was any place that was sheltered from the weather.

His coming to a backwoods cabin, heralded by a chorus of barking dogs—"Nawsuh, they won't bite, not them feist dawgs"—that jumped and snapped in the novel excitement of smelling a stranger, was a welcome moment for its occupants. Children were sent a-running to fetch those who were working in fields or wood, and soon the whole family pressed close around the peddler in joyous anticipation as he removed the oilcloth from his pack to reveal its wondrous freight. Two days' labor in the hot sun went for a dress length of gingham with thread to sew and rick-rack braid for trimming, and a day's work went for a dress length of yellow calico that sold for five cents a yard. Sometimes the customer requested a tiny sample. Then she chewed it and spat on the floor to see whether the cloth had faded.

When, after tramping the countryside for days, Tommy had sold most of his stock, he returned to Greenville. There he might buy more merchandise and re-joice and worship with his fellows who had come to town for the same purpose. Then he was out on the road again, back aching, legs numb with fatigue, and his mind was made vacuous by the weariness of the flesh.

Tommy and his kind endured hardships, asked help of no man and merely a memory of graying men. Years after they had vanished from the Delta, William Alexander Percy recalled them in his *Lanterns on the Levee:*

> Every American community has its leaven of Jews. Ours arrived shortly af-ter the Civil War with packs on their backs, peddlers from Russia, Poland, Germany. . . . They sold trinkets to Negroes and saved. Today they are planta-tion owners, bankers, lawyers, doctors, merchants; their children attend the great American universities, win prizes, become connoisseurs in the arts and radicals in politics. I was talking to one, an old-timer, not too successful, in front of his small store a short time ago. He suddenly asked in his Russian accent: "Do you know Pushkin? Ah, beautiful, better than Shelley or Bryon." Why shouldn't such a people inherit the earth, not, surely, because of their meekness, but because of a steadier fire, a tension and tenacity that make all other whites seem stodgy and unintellectual.

8

The River I Knew

"The People of the Delta fear God and the Mississippi River," Cohn wrote in God
Shakes Creation, *"for God and the river are immortal and immemorial." In this poignant
essay, Cohn discusses the Mississippi River's role in shaping the culture and society of the
Delta.* [1]

We were clearly and profoundly affected by cotton. But we were perhaps more subtly and enduringly affected by the Mississippi River.

The Delta was born of the river. Flowing down out of time, through countless
millennia, the Mississippi had built this earth, inch by inch, layer by layer, piling fatness upon fatness as it dropped its burden of loam gathered in its passage across half
a continent. The river's land nurtured the living. Our dead were buried in soil of the
river. The river was a god that gave. It was also a god that took away. And its mark
upon our community was pervasive and enduring.

The great age of Mississippi steamboating had long vanished when I was a boy.
Gone, too, was the gorgeous dynasty of the steamboat captains, imperial steamboat-
owning families such as the Lees, and the old Greenville that Mark Twain knew in
the 1870s. It had fallen into the river through the cavings of its banks.

(Steamboats had had firm friends in Greenville. When a meeting was called there
in the 1880s to discuss the building of a railroad through the Delta and speakers
described its advantages, a farmer arose and said:

> I am opposed to the railroad; there ain't no accommodations about them.
> When Captain White lands the *Pargoud,* you can go aboard and get a good drink
> of liquor with ice in it, and the captain will take one with you, and he ain't in no
> hurry. He will talk with you and give you plenty of time for your liquor to cool
> and to drink it, but them railroads come like a streak of lightning through your
> field, scaring your mules, killing your chickens and hogs, stopping about a minute
> for you to get off and on and nothing to drink aboard.
>
> I was going from Vicksburg to Edwards about a year ago, and I got off at Ed-
> wards and got a drink, and I told the cap'en of the train to wait a moment, I was
> going to get a drink of liquor, for I was mighty dry. Well, I hadn't more than

A portion of this chapter appeared in modified form as "The River I Remember," *Virginia Quarterly Review* XXXV (Summer, 1959), 393–405.

   1. David L. Cohn, *Where I Was Born and Raised* (Cambridge, Mass., 1948), 43.

touched the bar, hadn't even had time to order my liquor, when—off that train started. . . . No, sir; there is no accommodation in a railroad, and we don't want them things in the county.)

The Mississippi, to some extent, made each of us a world citizen. It therefore fostered an urbanity rare in the small, isolated town, kept it free of the more blatant crudities of the frontier, gave it an unwonted sympathy for alien men and alien concepts, redeemed it from many of the aspects of landlocked provincialism. For it had to do with one of the most potent influences in men's lives: communications. Long ago Pascal had observed that "rivers are roads that move."

Pioneering Americans were men against space, and they set out to conquer distances as though moving against a hostile empire. One of their picturesque instruments, of limited utility, was the pony express. Another was the widely useful Mississippi River steamboat. It enabled men to tap the rich resources of the Mississippi Valley and to trade with the world through an easily accessible southern gateway at New Orleans. But it also had other uses, less tangible but scarcely less valuable.

Men living along the river went downstream on palatial craft to New Orleans, a glittering city unlike any other on this continent, an outpost of French culture near the mouth of the Mississippi; Latin, Roman Catholic, French-speaking, wine-drinking, music-loving, it was an exotic, luxuriant Catholic-Mediterranean island in a Protestant, Anglo-Saxon sea.

Those who went there occasionally voyaged by steamboat to Louisville, St. Louis, Cincinnati, continuing overland perhaps to eastern or western cities and sometimes to Europe. They saw a bit of the world beyond their picket fences. They learned that there is more than one kind of people, one way of life, one code of conduct. From such a source springs the man who seems to me to be the flower of civilization, the Enlightened Provincial one who, loving his own soil and tradition, is moved by the informed mind and quickened insight toward a sympathetic comprehension of alien soils and traditions. I do not say that all our travelers returned with the wealth of the Indies. But only a leaven of such travelers may sweeten what would otherwise be a sour earth.

There were still a few steamboats on the river during my schooldays. Among them were the *Belle of the Bends* (pronounced bellathebends), the *Issaquena,* the *Kate Adams,* the *Verne Swain,* the latter our pride because it was locally owned and locally captained. Side-wheelers and stern-wheelers, unpretentious, bearers more of burdens than of passengers, innocent of the glorious legends that clustered about their queenly predecessors, they nonetheless quickened the beating of my boyish heart as they blackened the sky with smoke, breasting the swift upstream current or gliding in for a landing, bells clanging, paddle wheels throwing cascades of diamonds into the eye of the sun, Negro roustabouts poised with ropes in hand to jump ashore.

About them was the enchantment of distant places and the peril in the stormy night when, beacons obscured, the pilot desperately sought to penetrate the mystery that lay upon the face of the waters. How deeply I envied steamboat-men! Happy, unfettered, they led adventurous lives free of the chains that bound me, free of the hateful necessity to solve algebraic questions or recite *amo, amas, amat* when the fields called with a thousand voices and the woods beckoned and the river summoned me to drift upon its bosom far, far away.

The sight, sounds, and perils of the river during my childhood were much what they had been when Charles Dickens had encountered them seventy-five years before. In his *American Notes for General Circulation,* he said:

> What words shall describe this Mississippi, great father of rivers . . . an enor-mous ditch, sometimes two or three miles wide, running liquid mud, six miles an hour: its strong . . . current choked and obstructed . . . by huge logs and whole forest trees: now twining themselves together in great rafts . . . now rolling past like monstrous bodies . . . now glancing singly by like giant leeches; and now writhing round and round in the vortex of some whirlpool, like wounded snakes. . . . We toiled up this foul stream, striking constantly against the floating timber, or stopping to avoid those more dangerous obstacles, the snags or sawyers. . . .
>
> When the nights are very dark, the lookout . . . knows by the ripple of the wa-ter if any great impediment be at hand, and rings a bell . . . which is the signal for the engines to be stopped: but always in the night this bell has work to do, and after every ring, there comes a blow which renders it no easy matter to remain in bed.

Occasionally a snagboat run by the United States Army Corps of Engineers visited us. A big, powerful vessel, the engineers' castled insignia on its smoke-stacks, it discharged a specialized task: removing from the river menaces to navigation, including "snags." These were logs or trees embedded in the stream that became spears capable of ripping a steamboat's hull. Snagboatmen impressed me as less warmly friendly than steamboatmen. Perhaps it was because they represented the far-off "guvment" in a remote place called Washington, a shadowy entity whose works little concerned us. Or perhaps there was an effi-ciency about them that I found chilling by contrast with our easygoing ways.

Our elders felt otherwise. They said of the snagboat that "it's so clean you can eat off the floor." We boys thought this no compliment. What was wrong about eating off the floor? Beside, all this smacked of the distasteful maxim we heard at home: "Cleanliness is next to godliness." This was a doctrine that fell upon deaf and—when we had our way—not altogether shining ears. My com-panions and I therefore preferred the cozy disorderliness of the *Verne Swain* to the cold order and unearthly cleanliness of the snagboat. Besides, what price cleanliness? It was generally understood among the boys of Greenville, Negro and white, that you had to eat a peck of dirt before you died.

Sometimes the "guvment fleet"—also run by the Army Engineers—visited us for weeks or even months with a varied assortment of craft. Their crews lived in floating dormitories called "quarter boats," and they were primarily concerned with preventing cavings of the river's banks. For this purpose they constructed great "mats" of interwoven willows and sank them with layers of stone to prevent lappings and suckings of the stream against the banks.

When it was learned the guvment fleet was coming to town, there was a stir of excitement among townsfolk generally but especially among Negroes, merchants, and pleasure ladies of the two races. There was about guvment fleet men the aura of adventurousness that accompanies those who toil amid the mysteries of waters, and they were refreshingly new faces in a place where we usually saw only the same old faces. They were also aristocrats of labor and lordly spenders. Top men among them earned as much as $150 a month. And—astonishingly—common labor was paid as much as $1.50 a day. The fleet would, moreover, hire much local labor and thereby permit some of us to revel in Uncle Sam's largesse.

It was therefore warmly welcomed to town. Pleasure ladies, white and Negro, did a roaring Saturday-night business to the annoyance of the local regulars and steady customers who, disdained by the ladies for the fleet men, made futile threats of a future boycott. Hot-cat parlors, poolrooms, stores, gathered in money, and since the velocity of currency circulation among us was high, everybody in town benefited by the fleet's visit. We could also have our cake and eat it, too. While the fleet labored to prevent the town from falling into the river, its spendings were a factor in making it a town economically worth keeping from such a fate.

There were always tugboats on the river. They were squat, powerful craft, principally engaged in shepherding downriver huge rafts of logs from the forests where they were felled to local sawmills. I had a classmate whose father was a tugboat captain—a relationship that gave the son shining prestige among boys—and we were sometimes taken for a ride on the river.

Our most memorable trip was a visit to the U.S.S. *Wasp.* A tiny gunboat that seemed to us as mighty as the sunken *Maine,* it lay anchored off the Arkansas shore as it paused on its way to St. Louis. Here I encountered a novel breed more lordly than steamboatmen or snagboatmen: sailors of the Navy. Tattooed heroes every one, some had perhaps lived through the rain of fire that fell at Manila Bay. A few might even have heard given the immortal command: "You may fire when you are ready, Gridley."

Fighting men who could lick their weight in wildcats, I knew they could handle Gatling guns, one-pounder cannon, and Krag-Jorgenson rifles as easily as we shot our .22s. Yet, disconcertingly, while in high school I learned that a certain Captain Simms, USN, had said the Navy couldn't hit a brick wall. He added, unpatriotically, that 98 percent of its shells fired at Manila Bay missed the target. This struck me as a libel upon brave men, men like those I had seen on the *Wasp*. But President Theodore Roosevelt seems to have been taken in by it. For, not trusting the native, unerring marksmanship of Americans, he ordered that there should be constant naval gunnery practice even in peacetime. This meant, of course, all the time. What foreign foe would dare challenge Uncle Sam!

I left the gunboat proud to be of a country that could produce such a ship and such a crew. No other nation could match them. The next day I daydreamed about them in school, saying "boom boom" under my breath as I joined them in a wild sea battle. But I was rudely interrupted by Miss Barry, our geography teacher, who, just like a woman, asked me when I was directing our gunfire from a toppling mast to "bound" Louisiana.

If the river comes back to me bearing on its bosom an image of the redoubtable *Wasp*, it also comes back bearing the image of a woman. Her father was the tugboat captain who had taken me to visit the ship, and her brother was my companion. They lived in a house near the levee and but a little way from the school I attended. There I often went with my friend during "big ree-cess."

In this house I encountered a deliciously alien world: sweet-scented, cloud-nebulous, strangely disturbing. It was the world of my companion's sister. She always asked us in to see her, and she was always abed. Although she had reached the advanced age of at least twenty-five years, I thought her superlatively beautiful as she lay there in a halo of honey-gold hair, eyes as blue as the blue of robins' eggs, voice soft as April rain dropping mistily upon white clover.

The room fragrant with perfume, light falling upon her in tiny golden bars through partially opened slats of the shutters, she seemed both of the earth and the air, a hesitant angel, half ascendant, half descendant. In her presence I was filled with a sweet sadness, a strange exaltation. It was, somehow, rather like the time when I attended a classmate's funeral. Then I had wept without crying and mourned without grieving. But once outside the church, my homeward feet were light to the sidewalk, and in an abandon of joy, I chased the squirrels that played beneath the oaks before the Catholic convent school.

Miss Imogene, beautiful, gentle, beneficent, always offered us candy. My own favorite—a five-cent confection bought at Wichern's grocery on the way to school—was called "Johnny Crook," a large molasses bar striated with coconut. Teeth-clamping and therefore dangerous to eat in classroom, it was satisfyingly long lasting. But here were chocolates—high-toned folks called them "bon bons"—in a huge, compartmented box with each morsel, treasure that it was, wrapped in gold foil. My benefactress urged me to take more when with difficulty I refrained, in the name of manners, from taking several pieces. But in the end I left with a pocketful of candy. Manners can be pushed too far.

The room was filled with empty three- and five-pound candy boxes, their multicolored lids depicting lovers in gondolas, doves flying over a moonlit sea with wide bands of pink ribbon around them. These together with gilt-framed cellulo [*sic*] toilet things—mirror, brush, comb, nail file, shoe spoon, and box for "combings" to be made into "rats"—gave the chamber an elegance that accentuated my awkwardness and filled me with shame that I had entered it wearing muddy shoes. I had never before encountered such opulence of things or beauty of person, and if Miss Imogene had not been so terribly old, I might have dreamed of falling in love with her, princess though she was and I but a little country boy. Yet I liked her enormously and still remember her affectionately through a scented, time-entangled, honey-gold haze. My feelings are untouched by the irrelevant circumstance, learned long afterward, that in the days of my adoration the candy had come from her handsome Italian protector—to use the gallant Mediterranean term—who owned a local candy and soda-water parlor.

The river, in one way or another, affected everybody in town and from early childhood I heard it mentioned at our dinner table. Sometimes we talked about it to strangers who lived on streams they called "rivers" but which we regarded as little, ole, piddlin' creeks by comparison with the Mississippi. Then our enthusiasm for it approached that of the native son who exclaimed, "The great big rollin', tumblin', bilin', endless, and almost shoreless Mississippi! There's a river for you! There ain't nobody else but Uncle Sam as could afford such a river as that!"

In a more sober mood, we felt that the Mississippi was the dragon that sometimes pounced upon its victims in the night, the dragon that no St. George had risen to slay. The people perilously sheltered themselves against it behind the breastwork of earthen levees that ran, both sides of the stream, fifteen hundred miles from Cairo, Illinois, to New Orleans. Yet although the Mississippi drained half the waters of the nation, levees were built and maintained, not by the federal government, but by communities along the river. This made for heavy "levee taxes" and for urgent efforts on our part to persuade the guvment to shoulder part of the burden.

Our county had a Levee Board charged with maintaining the levees and keeping them from breaking in time of peril. Of all our public bodies it had perhaps the highest place of dignity and esteem among us and was notably free of politics. As nationally the guiding principle was that "politics stops at the water's edge," so among us, our lives at stake, politics stopped at the Mississippi banks. The position of our Levee Board, therefore, was comparable to that of the centuries-old Waterstraat in the Netherlands, a body of hydraulic experts charged with defending the country against the sea from which it had been snatched.

Dwellers on Vesuvius, the river's presence constantly reminded us of its terror and power, of our isolation and weakness. If it bred a certain fatalism among us and lent the community humility in the face of a terrifying phenomenon, men nonetheless pitted against it their strength and courage. Sometimes they lost. Perhaps, however, it was salutary for us that the river flowed by our door. For it gave the town the quiet dignity that attaches to danger, restrained it from the temptation to vulgar boastfulness, and kept it from getting too big for its britches.

For us boys the Mississippi was still what it had been to young Samuel Clemens of Hannibal, Missouri, a century earlier: a place of adventure, a wonderland that could never be fully explored, an asylum from adult tyranny and adult unimaginativeness. It was boundless, perilous, familiar, unfamiliar, forever changing, forever calling.

When I lived in a house near the river, its banks were my playground, the levee my other home. There I flew kites; watched floating driftwood and puffing steamboats; lay upon my back under a cloud canopy and drifted in fancy to seas that washed the shores of the farthest world. Spurning the sidewalk—a pavement without life, a road without springiness—I walked to school on the levee, an avenue high elevated in our flat land. Grasshoppers whirled from under my feet, crickets leaped, turtles sometimes waddled away, a bird took startled flight, a snake slithered into deeper grass. It was a path filled with secret life beguiling to a boy.

Going this way, the greatest of American rivers flowing below me under the wide sky and limitless horizon, quite subconsciously—like the slow sweepings of floodwaters into the body of the levee—I became dimly aware of the beauty of the world: of sun and rain and fog and tawny stream, of clouds and light and shadow and color. Oh, how I hated then to step from the lovely world, the wild, free, beautiful world, into the prison cell of my schoolroom. I was a boy, and my teachers treated me as a boy. But I was also something more than a boy. For the Mississippi was shaping me into premature sensory maturity and spiritual perceptiveness, a child still, but touched by wistfulness.

This did not, however, prevent me from sharing the full-bodied delights of the river. Its sandbars were perfect places from which pirates—as Huck Finn before us—could attack passing treasure boats, rob rafts, plan forays upon unsuspecting townsmen. In more lawful mood, a boy could fish in the mainstream, in ponds the river had scoured out when in flood, or in barrow pits—great water-filled holes dug when earth was removed from building levees. On hot summer afternoons I sometimes shot water moccasins with my .22 rifle as these poisonous reptiles lay in the shade of bushes along the water. In autumn I hunted rabbits in the no-man's-land between river and levee or wild ducks disporting themselves in ponds.

On one such occasion, being then in high school, I had a moving experience. Twilight merging into darkness, a lone duck arose from a pond and flew into the well of descending night. Then I began to understand—a heavy pressure on my chest—a favorite poem whose meaning had eluded me in classroom: William

Cullen Bryant's "To a Waterfowl." Walking homeward, the curtain opened a little way as I mumbled to myself the well-remembered stanzas:

> Thou'rt gone, the abyss of heaven
> Hath swallowed up they form; yet, on my heart
> Deeply hath sunk the lesson thou hast given,
> And shall not soon depart.
>
> He who, from zone to zone,
> Guides through the boundless sky thy certain flight,
> In the long way that I must tread alone,
> Will lead my steps aright.

Who comprehends revelation or its choice of instruments?

The river was unfailingly interesting. Sometimes I visited a floating fish dock
and watched fishermen remove "buffalo" (carp) from fishboxes in the stream
and, with deft movements of flying knives, dress them. On Saturdays they did a
flourishing business with Negroes. Come in from the country on morning
trains, many of them would go straight from the depot to the fish dock a mile
away, buy a big buffalo for four or five cents a pound, and run a wire through
its gills. Then they would drag the fish after them on the sidewalk and from store
to store as they did their tradin' until it was time to catch the late afternoon train.
Negroes, probably because of diet deficiencies, had an almost passionate longing for fish.

Huge rafts of logs—as in Huck Finn's day—were floated downstream, the
rude craft bound with steel chains. Occasionally I stood upon one tied up near
the sawmill—miles out in the stream it seemed to my landsman's eyes—and
watched rivermen as with shepherd's skill they detached a log from the raft and
maneuvered it with pikes to the sawmill landing. There it was dragged by a ca-
ble up a steel-shod way that shone silver in the sun, the log dripping water and
black as a whale, small branches lending it the semblance of fins.

Inside the mill, heroic figures, dimly seen through storms of aromatic sawdust, shuttled back and forth on moving platforms as their power-driven saw,
now screaming, now groaning, split the stout hearts of oak and walnut. Outside,
Negroes stacked sawn lumber for seasoning in the sun, children of giants playing at building castles of huge wooden blocks.

All this was like the circus, where one could not see everything that was happening in all the rings. But here nonetheless was a spectacular panorama of river
and sky and rafts. Here I first began to perceive a beauty that has ever since
claimed my attention: the loose-jointed, liquid grace of men working with pur-
poseful motion, men whose place of work in this instance was framed by a pillar of cloud by day and a pillar of fire by night as the tall steel incinerator of the
mill burned an endless supply of sawdust and slabs.

I met many kinds of men along the river. Some of them, although our town was just over the levee, were almost as remote from townsmen in their attitudes toward society as though they had come out of another time and place. There were boatmen, fishermen, lumbermen, hunters, loafers, trappers, farmers who tilled the soil between levee and river hoping to get their crops before the river got them. And there were "river rats."

People of Anglo-Saxon stock whose names rang English upon the oar, river rats lived in flimsy shanty boats, moving from place to place as whim or necessity dictated; rootless, acknowledging no jurisdiction of men or law and consorting only with their own kind, they were beyond the pale of the churches, the claims of other men, or of society generally.

They were, of course, fascinating to boys. Their lives, we thought, were enviably free of the impediments to joy that darkened our existence. *They* could hunt or fish whenever they liked. *They* did not have to go to school. And their fascination for us was heightened by something else. Gossip had it that many of them were murderous fugitives from the law, moonshiners, and, more darkly, incestuous. The meaning of "incestuous" was not clear to us, but suggesting something so rankly evil our elders would not talk about it, it raised river rats a notch higher in our esteem.

I made a lasting friendship among them. It was with the Harper family—father, mother, son. The elder Harper had a flowing patriarchal beard and long hair that cascaded over his shirt collar so that he came to be called Old Man Whiskers or, by the irreverent, Old Man Jesus. In my early maturity the Harpers had moved up in the world. No longer entirely nomadic, they lived in their shantyboat on an island in the Mississippi a few miles below town. I often stayed with them while hunting on the river, but however frequent my visits, I always took the precaution of hollering loud and long before approaching the island, of which they were the sole tenants. For Mr. Harper had a little patch of corn growing in his domain and, as befits a freeborn American, converted it into any form he chose: in this case "white mule" that he sold to townsmen. A crack shot with rifle or shotgun, my host instructed me to holler when I approached the island because, as he put it with touching solicitude for his guest's welfare, he "shore would hate to make a mistake and shoot a friend." Anxious to keep him from error, I hollered.

He ran off a little whiskey from time to time, fished a bit, piddled a great deal. His wife, Miss Ollie, was the mainstay of the family emotionally and financially, a woman of character against overwhelming odds. Slight of figure, weighing perhaps ninety pounds, hands gnarled and made horny by hard labor, face tanned, leathery, and intricately wrinkled through ruthless exposure to sun and wind, her gray eyes, steady and fearless within the frame of her gingham poke-bonnet, bore the wizened, crow's-feet look of seamen's eyes ever vigilant against the perils of great waters.

It was hard to tell at first glance whether she was male or female. The acid-eroding rains of hardship had stripped her to the bare bones of physical anonymity. She had the asexual appearance I have since observed among women in various parts of the world who lead lives of unremitting toil and gall-bitter deprivation. It is indeed only the well-to-do who have, or can afford to have, what one might call "racehorse women," women who are sleek, leggy, luxurious, fit more for pleasure than for toil or breeding.

Miss Ollie was a skilled operator of gasoline-driven small craft. So skillful was she that she had a government contract to "run the lights," to see that beacons along a defined stretch of river functioned at all times. Through sun, rain, fog, sleet, she kept the lights going and so moved nearer the fulfillment of her consuming ambition.

The Harpers loved their one child, Ben, but it was his mother who was determined that he should attend college. Bit by bit she saved money, and crushing as were her duties with the beacons and household, she took Ben daily to school in Arkansas, a round trip of thirty miles in her boat. Yet, with no sense of outlawry, she permitted him to help his father by taking skiffloads of white mule to the Arkansas or Mississippi shore, where he left jugs of it in the bushes for Pappy's customers.

Once, when I had not been to the island for a long time, I ran into Mr. Harper at the post office. Urging me to come and hunt wild geese, he offered, as a special hospitality, "a mattress that ain't got nair bedbug." Unable to resist this allurement, however it revealed me as a sissy, I soon went to the island, a lonely place whose silence was broken only by the roaring of the river and the soughing of the wind in the cottonwood trees. The shantyboat was scarcely visible against its overwhelming background of stream and bluffs, and my host's corn plot was a scratch upon the earth.

At four o'clock of a marrow-chilling morning, I was awakened for the hunt and went for breakfast into the tiny kitchen that smelled of kerosene and sour cornbread. Our repast lay upon the oilcloth-covered table: a cold 'coon, teeth grinning from its head, the carcass gray-white with coagulated fats; a layer cake, each layer of different color and flavor like the cakes that ladies bake for county fair contests; and a bottle of white mule. My host and his cousin from Carriola Landing lit into the food and whiskey with great gusto. But I, perhaps because of the disability of a certain town-bred effeteness—a recognizable flaw of character that had led my host to proffer me the insect-free mattress—skipped the mule and coon and ate only cake. Breakfast over, we went to the sandbar to hunt.

As time passed, Mr. Harper, whether growing older or becoming more triflin', put more of the burden of delivering whiskey upon Ben. One morning, as he was pushing off in his skiff from the Arkansas shore and still standing while it slowly moved out into the stream, two deputy sheriffs suddenly appeared from the bushes and shouted, "Halt!" Their shout was almost simultaneous with the crack of a rifle. Ben fell dead. The skiff drifted down the river.

Three months later Mr. Harper died. Miss Ollie soon followed him. Shantyboat people said, "They were heartbroke."

Growing into manhood, I continued to seek river and levee, their spell strong upon me. The levee was not, in the European or Latin American sense, a promenade. Nor was it a favorite walking place of townsmen and was little frequented by them. The river itself for perhaps subconscious reasons deterred them. For this was no quiet stream such as contemplative poets celebrate, a stream along whose placid banks men might tranquilly drift on slow currents of memory and reflection. Nor was it a brook burbling over rounded stones to make the tiny whitecaps of a nursery sea, a sea over which a child might assert sovereignty by launching the papal bull of a toy boat.

The river's awesome presence felt in his bones, Huck Finn tells us, "It was kind of solemn, drifting down the big still river, laying on our backs looking up at the stars, and we didn't ever feel like talking loud, and it warn't often that we laughed, only a little kind of low chuckle."

The Mississippi River was a wild and primitive force, a member of the monstrous family of cyclones, earthquakes, and tidal waves against which men assert in vain their vaunted authority. Maker of its own designs, it was the abode of a River God often malevolent and always inscrutable. Dun-brown, heavy-bodied, flowing eternally from an inexhaustible source, it almost compellingly suggested the transiency of human life, bringing one to meditate, however unwillingly, upon one's grasshopper moment in the sun and causing to reverberate in one's ear the Psalmist's query, "What is man that thou art mindful of him?"

It also suggested—this restless stream always seeking to break the bonds with which men tried to tame it—the immutability of struggle, the inescapable condition of naked, night-enshrouded man, forever attempting to return to the lost Eden whose gates are forever barred against him. An austere water, it demanded for its sympathetic comprehension some austerity of those who came to it, the wrinkled almond faintly bitter upon the palate.

Untamed, perhaps untamable, now roaring like a beast of Revelations, now going lamblike, the Mississippi was secretive and furtive, undermining its banks with subterranean suckings and lappings until they fell into the stream, taking trees and surface structures with them. Against it, as against the sinister sea, men had always to be vigilant.

Constantly trying to shift its channel, seeking out the levee's weak places, it treasured up the rains and snows of the Rockies, of the High Plains, of half the continent; the waters of great rivers and of lesser rivers; of thousands of creeks and lakes and billions of rills that emptied into it as it made its long way across the land. It contained them. Then it hurled them against the earthen levees. Sometimes it was victorious. Sometimes it was defeated. Its victories were expressed in men drowned, structures destroyed, roads and railroads undermined. In one place it heaped sand to bury the soil, but in another place, as by malefic caprice, it enriched the soil with loam looted from Iowa cornfields. These things our people knew and, knowing, feared.

In childhood I played along the river. In manhood I strolled with friends on the levee. There part of my youth lies buried. A man dies but once. Yet he has many graves. The more restless his spirit, questing his heart, the luck vaulting his mind, the more numerous are his graves, marked or unmarked, green or brown, so that his final interment is not a final summation but merely a putting away of the last remnant. His friends can mourn him. They cannot bury him.

I liked especially to walk along the levee when the winepress of autumn was stained purple with the lees of its grapes. The land's annual travail of life giving was over, and there was an ingathering of the fruits. There was then a winey headiness in the air that had been enervating during the long months of summer. Children, drunk with it, ran swiftly home from school on the pavement of Walnut Street that paralleled the levee. Field larks, released from their summer familial duties, drifted with joyous caprice on the flowing stream of the sky, singing as they soared. Householder's axes rang against firewood, the most domestic of sounds rich with intimations of warming blaze, bubbling pot, and contentment snuggling against the hearth.

From afar hunter's guns sometimes faintly boomed; how the spirit sadly turned in upon itself at this muted voice of death. Cottonwoods, leaves fallen, stood immaculate in the clean beauty of pure form, and the somber sun descending, the river poured into it a torrent of light. Overhead, southward and ever southward, flew wildfowl in the crystalline air, their cries thin against the great heights through which they moved. Sometimes, night come, wild geese, long necks outstretched, legs taunt against the body, plunged into the golden sea of the risen moon and swiftly beating its breasting waves emerged and were lost in the arching curve of the circling earth. The stroller stood still in the presence of this miracle, tides out of nowhere surging over his heart.

Since one must be part of what is forever part of oneself, I am indissolubly bound up with the river. Even now I cannot walk along it without a tightening of the throat, remembering the dear dead with whom I once strolled there. The ghosts of vanished sunsets are before my eyes. In my ears are the whimperings of the lost child. Darkness is falling, but no twinkling lights are coming on in the little town below the levee.

Cohn dined with many heads of state, including President Ramón Magsaysay
of the Philippines.

Cohn as a war correspondent

An avid outdoorsman, Cohn always tried to find time for a hunting or fishing
trip when he returned to the Delta.

Cohn also spent considerable time visiting with Delta blacks of all ages.

9

The Education of a Rounded Man

In this chapter (also titled in other versions "The Task Never Finished"), Cohn discusses the growth of his interest in learning, especially his desire to become knowledgeable about a wide variety of subjects—in short, to become a "rounded man." The disdain that Cohn expresses for specialists and specialization may result in part from the rough treatment he often received at the hands of the "specialists" (scholars in particular) who reviewed his books.

A little boy, wearing knee pants, homemade blouse, and black, ribbed cotton stockings, I entered Court School—the start of an endless pilgrimage in search of knowledge. Severe, totally lacking in amenities, smoothworn benches hard, the school was a small structure of crumbly red brick. Its classrooms were heated by potbellied stoves that older pupils stoked when Tobe, the Negro janitor, lost upon some obscure errand, did not appear to perform this important office.

Innocent of what are now elegantly termed "sanitary facilities," a pupil held up his hand, received the teacher's permission "to be excused," and went outside. His journey—its utilitarian aspects apart—could be an adventure.

Upon a rainy day he might wade through pools of water—what small boy ever went dryshod if he could slosh through water?—an avenging pioneer on Indian trails. Or, equally satisfyingly, he could become an escaped convict throwing bloodhounds off the scent. (Used by local police, these gentle, flop-eared, sad-eyed dogs were familiar to us.) Stumbling upon a rabbit, he could watch it run with white-rumped swiftness. Sleet falling, he might wish for the rarity of snow. Then classes would be dismissed so that all—including our teachers— might enjoy the fleeting pleasures of snow. Meeting another boy upon the same errand, he might trade agates with him or swap a magnet for a pencil sharpener; all American boys are traders at heart. Thus, "to be excused" in the pre-plumbing days of my childhood was often a passport to adventure.

Shading the entrance to school stood a mighty-limbed oak under which we played. It was host to squirrels that moved with acrobatic grace, to birds, to ants that had colonies in its roots. The wind spoke with many voices among its cathedral branches. From it in autumn fell the intermittent, crackling rain of ripe acorns.

Through classroom windows—when the teacher's head was turned—we watched the pageant of mule-drawn wagons creaking along a dusty road bringing cotton to the gins, cordwood to householders, or Negro families to town to do their tradin'. There were white men and Negroes on horseback, and sometimes many people come to attend a funeral in the graveyard that lay just beyond the road.

Occasionally, frightened and wondering, we stole into the little graveyard where local Chinese deposited their dead until the bodies could be sent to lie in China's hallowed earth. On the graves we looked for the bowls of cooked rice that people said were placed there so the dead might arise and eat at night pending their long trip home, but we never found any. There, in that still place, the humming of yellow-and-black bumblebees in our ears as they emerged nectar-dusty from tiny tunnels of blue clover, some vague notion of the wonder and solemnity of death entered our child minds. But we did not linger long. Play called. We hunted crawfish in wet ditches or raced in colts' abandon around the school grounds.

There was a general prejudice in town against "night air," the alleged source of fevers, but if windows were shut at night, few contracted "consumption." Some children wore a tiny bag of asafoetida attached to the neck by a string, a preventive of colds. We all believed that contact with a toad frog would cause warts. Our elders, ignorant of vitamins, did not give us orange juice or demand for us hot lunches at school. Yet we were lustily healthful. Food cheap and plentiful, boys' appetites keen, we ate all the time.

There was no notion in that pre-Freudian day that if Papa should tan Junior's behind in the woodshed, this would cause Junior to become a monster, or that Papa was moved less by a sense of parental discipline than by his own subconscious brutality. Nor did anyone talk about a "guilt complex" on Papa's part when, after the tanning, he and Junior went fishing together.

We had no "supervised play." Such a notion would have astonished our elders. Whoever had to teach lambs, kids, or children how to play? Given the animal spirits and inventive imaginations of children, our parents thought it enough merely to turn us loose on the levee or an empty lot. There we would play to the point of exhaustion, returning home with blackened hands and faces, pants torn, stockings ripped, ready for bed after a scrubbing and supper.

Our teachers, born when phrenology was more the rage than psychology, were firm disciplinarians. They were unaware that if we were kept from doing whatever popped into our (to us dear little) heads, the effects of restraint would ultimately prove disastrous. Nor did they believe that the fostering in us of anarchic individualism prepared us for living in an ordered society. On the contrary, they kept handy a peach-tree switch or other weapon suitable to a lady's strength and used it whenever anarchy threatened the scene. Its frequent herald, in springtime, was the flight of chinaberries ejected from popguns that we whittled from cane.

Archer High School, which I eventually entered, was as simple as Court School. Built of crumbling red brick, it was stocked with instruments of teaching and nothing else. It had neither auditorium, gymnasium, nor stadium. I was a member of our football and track teams. But athletes were not exalted over other students or the teacher-coach over other teachers. A truly amateur sport and therefore unselfconscious, football little interested the public. Star players did not expect "scholarships" from colleges, so-called institutions of learning clamoring for their services as meat-packers clamor for hogs when the runs are small. For colleges had not yet adopted the totalitarian principle of winning (football games) at any cost—the end justifying the means—and subtly corrupting youth upon the campus. This attitude—dictated more by alumni than students—perhaps led Warden Lawes of Sing Sing prison to say that he could run a good institution because he was unhampered by its alumni.

(It is evidence of the antiquity of my times that when I was a student at the University of Virginia, football players were bonafide students and the coach an unpaid alumnus serving for love of alma mater. Obviously such a point of view is "impractical," and so it had to yield in time to "progress.")

Archer High had no cheerleaders to generate a synthetic enthusiasm that seemed more proper to Germany than to us. There, as I learned from reading Stephen Leacock, birds sit on branches, never more than three to a branch, singing in unison, while below them peasants pick up leaves and put them into neat packets none containing more than thirty. We had no school band. One happy result of this was that we had no drum majorettes, adolescent girls preposterously got up in eighteenth-century guardsman's shakos, ballet skirts, and Russian boots, proper smiles filtering through dental braces on their teeth: youth immolated by their parents and community on a pyre of vulgarity.

Our school was without vocational training classes for boys or business classes for girls. We had not yet become so prosperous that our girls had to work outside the home to keep prosperity inside the home, while our superintendent of education, Mr. E. E. Bass, clung to the quaint belief that education was a training for the mind and spirit rather than the marketplace. One day he came upon me reading about personal immortality in the *Encyclopedia Britannica* when I ought to have been doing my lessons. He read briefly over my shoulder and then tiptoed away, leaving me shaken but grateful.

Tall, spare, with a halo of reddish hair, blue-eyed, smiling and intricately wrinkled, moving gracefully with a loping walk that covered much ground quickly, a lover of birds, flowers, and children, he looked sometimes a benevolent Silenus as he stood before us to make his weekly talk. Whimsically humorous, a disciplinarian without being a martinet, he lent me books from his own library—I remember especially William James—and being a various man, he once publicly commended me and a classmate for what might have been regarded as unruly conduct.

We had had a fistfight on the school grounds, but when it was over we impulsively shook hands and entered class together. Neither of us knew that Mr. Bass had been an onlooker. But at the next assembly he congratulated us because, the fight ended, we bore no grudge against one another. Sometimes, he said, a clash between evenly matched boys is good for the spirit and becomes harmful only when resentments are nursed by the combatants. I learned much from this old-fashioned educator—more from the man than from the instructor. The "facts" learned faded in time, but the example endures.

Most of our teachers were good. Some were bad. One of the latter punished us for misconduct by compelling us to copy a poem twenty times, a crime against beauty. Such a discipline might have made me abhor verse, but my love for it was proof against almost anything. This teacher had a sister in obtuseness who once publicly humiliated me because, a ninth grader, I had properly used the word "evince," a word, she announced to the class (to my crimsoned pain), that must have been supplied by my elders.

It was clear, even to my untutored mind, that some of our teaching was poor, and fond of "history," my notions were strengthened by a passage in Herbert Spencer, with whom I sometimes struggled on my own. History, he wrote, was taught as a "meaningless tissue of names, dates, and places." He had clearly said what was inchoately in my mind. Then I determined, with the humorless seriousness of an adolescent, that my "essay" to be read at our graduating exercises in the Grand Opera House should be a review of my education, a thanksgiving for it, and some statement of what appeared to me to be its defects.

Miss Carrie Stern, our "art" teacher, dissuaded me from my course. It was not, she said, that my charges were without foundation. But it would be "ungracious" of me to air them at the graduation exercises. Devoted to her and seeing merit in her words, I abandoned my plan, but not without an inward struggle. For I vividly remembered the words of Romain Rolland that I had just read in his recently published Jean Christophe: "When a man is young he must be under the illusion that he is recreating the life of humanity."

Long after her [*Miss Carrie's*] death, I delivered my graduation talk, however changed it was to meet changing circumstances. My audience was the Southern Governors' Conference meeting in New Orleans, and I spoke on southern education somewhat to this effect:

If the South is poor and proud, it is also prolific. It overproduces cotton; that keeps it poor. It overproduces children; that makes it difficult for poor communities to educate them properly. But it doesn't overproduce horse sense. On the contrary, we compound our idiocies.

Every June our newspapers announce, for example, that "graduating exercises will be held in the $500,000 Oakdale High School." Everybody knows that Oakdale has been living on whippoorwill peas and cornbread for fifty years. But that doesn't keep its people from building a fancy school whose construction and maintenance costs just about break their backs. The only thing they can do to keep the school open is to strip it of all that makes a school meaningful. They skimp on libraries, equipment, laboratories. They "save" on teachers' pay.

Gigantism, however, isn't confined to poor southern towns. It is a national malady. Consider Yale University with its "$15,000,000 Stirling Memorial Library." What happened there?

When Yale's income from its endowment securities sharply dropped in the depression of the 1930s, it balanced its budget by firing young instructors and cutting down the salaries of professors. You may blight a man's career. You may bring hardships to others. But you may not neglect to maintain in style a $15,000,000 library. Thus a university becomes a collection of costly buildings rather than a company of scholars.

As for teachers' salaries, I suggested they be raised. But the chances are that you won't get the best men and women to teach until society raises their *status.* Teachers have a low status among us, as do preachers and everyone else whom we do not regard as producers: salesmen, engineers, businessmen whose efficiency may be measured in terms of dollars earned. Yet we might procure a number of better teachers by offering them more pay. Certainly, I said, I'd rather sit at the feet of a great teacher in an outhouse than to sit at the feet of a fool in a palace. I suggested that the South build some schools of the plainest kind at the lowest cost, stock them with first-rate equipment, and hire the best teachers money can buy. Then, after watching the schools for a few years, determine your course.

The governors listened politely. The South went on its way. For it, too, had adopted the slogan of the house-paint industry that dominates much of our national life: SAVE THE SURFACE AND YOU SAVE ALL.

Miss Carrie, who beneficially affected life, was a tiny figure of a human whose fragility seemed to exaggerate her great brown eyes so that when I went to see her as she was dying of cancer and had become the mere shadow of a woman, I was conscious only of the deep pools of her eyes. Her face was not beautiful, but it was an intelligent face lighted by her spirit; her small hands had the grace of birds' wings, and her expressive voice lent drama and color to the stories that she read for thirty years to the children of Greenville, who year after year clamored, "Miss Carrie, please read us a story."

The tiny, bird-boned woman with great brown eyes whom we called "Miss Carrie" left me deeply her debtor. A lover of painting—particularly that of the Italian Renaissance—and English verse, she painted and wrote verse. But the creative spark glowed only faintly within her. Yet her victory was summed up by her beloved Browning—to whom she led me—as he causes Andrea del Sarto, "the perfect painter," to say of his less gifted colleagues:

> Their works drop groundward,
> Themselves reach heaven many a time, I know.

Miss Carrie's infectious love for the Italian Renaissance communicated itself so strongly to me that, in the latter years of high school, I led an enchanted double life. One part of me resided in Greenville amid its familiar people and places. Another dwelt in an alien place at an alien time. Moving between an inner and an outer landscape, I lived almost as much in the Rome, Florence, Venice of the fifteenth and sixteenth centuries as in my twentieth-century Mississippi town. Many of their famous men became almost as familiar to me as my neighbors through the somewhat similar process by which great fictional characters become more "real" than one's neighbors. Thus, Savonarola's immediacy for me was little less than that of Sam Jones, the evangelist who thundered against sin and brought sinners in droves to repentance.

The gossip and intrigues of the period, the silken skullduggeries that marked it, the Herculean quarrels of the Pope and Michelangelo were as though they had been of my time and place. Straying into areas where, I am sure, the gentle Miss Carrie never wandered, I came to know such figures as Aretino, Caesar Borgia, and Pope Alexander VI in whose glittering sins I vicariously reveled. They were more exciting than the most purple screen melodrama offered by the Dew Drop Inn Movie Theatre.

Intoxicated by the heady wine of the Renaissance, I read everything about it that was available to me, ranging from Vasari to John Addington Symonds. My familiarity with its artists increased after I saw inexpensive reproductions of their works that Miss Carrie ordered from Boston.

My other affection, touched almost to adoration by Miss Carrie's love of it, was for English verse. Here the Greek mythology that I had read for an understanding of the Renaissance painters helped me to understand the English poets, while my limited perceptions of the Renaissance later brought me a clearer vision of the Elizabethan Age, which was so Italianate in many ways.

Editions of the "standard" poets were readily available to us at modest prices. Sears and Roebuck then sold them through its catalog. (But it no longer does.) Carter, our dignified Negro bookseller and stationer on our principal street, also stocked the standard poets. And while I was in high school, the local Jewish congregation called to its pulpit Rabbi Emanuel Sternheim. English-born, English-educated, a scholar and lover of books, he led me into new avenues of reading. We had no public library. But Sternheim and Will Percy took the lead in establishing one that has since become the creditable William Alexander Percy Memorial Library. Now another window upon the world was opened for us.

Our sky was unsmudged by factory smoke because we had no industries except a few small ones that stemmed from our soil: cottonseed oil mills, cotton compresses, sawmills. No one wanted industries in that day before the arrival of the booster, promoter, and chamber of commerce. Our elder statesmen held that factories would "ruin a nice town to live in," "stir things up," bring down upon us a "lot of riffraff." If boosters had shown their heads, they would have been derided as noisy, quarrelsome jaybirds.

Animated by the antebellum southern prejudice against industry, our elders were in harmony with Colonel Carter of Hopkinsville, Kentucky. After The War, progress having infected with its virus some of the town's young men, they were eager to build a hotel and called a meeting of citizens to consider it. But the Colonel—a man who had left an arm at Chancellorsville—opposed the project. "If a man gets off the train here," he said, "and he's a gentleman, he will be welcome as a guest in my house. If he isn't a gentleman, we don't want him in town." [*This story is, of course, apocryphal. The same tale circulated in postbellum Georgia, with General Robert Toombs as the protagonist.*]

(Yet progress eventually stormed Greenville, and the measure of change is this. In the 1870s, its people had fought carpetbaggers. But by the 1950s it had inveigled a northern carpet mill to come to town, heavily subsidizing it to do so.)

In other fields, we stubbornly resisted change. When the tiny British ship *Beagle,* bearing a young scientist named Charles Darwin, made a nineteenth-century journey, it set in motion tidal waves that broke violently upon Europe's shores. But it caused not even a ripple in the Mississippi River. No one could have convinced us that our remote kinfolks were monkeys or, contrary to the Bible, that the world had not been created in the year 4004 B.C. Most of us said, "I'd believe it if it's in the Bible, even if it ain't so."

Yet the town's small group that was somewhat traveled and college educated, while maintaining the forms of traditional religious faith, was touched by an amiable agnosticism. Its members held easygoing attitudes toward "sin," especially sins of the flesh. Some even took a pagan pride in the fact that a minister of every denomination represented in Greenville's white pulpits had been "messed up by a lady." Sinners rejoiced that even sin-splittin' preachers had sinned. But the godly drove from town ministers who had "fallen by the wayside." Negroes, more charitable than whites, put the case with mercy. "Even a preacher's liable to do bad," they said. "So let's pray a prayer for him."

Most of the white people and Negroes remained fundamentalist in their religious beliefs. For them Noah's Ark sailed on, Jonah rode inside the whale, Joshua fit the battle o' Jericho, and the wicked boiled eternally in oil. Religious fundamentalism was accompanied by political fundamentalism. We were untouched by storms of political doctrine blowing across the Western ocean, by Populism that shook some of the country, or by the struggles of trade unionism for a place in the industrial sun. In terms of today's political jargon, we were right of right. The world peaceful, white supremacy unquestioned locally, we sought little more than the triumph of the Democratic party and a good price for cotton.

But no community, however remote from the mainstream of intellectual life, is impervious to the dust-siftings of ideas. Somehow I became dimly aware of stirrings beyond our cotton-encompassed horizon. One clue led to another, and I felt a mounting excitement as the chase proceeded. Untutored, unguided, confused, my mental equipment inadequate to the task, I desperately tried to understand socialism, anarchism, syndicalism, the cooperative movement, and the "modernist" effort, largely centering in France, for reforming the Catholic Church. In my efforts to understand I sweated—literally sweated—during the hot days of school vacation over books available to me bearing upon these things, encountering such strange names as Proudhon, Bakunin, Kauntsky, Loisy, Kropotkin. My heroes—as befits a schoolboy—were men of action such as soldiers, adventurers, and explorers, but if I failed to understand all that I read, I began to perceive that the movers and shakers of earth are men of ideas.

I could not then know that my adult life would be profoundly affected by earth-shaking ideas coming from overseas, and I would live in an almost unbroken era of wars and revolutions. Yet, for no explicable reason, I was drawn to writings about international affairs, reading anything that would tell me about them, ranging from the *New Republic,* then just appearing, to the *Encyclopedia Britannica.* Boylike, I reveled in Mahan's *The Influence of Sea Power upon History,* because its dryer passages were relieved by narratives of sea battles.

These extracurricular researches did nothing to improve my lamentable standing as a high school student who was obtuse at mathematics, substandard in Latin, and bewildered by English grammar. Nor did I get much from my adolescent probings into the unknown except the headily stimulating knowledge that the sky, once empty to my eyes, swarmed with whirling planets.

My frenzied reading failed me at a critical moment, an early intimation of the Preacher's fiat that "he who increaseth wisdom increaseth grief." For once, when one of the prettiest girls in school, sweetening up her voice, asked me to give her the outlines of a popular novel or two so that she could knowingly mention them at dinner parties, I miserably failed her—and myself. Then I upbraided myself for having wasted time upon Friedrich Wilhelm Nietzsche when it might have been more fruitfully employed reading Harold Bell Wright, a popular novelist of the times.

Remote from the mainstream of Western intellectual life, Oriental thought for us—as for most Americans—was a closed book that we little cared to read. Yet we had firm convictions that we shared with our countrymen elsewhere in the nation.

We believed that man was essentially good, that his heart would mellow, religion would dissipate his evil impulses, and he would eventually come into a spiritual state of near perfectibility.

We shared with our nineteenth-century countrymen—the century that did not end until 1914—an unshakable belief in progress. We believed in progress as sure, unbounded, limitless; in progress by evolution rather than revolution; in the ultimate triumph of right over might, of truth over falsehood, of virtue over vice.

(No one told me that in the first year of my life and the last year of his life, in a book forebodingly entitled *Nemesis,* Alfred Nobel, inventor of dynamite and founder of the Nobel Prizes, had written, "The so-called Christian world is still little more than a battlefield.")

Inextinguishably hopeful, we looked forward to a wider application of human brotherhood than man had hitherto known. There were no limits, we assumed, to which men might not reasonably aspire in their search for happiness and prosperity. So believing, we found our convictions strengthened by the books we read, the political pronouncements we heard, the plays we saw, and, even, sometimes by the songs we sang.

The time seemed short between the period when the Continental Congress, the colonies still at war with Britain, considered a resolution stating that this was the world's greatest country, to the moment when a president of the United States was photographed sitting on a dredger in the Culebra Cut. The Panama Canal, under American impetus, was going forward despite yellow fever and landslides; a triumph somewhat the sweeter because there a foreign nation had failed. There was no doubt about it: we were going places. How far no one, seeing the distance we had covered in so short a time, was rash enough to say.

The War was ever receding into the past, its wounds healing with time. Confederate veterans walked our streets with veterans of the Spanish-American War. That conflict, shameful and foolish, had done much to unify the sections that only a generation before had been at one another's throats.

The world, with the exception of such localized wars as the Crimean, Franco-Prussian, South African, Russo-Japanese, had had peace for nearly a century. Foreign wars, in any event, little disturbed us. Indeed they seemed dashingly romantic as described by the handsome war correspondent, Richard Harding Davis, who continued to look an Arrow-collar man amid shot and shell.

Nations in the future, we believed, would honorably adjust their differences without wars, just as we settled our claims for a railroad-killed mule in our circuit court. A tribunal for this purpose was convoked by the nations at The Hague, a prime mover in its establishment being Nicholas II, Czar of Russia, and I felt personally indebted to His Imperial Majesty when I won a $5 "essay" contest prize on the subject of the Hague conference.

Common sense, restraint, and moderation seemed to govern an age in which mankind was given to reason and the reasonable. Who could doubt, therefore, that, having reached this plateau after centuries of plodding, it would go on to the peaks where blow the clean airs of truth?

Within our little province of the Delta—the world peaceful—men, if not avid for machine-made progress, were sanguine of the future. They faced difficult problems concerning the eradication of malaria, the draining of low-lying lands, constructing hard surface roads, the everlasting struggle with the river, and the price of cotton. But nothing so pleases Americans as problems. "Yessir, that sure is a problem!" we happily exclaim, licking our chops over the prospect of settling it and looking forward to another when that one is no more. Pioneer maxims are still high in our sky—"Paddle your own canoe"; government would, or should, help men to solve problems they ought to solve for themselves.

Thus it was that, genially improvident, optimistic, slow-paced, pleasure-loving, politically and religiously conservative, Greenville scarcely stirred in its nineteenth-century dreams as German lancers, upon a summer morning of 1914 when the lands of the Delta were beginning to run white to the farthest horizon, galloped down the Roman roads of Belgium.

[*However sleepy, isolated, and out of the mainstream Greenville may have seemed, its plantation tradition of at least lip-service support for literature and the arts, as well as the influence of individuals such as E. E. Bass, Carrie Stern, and Rabbi Sternhein, clearly inspired Cohn to broaden his intellectual horizons.*]

Now there began to form in my mind a not uncommon ambition—to become a rounded man. But I soon found I had committed myself to a project that, never completed, would always be a work in progress. How often since then have I awakened in the night and entered the rafted studio of my mind to undo what I had done during the day or to do what I had left undone. I removed the damp cloths from the clay of the unfinished sculpture, smoothed out a line here, erased one there, touched up the corner of the mouth too greatly drooping, tilted downward the upward, arrogant nose. Yet in the morning I found that my work was not good.

Paul Valery has it that "plays are never completed; they are abandoned." The playwright, after so much writing and rewriting, finally commits his play to the stage, heavyhearted perhaps because he had not bridged the gulf between the vision seen and that committed to paper. Thus he is doomed to failure as, in a similar sense, are all men.

These were conclusions I had glimpsed through association with Miss Carrie Stern, who was wise with the wisdom of the poet and visionary. They also came to me through her from another poet, the now neglected Browning, whose verses she read to me before many a winter's fire in her little house that was near mine. The words, dusted with sugar of the marshmallows that she toasted before the hearth, come back to me across the stream of time:

> What hand and brain went ever pair'd?
> What heart alike conceived and dared?
> What act proved all its thought had been?
> What will but felt the fleshly screen?

Yet the gulf between thought and act was no cause for despair. On the contrary, the concept of completion seemed to me chilling. I knew it had not validity in nature. There sea change is constant. Lillies spring from cow's droppings. Rotting fish emerge Pequod's corn. Man, manipulating the chemistry instinct in nature, so orders it that many a beautiful woman wears the distillation of stinking animals' organs become perfume sweet.

Men have long mused upon this phosphorescent mutation, among them Shakespeare. I knew that no housewife rivals nature in her use of leftovers. I also knew that as the earth is still "settling," so there are no finalities in the living organism of society, revolutions being the extreme manifestation of change within it. Certainly there is no completion in man's mind. It is animated by the principle of growth and change. Stultify the principle, and you produce dwarfs, monsters, or living corpses of men.

I was not fearful that I should never become complete. My fear was that of Rabbi Meir of Apt. "When in the world to come," he said, "I face my Final Judge, I do not fear lest he reproach me: 'Why haven't you been Abraham our Patriarch?' or 'Why haven't you been Moses our Teacher?' I only fear that he might ask me, 'Why haven't you been Rabbi Meir of Apt?'"

My goal was harmony—spirit, mind, body, moving to one music, the being fluent to the slopes of the hills. Each component of the trinity has its virtues and its claims, and often the claims clash. But none is completely separate from the other although there is a formidable body of evidence to the contrary. Who shall precisely define their boundaries? The doctor of medicine? The doctor of philosophy? The doctor of divinity?

I tried—and failed—to impose harmony upon disharmony. For while I am gentle, I am also brutal, and while I am capable of holy wonder, I am also capable of denying wonder.

Once I sat in a south Louisiana duck blind amid a landscape of the morning time of the earth, the sun rising for me alone and the day new for me alone and the world fresh for me alone as the sun rose new and the day was new and the world was fresh for Adam. So it must have been when being began and the Lord said, "Let the waters bring forth abundantly the moving creatures that hath life, and fowl that may fly above the earth in the open firmament of heaven."

The mist dissolving, the air wine, the pulse of the sea beating faintly in the tidal marshes, white galleons of pelicans sailed in the immaculate sky. Red-winged blackbirds sang from swaying balconies of cattails, muskrats trailed courtiers' capes of black velvet through the water, snakes patterned it with the evanescent rippling ribbons of their swimmings. Overhead, in twos and threes, hundreds and thousands, wildfowl, whose home is the earth and the sky above the earth and the waters that cover the earth, flew to their feeding grounds, the silken music of their beating wings drifting down through layers of light. It is not alone in vaulted cathedrals that the head is bowed and the heart makes its genuflection.

And yet, moved by the primitive desire to kill, I fired. The third in a string of five ducks crumpled in the air and spinning fell. Only once before, watching a Cardinal's procession in Seville, I sadly remembered, had I seen red so brightly, richly red as the red of the blood that flecked the green-blue of the duck's broken neck.

My goal being roundedness, I rebelled against the overspecialization of our times. Even at college I had seen men disappear into specialists. I had long observed that overspecialization produces a certain mental claustrophobia among its devotees. "Beowulf men" tend to associate with other Beowulf men, undertaker's beauticians with undertaker's beauticians, bolt-and-nut men with bolt-and-nut men, lawyers with lawyers, doctors with doctors. But the corporation lawyer ignores his criminal law colleague as the obstetrician avoids the internist.

The specialist looms large among us and is correspondingly dangerous because he is essentially illiterate. Thus, doctors of medicine are notoriously without social or political literacy. I cheered the words of Ortega Gasset, who said, "In politics, in art, in social usages, in the other sciences, he (the specialist) will adopt the attitudes of primitive, ignorant man. . . . By specialising him, civilization has made him hermetic and self-satisfied within his limitations; but this very feeling of dominance will induce him to wish to predominate outside his specialty. . . . Today when there are more 'scientists' than ever, there are much less 'cultured' men than . . . about 1750."

Everywhere I could note the sterile pedantry of the overspecialized pedant. He might have bored many of us, but he was in good case. For since numerous men regard dullness as synonymous with profundity, those who put their footnotes in their mouth when they speak or write are regarded as "sound" men and are in demand as teachers and writers of "authentic" texts.

One of the old conventions of arid scholarship is that college faculty members must "publish" at intervals. It does not seem to matter a damn what they publish. Here the lettered appear to be as much in awe of the printed word as the unlettered: "Dr. Hazenway is the author of *Dart Throwing in Eastern Northumberland, 1783–1786.*"

The teacher's chance of promotion on his own campus or of acquiring a better job elsewhere might hang upon "publishing." And the drier the writing, the more finespun the specialization, the more likely is the author to escape the damning charge that he is "popular." He is not to be confused, to his embarrassment, with such popular writers as Shakespeare, Cervantes, Tolstoy, Dickens, and Mark Twain, who have long been read with pleasure by ordinary men.

The nonspecialist is at a disadvantage in a society of specialists among whom, typically, the doctor who looks up your nose is unqualified by training or disqualified by law from looking down your throat. We are, moreover, a people uncomfortable in the presence of those whom we cannot pigeonhole. Hence manufacturers of pigeonholes, themselves specialists, have a potentially huge field for operations. In such an environment the nonspecialist lacks prestige and is unlikely to be employed except upon pedestrian tasks.

All this I knew. But I was prepared to pay the price for what I wanted: roundedness. I have not achieved it, but I have not regretted trying to achieve it.

10

Student of the Law

In this chapter, Cohn discusses his experiences with higher education at the University of Virginia and Yale and describes the process whereby he decided that "the law" was not to be his career.

Extremely young, I entered the University of Virginia law school, moved to do so for several reasons. It was the alma mater of LeRoy Percy, our leading citizen and leader of the Mississippi Bar. From it had emerged many distinguished southern lawyers, and it was widely regarded among lawyers as being the best of southern law schools. But the law was not to be my career.

When I enrolled at the University of Virginia, it had only seven hundred students. They were all male. Women clamored for entrance, but alas for southern gallantry, their efforts to invade the campus except as welcome visitors were regarded with abhorrence by faculty and students. We were neither a monkish community nor misogynists, but the feeling prevailed that for centuries universities, along with their other blessings, had been temporary male retreats—a boon not lightly to be abandoned.

The ladies, with some difficulty, were staved off, but the process was already under way by which many of our colleges would become educational mass-production factories. During my second year I called upon President Alderman at the beginning of term, and he wearily said, "All over the South today parents are putting their sons on trains to come to the University of Virginia. Many of the parents do not know why they are sending their sons, and the sons do not know why they are being sent." There was beginning to dawn upon him, apparently, the unhappy realization that while democratic education has many virtues, it embraces equality of idiocy as well as of opportunity.

The university's technical students knew what they wanted: technical knowledge and little else. They had what they regarded as a manly contempt for "culture," and many of them left college without being able to write an intelligible business letter. Upon their premises, the ruder the man the better the technician. One could depend upon them to keep alive the tradition of Philip Armour, founder of the great meatpacking firm, who said, "All my culture is in my wife's name."

Many in the college wanted a training in the humanities, and one hopes that their tribe will increase. It is part of civilization to bend nature's resources to the uses of man. But technicians alone have never made a civilization. Others sought the social or business prestige of a degree. Still others, a considerable number, found the university a pleasant place in which to pass four years. I am not unsympathetic toward their aim. But since no one can be denied an "education" in a state-supported institution and since no class can move faster than the wits of its slowest members, it has long seemed to me that the state ought to run two kinds of schools. For those who merely want a degree or desire to pass four years pleasantly on a campus, the state might set up schools in congenial places such as Capri, say, or Santa Barbara, where climate and environment tend to make living more attractive than at Charlottesville, Virginia, or Bloomington, Indiana. Nothing is too good for our boys. After so long a time, students would be awarded a degree and the community's thanks for not having cluttered up universities tenanted by those who want to work. Thus all the state's children might be equitably served.

Located in the foothills of the Blue Ridge, its climate pleasant, its campus symmetrically beautiful, the university was a delightful place in which to live. Washington, three hours distant by train, afforded metropolitan pleasures, while the valley of Virginia, dotted with girls' schools, was host to hundreds of southern belles. The university, going upon the sound assumption that students were no longer attached to their mothers' apron strings, placed few formal restraints upon their behavior. Neither drinking nor gambling were prohibited. Charlottesville was dry, but bootleggers sold legal whiskey or moonshine made by vigorous enterprisers in the nearby mountains. There was much drinking, notably on the part of those who came from homes where alcohol, except for rubbing purposes, was forbidden. A few students, ambitious for all-southern homes, drank themselves out of school, and there was but one rule to govern the sport: a student going to a college dance had to give his word that he had not touched liquor during the preceding twenty-four hours.

Gambling usually took the form of poker or dice. I had already absorbed some of the lore of poker that was immanent in Greenville's air and there taken a few desultory dice lessons. Now I undertook to improve my knowledge of this noble game to which I was much drawn because of the kaleidoscopic changes of fortune that it permitted. The lessons were sometimes costly, but they proved to be invaluable later at Yale where I played with less-knowing players.

Dice shooting rose to its heights on the eve of the annual Virginia-Carolina football game. Then, night and day for forty-eight hours, the "Carolina tryouts" took place on the campus, faculty and students passing it on their way to classes. Dice, among its other charms, gives the player the illusion that mind may influence matter. Hence the players, on hands and knees, nerves and bodies taut, implored the galloping cubes to favor them with loud and fervent cries of beseechment: "Eighter-from-Decatur!" or "Joseph of Arimathea come forth!" or "My baby needs shoes, and I don't mean maybe!" Winners went to Chapel Hill for the game. Losers stayed home and borrowed money for meals.

In this nation devoted to risk capital, it seems anachronistic that we should have a bluenose attitude toward gambling. The country owes much to men who took great financial risks—even if they were often taken with other men's money. We used to say, "Well, Brodie took a chance," the implied corollary being that when there were no more Brodies to take chances, freewheeling America would cease to be. (For the benefit of those less antique than I, let me say that Brodie, just for the hell of it, jumped from the Brooklyn Bridge into the water and lived to tell the tale.)

Rigorous disciplines of scholarship did not exist except for the minority in the technical schools. Students were occasionally "shipped" for various reasons, but there were only a few perverse geniuses who were unable to keep up with their classes. The amenities of the university and its amiable attitude toward scholarly disciplines annually brought us a number of eastern students. Refugees from the rigors of work at Yale, Harvard, Princeton, who had flunked out, they came to pass a few pleasant years in Virginia. Conveniently near their homes and former classmates, the surrounding country superb for riding and fox hunting—plutocratic sports to which Democrats attach a high value—the university, although a state institution, was free of the taint of the freshwater. These factors made a great appeal to the sons of successful manufacturers of the East. Wealthier than most of us, possessing cars and extensive wardrobes, our refugees were baroque ornaments of the campus who gave the university the undeserved reputation in many places of being a "country club school."

The University of Virginia, conceptually and architecturally, sprang from the myriad mind of Thomas Jefferson whose mountaintop home, Monticello, still stands a few miles from the campus. Universal genius, author of the Declaration of Independence, signer of the Constitution, secretary of state, ambassador to France, and president of the United States, Jefferson left a sketch and inscription for his tombstone. He wrote:

> . . . On the face of the obelisk the following inscription and not a word more:
> "Here was buried Thomas Jefferson
> author of the Declaration of American Independence
> of the State of Virginia for religious freedom
> and Father of the University of Virginia"
> because by these, as testimonials that I have lived, I wish most to be remembered.

His school, however, was not Jeffersonian; nor is the sun's afterglow the sun. The mood of a lately revolutionary country—of Congress at least—became timid and even anti-Jeffersonian soon after Jefferson's great labors. When Congress returned to Washington after the War of 1812, its members fell into furious debate upon the question of accepting Jefferson's library as a gift to the nation. It was said to contain "subversive books," volumes by Newton, Locke, Voltaire.

It is perhaps not unnatural then that one found at Jefferson's university little of the founder's love of intellectual inquiry, his fluidity of mind, his emphasis upon the fact that society, as a living organism, must constantly change or become ossified. There was, instead, merely a pale ancestor worship and a sacrosanct reverence for the past with little excitement about the present or the future. Jefferson was a great theoretician of "natural rights." But it was only in the law school that I one day heard Professor Raleigh Minor—a silver-maned Virginia gentleman of the old school—quietly say with simple conviction what Jefferson had said: "Revolution is the ultimate right of the people." Here was a harking back to the "higher law" so effectively used by Jefferson in the colonies' quarrel with Britain.

In the university, the gentlemanly tradition stripped of nearly all but form had, it seemed to me, degenerated into the genteel tradition, entities widely separated. In such a tradition, there is no passion. The mood among "nice people" becomes diminuendo; the highest desideratum "objectivity." Hence there was little passion of ferment on the campus or in the classroom. There was small concern even with perplexing questions of the changing South. There was not even an earnest attempt to collect the "facts" of the section, a task not unbecoming a regional university. The important work of gathering and interpreting the facts was largely left to the University of North Carolina.

Aside from its gentility, the school suffered from the homogeneity of its student body. Its members, coming predominantly from middle-class families of Anglo-Saxon stock, were too much of a kind to generate a stimulating friction. There were few foreign or foreign-born students greedily hungry for knowledge and debate such as one found in the great northern universities, men who, themselves afire, struck fire from others.

There was an appalling immaturity among the students generally, the sins of their fathers visited upon them. But this is a national, not an exclusively Virginia, phenomenon. The fathers had been corroded by the widespread installment-plan mentality so common among us. It dictates that you yourself do not have to do anything provided that you can spend ten cents to cover the cost of postage and wrapping or put a dollar on the line and make the rest in "easy payments." Hence the fathers, having done little to stimulate the intellectual curiosity or intellectual processes of their sons, thought it was enough to send their sons to Virginia when they became eighteen. The university would do the rest. Of course, the university could not do it, however valiantly it tried. How could it in a country where, as in 1949, we spent $400 million for books of all kinds, and at the same time spent $200 million for potato chips?

It was, however, fortunate for me that the university was not intellectually dynamic. Extremely intense, devoured almost by a passion to know and understand, I worked hard at the law and simultaneously read widely in politics, economics, sociology, anthropology, history, international affairs, literature. But of all the reading of that far-off time, I still remember vividly when, for the first time and unforgettably, I came to the fog-enshrouded, ocean-sea of Russian literature and ventured into its depths. I admired the great English and French novelists, but to my juvenile judgment they seemed too rational, too lacking in chaos themselves ever to penetrate the dim chaotic recesses of the human soul. I admired them, I repeat, and took pleasure in them and found them, at their best, filled with wonder, but it was the Russians who gave me intense pleasure and intense disquiet. So it was that they became my constant companions—Gogol, Tolstoy, Dostoevski, Chekhov, Turgenev, Goncharov, Gorky, Andreyev, and even Pryszbyweski, whose *Sanine* was published here during my freshman year.

If in my youthful gropings I did not always completely understand them, they often profoundly moved me, stirred depths hitherto untouched, gave me awesome insights into the human spirit. But of them all, even if perhaps of the second rank, Turgenev most engaged my affections, while of all of their masterful portraits, Goncharov's portrait of Oblomov gave me the greatest delight. For Oblomovism was no phenomenon alien to the Deep South of my youth, and Oblomov was not unlike southern plantation owners whom I had known: dreaming, tender, humane, the springs of action within him broken.

The while new and exciting names in the arts constantly came to me through the medium of James G. Huneker, who sometimes called himself a "steeplejack of the arts." Primarily a music critic, but rejoicing with almost Dionysian frenzy in all the arts and shuttling between New York and Europe, he first made familiar to me such men as Shaw, Huysmans, Flaubert, Stendhal, the brothers Goncourt, Ibsen, Strindberg, Schnitzler, Nietzsche, and many more in literature, painting, sculpture, theatre, and the ballet. He sent me running down a dozen paths simultaneously, and as his books and magazine articles appeared, I fell upon them eagerly. It is unfortunate that there is no one quite like him to serve the present generation.

The upshot of all of this—of hard study and hard reading and of a too constant state of exaltation—was that, as I later realized, I came near to a "nervous breakdown." Quite unconsciously, however, my equilibrium was preserved through the music and rhythm of words, specifically of verse. I did not at all know what I was doing, but when I became almost unbearably lonely or restless, I instinctively recited verse to myself, sometimes annoying my friends. Once Alfred Noyes read his poems at the university, and never before having heard a poet recite verse, it was an evening of high pleasure for me. Thereafter I added his "Barrel Organ" to my repertoire. It did not matter to me what the verse was so long as it was rhythmical and fell easily upon the ear. In the shower I murmured to myself:

> The linnet and the throstle too,
> And after dark the long halloo,
> And golden-eyed too-whit too-whoo,
> Of owls that oggle London.

One night, as I was leaving the Charlottesville railroad station in a dark mood, a train arrived. Its two Pullmans were named Hyacinth and Columbine, and I immediately felt more cheerful. For, aside from verse, single words were enough to compose my nerves if they were of a certain shape and color, and they were especially soothing when, as in this case, they evoked pleasurable images or connotations.

It is part of the wonder of words that their appeal is both mental and sensory. Seen by the eye, heard by the ear, perceived by the mind, they may, almost, be felt with the hands and rubbed to a soft patina, as Orientals rub cherished ivories until they color to mellowness. The lover longing to touch his beloved, so the lover of words has a compulsion to touch them and to feel their texture and linger gently on their surfaces, touch being not only the most primitive of the senses but also one of the most perceptive. There were glowing sunset words as burnish, night-descending words as landfall, mournful words as dust, drowsy words as twilight, bird-song words as cello, drum-beating words as bassoon, slithering serpent words as sibilant, and words wearing a stiff, high collar as circumstance. There were words—place names—that smelled of sandalwood and cinnamon and sounded like the slap slap of Eastern seas upon the sands of Eastern shores: Rangoon, Colombo, Singapore, Zanzibar, Malaysia.

Seductive words with the dark sweetness of sleep upon them, words that danced to the music of flutes, and words that shone with opiate brightness saved me from what might have been a physical debacle.

Soon after entering the university, the shadow of the Great War, as we later called it, fell upon us. Many students and faculty members were for immediate participation in it on the Allied side, but they represented the point of view of a minority of Americans. There was a strong pro-German sentiment among the people; there was an urgent desire to stay out of "European squabbles." Few believed that we would enter the war, and as we read of the great battles in France, we read also of the rise of "prosperity" in this country where business had been poor in 1913 before the outbreak of the war. War was good for business, while at the same time it was no business of ours: an ideal combination.

I spent the summer following my graduation from the university's law school at the University of Wisconsin in order to supplement my meager knowledge of men and society by sitting briefly at the feet of Edward Alsworth Ross, who then presided with gruff, walrus majesty over its department of sociology. In the autumn, candidate for the degree of Master of Laws, I entered the Yale Law School.

Some of my work was done there under William Howard Taft, former president of the United States, for whom I came to have much affection. A mountain of a man, often wreathed in smiles and given to an infectious chuckle, I found him a fine teacher, modest, gifted with a superb sense of humor. Once, talking about Theodore Roosevelt, his eyes crinkled with laughter as he said, "Mr. Roosevelt, after I became president, thought of me as being the kind of man who, if I were the Pope, would appoint Protestant cardinals."

I had to write a thesis to qualify for my degree, but having nothing particular in mind, suggested to Mr. Taft that I might investigate some phase of the law that he had had little time to explore. "There is one," he said. Then, smilingly, he added, "I lectured on it last night at the Johns Hopkins, but I really don't know much about it: federal incorporation of railroads." The point, in part, was that a train going, say, from New York to Alexandria, Virginia, was subjected in the course of this short journey not only to the federal jurisdiction governing interstate commerce, but also to the complex and often conflicting jurisdictions of five states and the District of Columbia. These threw a heavy burden upon railroads. After I had done my thesis, Mr. Taft was pleased when I suggested that we were now upon terms of partial equality since neither of us knew much about railroads as federal corporations. "Well," he chuckled, "for an ignorant man you are not so ignorant," and then he told me how he had once been paid a similarly dubious compliment.

When he had been secretary of war, he said, he had succeeded in reinstating, at the urgent request of the cadet's mother, a young man who had been dismissed from West Point because of weak eyesight. The grateful mother, a handsome woman, came to Washington to thank him, and, said Mr. Taft, his face suddenly rippling with smiles, "I'd have you know that I am not insensitive to physical beauty." The lady chatted a while with the secretary, who then weighed over three hundred pounds, and rising to go, in her gratitude paid him what she thought was the ultimate compliment: "Mr. Secretary," she said, "for a fat man you are not so fat."

My life at Yale was quite unlike my Virginia years. There I ventured outside the library, outside books and reading, into a world of which I knew next to nothing, a venture made possible by the proximity of New Haven to New York and a facility with dice that I had acquired at Charlottesville. My classes coming early in the week, I often spent the remainder of it in New York. There I haunted the Museum of Art, picture galleries, and the theatres. Music, pictures, and the theatre, so long inaccessible to me, were at last accessible. I gulped them with the insatiable appetite of a healthy, hungry country boy.

These were, however, only part of an exhilarating new world that was now opening to me. My curiosity about men as great as it was about the arts, I took long walks in various sections of New York—especially the "foreign" sections. Their people were the more exotic to provincial eyes that had largely looked only upon southern whites and Negroes. I loitered in the vibrant streets of the lower East Side, sampled strange food and drink, and returned to New Haven broke but tingling with excitement. I studied at Yale. In New York I got an education.

My forays were made possible by dice shooting. Yankees were easier game than the southerners with whom I had competed in Virginia. My ambitions were, however, modest. I simply tried to win enough to finance an expedition to New York. Then, that having been done, with a polite bow I made a little speech to the losers telling them to have no regrets since I had not played merely for vulgar gain, and their money would be devoted by me to higher use. This crocodile speech, far from assuaging the unhappiness of the losers or melting their hearts toward me, made them the more avid for revenge, and the next week we were hard at it again.

The while the war went its way in Europe and a faraway place called Mesopotamia. The *Lusitania* was sunk by a German U-boat with a large loss of lives, including many Americans. German submarines were halting our ships, and it began to be evident that we might soon be in the war. One day early in 1917, Mr. Taft said to us with a grin: "Gentlemen, I hope to make lawyers of you before you become soldiers." But this was not to be. By April of that year the United States was at war with the central powers. My brother in Greenville had joined the Army, but I liked the Navy, influenced perhaps by my reading of Mahan in high school, and I joined it at Hampton Roads, Virginia. There I had an utterly ignominious career. Far from seeing the world through a porthole, my Navy seemed not even to have a porthole. A lowly bluejacket, I was kept in the vicinity of Norfolk for nearly a year. Then, the war over, I returned to New Haven and got my degree.

I had planned to be a county-seat practitioner in Greenville, yet following the plan would have been ruinous to the serenity that I sought. In my youthful, perhaps over-romantic imagination, I had pictured the lawyer as a fierce individualist, ideally as the learned rebel. I soon saw, however, that most lawyers were neither learned nor rebels but were mere unlettered tame technicians. It became apparent even during my college days that lawyers were increasingly becoming fetch-and-carry boys of business. "This is what we want to do," said the corporate executive to the lawyer. "You find the way to do it." The process accelerated as business extended its sway over a nation that had been largely agricultural from the founding of the Republic until after The War. It offered the most dazzling money rewards in our economy, businessmen ascended to the peak of our hierarchy, and if a man made a fortune manufacturing disposable diapers, the press sought expressions of his opinion on subjects ranging from personal immorality to the Tacna-Arica dispute in South America. But no one asked the learned Bishop Gailor of Tennessee whether he thought October cotton futures were a good buy.

The dominance of the corporation could be seen in Greenville. When I was a child there, all the stores along Washington Avenue were home owned and home run. Their proprietors were true proprietors—a rapidly vanishing class among us—because they not only managed their businesses but also owned them. Everybody knew Mr. Charley Hafter, Mr. Sol Brill, Mr. J. P. Greenley, Mr. Meck Reid, Mr. Joe Herbison. They had been born in the town. They had spent their lives there and were in all things—including their businesses—three-dimensional. If you called on them for a contribution to the Red Cross or for money to pay for a poor widow woman's surgical operation, they did not have to refer the matter to a branch manager in Atlanta who referred it in turn to the general manager in New York, the while the local chapter of the Red Cross languished or the widow woman died. One could talk with them, plead with them, berate them, and—most important—get credit from them.

All this was changing even while I was a college student. Now the change is great. A high proportion of the stores on Washington Avenue are owned by corporations domiciled elsewhere, their transient managers transient in the town. These stores are run with a chilling efficiency. Their operations are standardized. The invisible strings that pull them are manipulated by unseen hands in distant New York. You cannot loaf in them. You cannot get them to close for an afternoon because the fish are biting. You cannot be cozy with them because, as corporations, they have no flesh and blood. So disembodied are they that their employees are only vaguely conscious of their employers. Rarely do they know the names of their ultimate bosses. I have asked many a clerk of the A&P, a company owning thousands of stores, to tell me the name of the president of the firm, but I have yet to find one who knows it. Washington Avenue, in short, is now largely a street of anonymous corporations and faceless clerks.

Many celebrated lawyers were little more than "fronts" for business, bound-in-calf promoters, or men who grew rich from crumbs left on the table by their corporate employers. They would have regarded you as naïve to the point of feeblemindedness had you suggested that traditionally the lawyer was an "officer of the court," one whose profession was charged with a public responsibility.

Yet Greenville and every Mississippi town of my acquaintance then had at least one lawyer who responded to these ancient canons. Stubborn, "cranky," a nonconformist, animated by a passion for justice, he would espouse so-called unpopular causes and, going upon the assumption of our jurisprudence that every defendant however wretched or wrong is entitled to a fair trial, would defend a man regardless of fee or public opinion.

Often this lawyer was the most learned—and sometimes the only learned—man among us. This, however, was not held against him, since that swinishly boorish blight called anti-intellectualism had not yet descended upon the land. Touched with a classical education, grounded in Coke, reverential of the Anglo-

Saxon law born of centuries of struggle, given to "plain living and high think-ing," he was at once useful and an austere ornament of the community, a strong Doric column.

Sometimes the community disapproved of him and banished him, tem-porarily at least, to that Gethsemane which every community maintains in a cor-ner of its mind. But it secretly admired and often came at last to love him be-cause he personified in his living that most profound of American rights which underlies all the others: the right to look every man in the eye and tell him where to go. Yet fiercely determined to be his own master and notoriously lacking that "cleverness" which we came to esteem so highly, it was inevitable that he should disappear.

The practice of "corporation law" became the most lucrative of practices. It endowed the practitioner with the highest prestige. At college we heard with awe of the million-dollar fee said to have been earned by the lawyer who drew the charter for the United States Steel Company in the early 1900s. But one also knew that those who serve great corporations are necessarily less concerned with broad human rights than with narrow corporate rights. Few things indeed have more affected the nation's course than that, in time, the Supreme Court has endowed anonymous corporations with nearly all of the "rights" that pertain to flesh-and-blood persons.

I felt that it was one thing to be the servant of a king, a cause, or even of one's vices, but it is another thing to be the servant of a shadowy entity that is a per-son only by a fiction of the law. A similar conclusion later caused Will Percy—a lawyer sprung of a long line of lawyers—to advise his adopted sons against en-tering the family's ancestral profession.

It soon became clear that I was not to be a lawyer. Shortly after the end of the war, deaths in my family and financial reverses threw heavy responsibilities upon me. I could never have discharged them as a novice lawyer. So I got on the train and went to New Orleans, the nearest metropolis to Greenville. There, as many a country boy before me, I tried my luck in the city.

11

Where Is the Way?

Although Cohn's Jewish heritage was a vital part of his identity, he ultimately rejected religious orthodoxy of any sort. In this chapter, he describes the spiritual and intellectual odyssey that led him to this point.

One of the first acts of men come to this country is to build a place of worship. Thus the Jewish pioneers of Greenville built a synagogue (or "temple" as it is locally called). While it was under construction, services were held in the Methodist church. (Years later when the Methodists built a new church, they temporarily worshipped in the synagogue.) My parents, continuing to be members of the Jewish community, kindling Sabbath candles in accord with the ancient practice and fulfilling the numerous precepts with respect to good works, were not actively of the congregation. But I attended religious services and Sunday school. I was even—despite my spiritual unworthiness—awarded a prize for excellence in Sunday school. It was a little book entitled *Gems from the Prophets.* Yet I never came into full possession of the gems because the book's print was so tiny I gave up trying to read it.

A small boy, scrubbed and polished almost beyond endurance by my mother before she would let me leave home, I attended religious services on Saturday mornings. (As a master's painting is sometimes found under overlays of lesser painters, so it is the continuing miracle of small boys that they are daily discovered anew by the removal of overlays of dust, mud, or tar.) But I took little pleasure in the services or even in the joyous festival of Passover, and I remained unimpressed by the fact that it had been unbrokenly observed for thirteen hundred years before Christ to date and is perhaps the oldest religious festival that men celebrate.

It comes in the spring at about the time of Easter. What small boy could then sit quietly in a synagogue while spring was swelling his heart to bursting as it swelled the buds on the bush? Once I sat at a window close to which grew a locust tree. April stirring its branches, a frond broke in soft pink waves upon the window sill: broke, retreated, and came again. I sadly watched it. I felt sorry for myself and wished that I, a prisoner, were the locust, free and bending to the breeze.

Yet I was joyous at Succoth, the feast of the harvest, perhaps because of some pantheism strong within me at an early age. The Lord had commanded the Israelites, saying, "And ye shall take you on the first day (of the seventh month) the boughs of goodly trees, branches of palm trees, and boughs of thick trees, and willows of the brook; and ye shall rejoice before the Lord your God seven days. Ye shall dwell in booths . . . that your generations may know that I made the children of Israel to dwell in booths, when I brought them out of the land of Egypt."

There were no palm trees around Greenville, and the Lord could hardly blame us for disobeying him with respect to them. But there were other trees: "goodly trees," "thick trees," "willows of the brook." Branches of these were gathered and fruits of the season. They were placed before the pulpit, and these symbols of the harvest gladdened my heart. I have ever since rejoiced in autumn's dark-eyed, tawny child.

Living in a small town caught within the green embrace of trees, the town surrounded by forests slowly being cleared, and loving the sight, sound, and smell of trees, I was pleased that the Hebrew prayer book contained benedictions thanking the Lord for his gift of trees to men.

One was grateful for the scent of fragrant woods: "Blessed art thou, O Lord our God, King of the Universe, who createst fragrant woods."

On observing the miracle of trees blossoming in spring, one said, "Blessed art thou, O Lord our God, King of the Universe, who hast made thy world lacking in naught, but has produced therein goodly creatures and goodly trees wherewith to give delight to children of men."

Ours was a whiskey-drinking, Bible-reading, church-going society. A man among us was expected to belong to some church, to "stand up and be counted." In business and social circles it was accounted a good thing to be a member of a church and so, whether we wanted to acknowledge the goodness of God in common worship with our fellows or whether we wanted to be counted "present" by them, most of us belonged to some church.

When Greenville's church bells rang on Sunday mornings—Jewish religious services were held on Friday nights and Saturday mornings—and I saw members of the various denominations entering their churches, I wondered as many men before me had wondered. To whom is it given to know God's mind? Who possesses the sovereign recipe—the one and only recipe—for attaining communion with him? The recipe exclusive, communion becomes the dearer. Worshippers cuddling up to God, sole possession of him brings a not unwelcome touch of the voluptuous.

One could, it appeared, enter into communion with him by performing certain rites, ablutions, incantations. The minutiae of the rites were sometimes such that God seemed enamored of protocol and peacock proud of his prerogatives as though he were chief of state of some flea-bitten, jungle republic. There were those who felt that theirs was the right way. There were also those who maintained inflexibly that there was no other way except their own.

Still others—rites, ablutions, incantations being deemed insufficient—
rolled upon the floors of their churches, heads jerking, bodies writhing, eyes
bulging, mouths twitching, spittle flecking their lips: so they plucked at God's
sleeve to draw his wayward attention to them.

These were whites. Many Negroes also howled and became convulsive at
worship. But they, by way of saving grace, erected golden columns of song in
their adoration of the Lord.

(But I never heard a white or Negro preacher introduce commercial cate-
gories into his religious thinking. None used words such as these of Bishop
Sheen: "Our reason tells us that if anyone of the claimants [for the role of God's
son] came from God, the least that God could do to support His Representative's
claim would be to preannounce His coming. Automobile manufacturers tell us
when to expect a new model."

Nor did any talk like Billy Graham, who said, "I am selling the greatest product in the world; why shouldn't it be promoted as well as soap?")

In churches where our poorest white people worshipped, the most constant
themes were sin and death. Love was seldom mentioned. The people cried aloud
to God in their fear and pain, while their preacher repeated over and over the in-
effable name:

> The wages of sin is death! We don't want that kind of death, praise God, amen.
> Someday we'll meet God, face to face, and uh, we want to be ready for him, praise
> God, amen. You may die tomorrow, praise God, glory be to God. [Congregation:
> "Yes, that's so, praise God, glory be to God!"] You may die as you're leaving this
> church, praise God, and walking up the street. You may not get home for dinner,
> praise God, glory be to God.

How can a man "overcome" death? The preacher, shaking with fervor,
continues:

> I can meet Jesus, praise God, in peace, amen, if I go tonight, praise God. I over-
> come death and I ain't afraid of it, glory be to God. Jesus conquered death, praise
> God, amen, glory be to the Lord. He forgave the thief on the cross, praise God,
> showed no pain, glory be to God, praise the Lord. Did death conquer? No,
> praise God, and all the devils in hell couldn't keep Jesus in his, praise God,
> tomb, praise God, amen. He said he'd arise the third day, uh, the stone was
> rolled away, praise God, glory be to God, thank God.

Finally, in a state almost of catalepsy, the preacher concludes:

> Death, where is they [sic] sting? There is no sting in death 'cause I'm ready,
> praise God, thank God for it. Yes, I'm ready, praise God, amen. When my father
> died, praise God, glory be to God, he made me promise, glory be to God, thank
> God, to meet him on the other side, glory be to God, thank God. So I had to lead
> a good life, thank God, glory be to God.

The sermon preached, many of the faithful, at the preacher's invitation, went
to the mourners' bench. There they knelt and confessed their sins to God. Then

the congregation sang one song, clapping hands in rhythm with the music. Now there was a prayer and the service ended.

In this manner hundreds of thousands of us sought God. The preacher felt that, if his was not the only way, it was certainly the right way. Indeed an old song illuminated the certainty that your sect is right and the others wrong:

> Methodist preacher you are dead,
> You poured water on the baby's head;
> Baptist preacher you are right,
> 'Cause you take them candidates out of sight.

(These are what H. Richard Niebuhr calls "churches of the disinherited." "The religion of the untutored and economically disinherited classes," he notes in his *The Social Sources of Denominationalism,* "has distinct ethical and psychological characteristics, corresponding to the needs of these groups. Emotional fervor is one common mark. Where the power of abstract thought had not been highly developed and where inhibitions on emotional expression have not been set up by a system of polite conventions, religion must and will express itself in emotional terms. . . . From the first century onward, apocalypticism has always been most at home among the disinherited.")

A day came when I no longer attended religious services. I do not yet know why. But I am not for this reason chagrined. One is dealing here, in part, with a man's life. It is of necessity tremulous, marked by strange disproportions and ambiguous shadows, the dream real, the real the dream. ("A man walked, as it were, casting a shadow," wrote Yeats, "and yet one could never say which was man and which was shadow, or how many the shadows that he cast.") It happens to be my life but inevitably it is also, in some degree, your life. Nothing of you is alien to me as nothing of me is alien to you. What concerns the one must therefore be of concern to the other.

Aware of catalogs of "facts," I found none of them light giving. But there were also intimations, intuitions, perceptions, whisperings, insights, world and beyond-world meeting, merging, drawing apart, meeting again. My ship having all day descended the Mississippi River to its mouth, at nightfall there was suddenly beneath me the surge and thrust of ocean and I felt a sense of oneness with the immanent.

Is not the lost the found, the detour the shortest distance between two points? The young shepherd whom I saw that late afternoon in the mountains of Persian Khuzistan, piping as he went, his flock skipping over rocks to the notes of his flutes, a wan sun lighting their way—whither was he going? To his village? Yes. But was he not also going into me and through me into you and so into all of us, his music forever upon some distant air, the wan light of that waning sun yielding to no darkness, the flock skipping eternally over alien stones?

Shall I be dogmatic about God? Shall I arrogantly insist that my deity be your deity? Shall I, to paraphrase Thoreau, force God into a corner and shake out of him the meaning of life?

I have not tried to reach knowable conclusions about those things that impress me as unknowable; nor am I convinced that any religion is the custodian of absolute truth. I not only have no desire to bring anyone to my way of thinking but would shrink from it. Should I, for example, have tried to "convert" Raiere, the Polynesian chief, when I lived in his little house at Tautira by the green Pacific lagoon, he who led a life of lamblike innocence and called God the "Parentless one"?

The more I thought about formal religion, the more I agreed with Benjamin Franklin. Saying that the older he grew the less faith he had in the infallibility of his own judgments, he continued: "Most sects . . . think themselves in possession of all truth, and that wherever others differ from them it is so for error. Steele, a Protestant, in a Dedication tells the Pope, that the only difference between our churches in their opinion of the certainty of their doctrine is, the Church of Rome is infallible and the Church of England is never wrong."

The sects held all men to be God's children. Yet he seemed a cruelly capricious parent. To some he gave bread; others a stone. Some would stand beside him eternally. Others, for the error of birth or creed or neglect of protocol—the error assessable against infant as well as graybeard—would burn in hell or linger in limbo, their misery deepened as others winged by to paradise. The while, on earth, the children's struggle to gain God's favor or exclusive possession of him often had about it the obscenity that flowers when the offspring of a rich, senile parent clamor for favor in his will.

Many of God's Jewish children felt they had an especial claim upon him. Had they not come a long way together? Had not God, through them, given mankind the moral code of the Decalogue? Was not theirs a universal mission, decreed by God, so that they should be "a light to the Gentiles . . . my salvation unto the end of the earth"?

(Heinrich Heine observed that God was angry with the Jews. He was angry, said Heine, because they had started out together when he was but a tribal god and the Jews a group of small tribes of the desert. They had then called him "the God of Abraham, Isaac, and Jacob." But, said Heine, God is displeased with the Jews because although half the world now acknowledges him as the supreme deity, Jews still call him "the God of Abraham, Isaac, and Jacob.")

God, moreover, had made a covenant with them, and they had worshipped him as the One and Only God and exalted him above the myriad gods of their pagan neighbors. Thus they committed the sin they have never been able to expiate, the perhaps unexpiable sin of being "different." What so arouses the fury of the tiger, longitudinally striped, as the Zebra wearing stripes reticulated?

Judaism and its foster children—Christianity and Islam—proclaim an all-loving God. But each holds its truths to be generally incompatible with the truths of the others. Co-belief and co-worship among their adherents is impossible. Those who "believe falsely"—the other fellow—are "God's enemies." Hence Biblical Hebrews killed "heathen" to the greater glory of God. Centuries later when, as Disraeli put it, "half the world worshipped a Jew and the other half a Jewess, Christians slaughtered Jews in Christ's name."

Even God is hard put to pound into men's heads a sense of respect for the other fellow's religious point of view. It is said, at least, that Abraham once invited to his tent an aged man, but the guest refused to join him in prayer to The One God. And when Abraham found that the man was a fire worshipper, he drove him from his tent.

Then God, a little wearily perhaps, appeared to Abraham in a vision and said, "I have borne with that ignorant man for seventy years. Could you not have patiently suffered him for one night?"

God has not had much success with his religious-toleration program. Some seven hundred years after Godfrey of Bouillon sacked Jerusalem, killing seventy thousand Muslims and burning the Jews in their synagogue before "the bloody victors ascended the Hill of Calvary, amidst the loud anthems of the clergy," I visited Palestine. So venomous were the hatreds between sects contending for possession of the Church of the Nativity that at the Christmas Eve midnight mass the British sometimes had to send troops to keep them from one another's throats. Nor was this all the discord between God's children. At the Wailing Wall in Jerusalem, there was a constantly manned British sentry post. Its duty was to prevent Jews and Muslims from maiming one another.

Sad was the lot of the British Governor. He had, so to say, to apportion Christ among a host of claimants and simultaneously keep Moses and Mohammed in stable equilibrium.

Hope of a life after death—to return to my hometown—was held out to members of the Greenville synagogue by the rabbi. Yet it is only vaguely promised in the Old Testament. Job indeed said, "So man lieth down, and riseth not: till the heavens be no more, they shall not awake, nor be raised out of their sleep."

The Psalmist, in that superb poem of despair—"Before I go hence and be no more"—states the same concept but more poetically than Job:

> And now, Lord, what wait I for?
> my hope is in thee.
> Hear my prayer, O Lord, and give ear unto my cry:
> hold not thy peace at my tears.
> For I am a stranger with thee,
> and a sojourner, as all my fathers were.
> O spare me, that I may recover strength,
> before I go hence and be no more.

Whence came the yearning of my Jewish neighbors for a life hereafter even though the doctrine of immortality is omitted in the law of Moses and is only dimly insinuated by the prophets while, as Gibbon notes, "during the long period which elapsed between the Egyptian and Babylonian servitudes the hopes as well as the fears of the Jews appear to have been confined with the narrow compass of the present life."

The source of the yearning evidently lay in the long, tragic Jewish history. When wars or natural catastrophes threaten a group, men pray for deliverance. Yet these, however appalling, are relatively transient. But when the very existence of a group is threatened century after century, the transient takes on the aspect of permanency. (Twenty-five hundred years after King Nebuchadnezzar of Babylon, there arose Adolf Hitler of Germany.) Then, hope on earth waning or lost, men begin to yearn for the blessings of a life hereafter, blessings secure against the tamperings of mortal hands. So it was with many post-exilic Jews.

Even if there had been no other evidence, this was a conclusion bolstered by environment. Centuries ago a Jewish poet sang one of the world's great songs. It was about the captivity of his people:

> By the rivers of Babylon, there we sat down, yea we wept when we remembered Zion.
> We hanged our harps upon the willows in the midst thereof.
> For there they that carried us away captive required of us a song; and they that wasted us required of us mirth, saying,
> Sing us one of the songs of Zion.
> How shall we sing the Lord's song in a strange land?
> If I forget thee, O Jerusalem, let my right hand forget her cunning.
> If I do not remember thee, let my tongue cleave to the roof of my mouth; if I prefer not Jerusalem above my chief job.

All around me were Negroes. Their ancestors had been torn from Africa and sold into slavery. They had not yet found a secure home upon this alien earth, and as the dispersed of Judah had wept by the waters of Babylon, so they wailed by the waters of the Mississippi and sang hauntingly sad songs of the good life that would be theirs in the hereafter: "When I get to heaven, gwine put on my robe and walk all over God's heaven." In the sermons of their preachers, the name of Nebuchadnezzar, enslaver of the children of Israel, occurred again and again.

Perhaps the one part of American life that appealed to the Negro slave was the Christian religion, just as it had appealed so strongly to slaves of the Roman Empire that numbers of them became converts. Here where the enslaved Negro had little hope of improving his earthly lot, he embraced a religion which promised the overthrow of the mighty and eternal life for the meek in a glorious land beyond the skies. Such promises gave a meaning and purpose to the lives of American Negro slaves.

I clung to the concepts of my most ancient ancestors and did not yearn for personal immortality. They had taught the bleak doctrine of doing right for right's sake without respect to, or hope of, reward here or hereafter. I found myself in accord with it. It had for me an austere beauty more attractive than that of some baroque heaven. And from a worldly point of view, it worked a welcome change in the stubborn donkey. Under the given theorem, he need neither be beaten with the stick nor coaxed with the carrot.

The ancient parable appealed to me. A visitor to Paradise found no angels but only old men studying that vast compendium of Jewish religious and secular lore called the Talmud. The visitor, surprised at finding men in Paradise, turned to his guide who explained: "You have the mistaken idea that the men are in heaven. Actually, heaven is in the men."

In the absence of promised certainty hereafter I did not find the prospect altogether bleak. The particle becomes part of the whole and the whole a sea whose waves break upon the violet shores of wonder. Is not movement itself wonder in wind-rippled wheat or in the immortal procession of men and horses and chariots that moves cross the pediments of the Parthenon? Surely the earth is filled with wonder, and one holds one's cup to catch it till it is running over, a cup as large and as round as the eyes of a Gypsy child that I saw one night lying dreaming while awake upon a bench in the Vicksburg railroad station. Wonder being imperishable, do not those touched by it partake of its eternal substance?

There were other alternatives to negation. One could identify oneself with timeless values. If they can never be realized, they can never be destroyed.

(While considering this chapter, I came across a touching passage in Stendahl's *The Life of Henri Brûlard:* "My grandfather . . . took religion very gaily. . . . He became depressed and rather religious only after the death of my mother . . . and even then, I think, in the uncertain hope of meeting her again . . . in the next world; like M. de Broglie, who said of his charming daughter who died at the age of thirteen: 'I feel as if my daughter is in America!'")

A central device of orthodoxy repelled me. I had no faith that the mechanical repetition of ordained ritual—the prayer wheel spinning constantly at the pressure of an abstract thumb—would bring me closer to God. The face may turn to Mecca five times a day or fifty. The heart turns on its own axis.

I asked myself: Is God a reluctant djinni to be summoned only through the ritualistic rubbing together of persistently ritualistic pebbles? Shall I gain his ear only by reciting formalized words to him as though I were a child presenting posies to a state senator? Shall I, his son, to whom he has given a spirit so various that its facets are beyond counting, always approach him with "a contrite heart"? Is it forbidden me that I should strike in impotent fury against heaven's ramparts, cry out in anger, rend my clothes in misery? Brother to the worm I may be, but in that fearful oven where I was fashioned, I was not fashioned as a worm.

Yet I was often touched by ritual. I knew its place in religious experience—

how it has marked the path of peace for many men and is symbolic of the con-
tinuum of which every man is a part: the wave blowing in spume and the spume
returning to the wave.

But the hair-splittings of theology wearied me. How is the simple Christ lost
in the jungles of his "interpreters" to be found? Who shall lead one to the
heart of Judaism through the mazes of rabbinical interpretation and disputation?
Yet when a disciple of Hillel, the great rabbi and sage of the first century B.C.,
asked if he could tell him all there was to know about Judaism while standing on
one foot, Hillel replied, "Do not do unto others that which you would not have
them do unto you; all the rest is commentary."

The ruling out of skeptical inquiry about religion seemed to me the substi-
tution of bias for belief. Faith, I felt, is the indissoluble love-marriage of intuition and reason, the mind confirming what the heart postulates. Certainly denial of the right to doubt in one field may lead to tyranny—denial of the right
to doubt in all fields.

Man is a parvenu on this earth. His behavior is often that of the outrageous
parvenu. Blind, destructive, and cruel as he often is, there is yet a shining glory
about him. His greatest glory is that he is forever Queequeg, "holding up that
imbecile candle in the heart of the almighty forlornness."

His time short, his way hard, his destiny dark, there is about man a sublime
impertinence. For this fragile animal dares to tilt with time, sport with space,
sound the seas, weigh the bauble earth, spy upon the stars, register the fevers of
the sun, and seek the source of life itself in the perilous jungles no matter where
lies the cub-nursing tigress, crying out in his agony to know: Why? Why? Why?
Surely God is not a fairy tale whose enjoyment demands the suspension of
subjective judgment in the reader.

Some years ago, a friend induced me to attend religious services in a great
New York synagogue. I thought it repulsive that houses of worship should be
built in streets that are luxury shopping locations and were what society editors
called "fashionable." One derived prestige by attending them. So also, I supposed,
did God. Yet as fashionable as were these churches and synagogues, Christ, a Jew,
was hardly eligible for the Social Register, while Moses was poor "club material" for the Country Club.

(Outside the cities, many country churches were relocated when the automobile came to America. They were put upon main highways. The patronage
of God, as that of hot-dog stands, seemed to depend upon the best locations.)

Soon I fled the fashionable synagogue. To me it was filled with emptiness.
There I could detect no scent of incense above the reek of perfume.

I recalled another synagogue I had visited in a village sixty miles from Warsaw. I had driven to it upon a cold, foggy, mournful winter's day through a snowy
landscape made the more funereal by thousands of black crows in the muddy-
white fields and shawl-enshrouded figures of peasant women drifting by wraith-

like in the northern dimness.

The village, largely Jewish in its population, was a poor thing of wooden shacks that seemed afloat in a sea of mud, the marrow-chilling breath of poverty frosting its surface. Remote and dreaming, it was only sixty miles distant from the capital—the capital with its schools, libraries, museums, theatres, motion picture houses; its cafes smelling deliciously of aromatic coffee and spiced cakes; its restaurants with their superb cuisine that was a mixture of French, Polish, and Russian cookery; its shops stocked with all manner of things useful and frivolous; and above all perhaps, its light: torrents of light flowing down the streets, the avenues deep in rivers of light. But the village I visited seemed to exist upon another sphere, the condition being as Sara Teasdale put it in a poem: "Warsaw in Poland is a thousand miles away."

I found two of its elders through my guide and interpreter, a Warsaw Jew of about forty years of age. A young boy at the time of the first world war, he sold newspapers in the capital's streets to occupying German soldiers and learned something of their language. Afterward, already knowing Polish and Yiddish, he acquired English at a night school. These accomplishments did not go unrewarded. The war over, they enabled the linguist to become a porter at the central railroad station. But all paths open to the learned, he had now, after years of waiting, arrived at an undreamt eminence. As its badge he wore a cap bearing the legend embroidered in gold: THOMAS COOK & SONS. He removed it constantly while we were motoring, looked wonderingly at the legend, ran his fingers over the threads of the embroidery. It was as if His Majesty had yesterday decorated him with the Order of the Garter.

The elders were small, pale, bearded men, their wafer-thin hands almost transparent in the light, mirth dancing in their luminously sad eyes, jokes upon their lips. Humor is the temple of the tragic, and Eastern European Jews, for centuries intimate with tragedy, had invented a rich, warm, prolific humor. Humor indeed belongs to an ancient Jewish tradition, the joke uncorrupted by blood bubbling in the throat. These are a people who have learned to take themselves and their troubles less seriously by laughing, not at others, but at themselves. "I do not know," wrote Freud, "whither one finds a people that makes so merry unreservedly over its shortcomings."

Any stranger was welcome in this village that seldom saw strangers. The stranger "from America"—fabled, thrice-blessed, free America—was feverishly welcome. I had come upon a cold day, yet the elders had no fire in the glacial room above the little store where one of them lived. They could not afford fire throughout the day. But there were the obligations of hospitality. A child was sent to buy a bundle of twigs and tea was brewed. We sat there talking, I wearing overcoat and gloves. After a while my hosts took me for a tour of the village, a promenade through a frozen inferno of poverty.

In the street we met a giant with two buckets on a pole swung over his shoulder. He was a water carrier. There was neither plumbing nor running water in the village. At dawn he filled his buckets at the river and trudged until darkness selling water. He earned perhaps the equivalent of $3 a week. But it was clear, as we talked, that he was not unhappy. Did not God watch over him? Had he not given him a good wife ("A woman of worth—who can find her? For her price is far above rubies. The heart of her husband trusteth in her."), obedient sons, comely daughters?

Suppose a man did work hard all week until his back was a sea of pain and his legs wobbled from weariness? Did there not then come the Sabbath; the holy, blessed, day-of-rest Sabbath, ordained of God amid the clouds shrouding the summit of the Mountain of the Law?

Did not everybody know that God had said to Israel, "If you accept my Torah and observe my Laws, I will give you for all eternity the most precious thing I have in my possession."

"And what," asked Israel, "is that precious thing?"

God: "The future world."

Israel: "But even in this world should we have a foretaste of that other?"

God: "The Sabbath will give you this foretaste."

On the Sabbath a man washed himself clean, put on fresh clothes, and went to the synagogue. There, standing amid his neighbors, he reaffirmed his love for the Lord saying:

> Hear, O Israel, the Lord our God is one Lord: And thou shalt love the Lord they God will all thine heart, and with all thy soul, and with all thy might. And these words which I command thee this day, shall be in thine heart: and thou shalt teach them diligently unto thy children, and shalt talk of them when thou sittest in thine house, and when thou walkest by the way, and when thou liest down, and when thou risest up. And thou shalt bind them for a sign upon thine hand, and they shall be as frontlets between thine eyes. And thou shalt write them upon the posts of they house, and on they gates.

The worshipper came home to find Sabbath peace in his house, Sabbath candles glowing, the children scrubbed, their mother in her black silk dress. As the sun sets, and Queen Sabbath enters the little houses of the village, the woman of the household lights the candles, praying as she does so, "Blessed art Thou, oh Lord our God, King of the Universe, who has hallowed us by His commandments and commanded us to kindle the Sabbath light."

The Sabbath meal begins with the blessing of the bread—today the family eats *white* bread—and slowly goes its way through the chicken soup, the chicken, the fish. Is not all this, the Sabbath peace, the family gathered together in love, the guest partaking of the family's joy, a foretaste of the life to come that the Lord promised those who obey his Laws? And if the fare on the table is but meager? If times are more than ever hard, sickness has depleted the family's purse, and there is not even a fish? Does it really matter? One blesses the Lord's name and turns to the pot of soup and loaf of bread.

A young cobbler sat at his bench in a one-room house. It was his workshop, home for himself, his mother, and five small brothers and sisters. Competition was savage in the poverty-stricken village. As I stood there, the cobbler was paid one zloty—twenty cents—for half-soling a pair of shoes. His profit was about two cents, a profit that a competitor would have welcomed. He himself had recently been released from the Polish Army to come home and support his family, his father having contracted tuberculosis. This disease sometimes afflicted 80 percent of the undernourished, ill-clad Jewish children of the village.

The "stranger from America" was, I repeat, doubly welcome in the village, but as I talked with the cobbler there sat on a bench near him one who was unconscious of, or oblivious to, my presence. A beautiful old man with finely drawn features, long silky white beard, and sea-blue eyes, he was lost in dreams. The cobbler's mother told me—speaking as though the man were absent—that he had been a hosiery worker in Warsaw, had lost his job, and now trudged the countryside teaching Hebrew to children. Tutor to the poorest of the poor, they paid for his services with a few pennies and a piece of herring and black bread for his meals. "But," said the woman, her eyes bright, "with the money the old man pays me to sleep on this bench, we can pay the rent for this whole place," her gesture going out to describe the little room as though it were a wing of a Faeroe palace. "God takes care of us," she concluded.

Accompanying the miseries of poverty and disease there were persecutions and pogroms against the Polish Jews. In part they stemmed from an anti-Semitism that was an endemic illness in devout, churchgoing Poland, where the sorrowful figure of Christ looked upon the road from many a wayside shrine and upon the fields whence the people drew their life. But in part the persecutions and pogroms were a manifestation of that most pathetic of struggles: the poor against the poor. The poor white against the poor Negro in Mississippi, the poor Pole against the poor Jew in Poland.

The leaders took me to see the glory of their community: the synagogue. We approached the tiny, weather-beaten, wooden structure through a muddy morass. Innocent of paint, bleak, bare, cold, it had hard wooden benches and an unadorned altar. But painted upon the walls in garishly violent colors—an affirmation of joy amid despair—were violins and mandolins.

The eyes of the elders shone with love. God was good. Here, I felt, that quintessentially Jewish Jew called Jesus Christ, no stranger to the synagogue and no stranger to sorrow, would have felt spiritually at home, he and the elders one in commonalty of pain. There was another bond between them. As the suffering Christ had loved the anemones that flood the Palestinian hills in spring, calling them more gaily attired than "Solomon in all his glory," so the Jews of this poor village, in their agony, had illuminated the walls of their bleak synagogue with painted instruments of tinkling music.

Though our mouths were full of songs as the sea (They had prayed at morning), and our tongues of exultation as the multitude of its waves, and our lips of praise as the wide-extended firmament; though our eyes shone with light like the sun and the moon, and our hands were spread forth like the eagles of heaven, and our feet were swift as hinds, we should still be unable to thank thee and bless thy name, O Lord our God and God of our fathers, for one-thousandth part of the bounties which thou hast bestowed upon our fathers and upon us.

The elders are in all probability dead. Dead, too, are the giant water carrier, the cobbler, his mother, sisters, brothers, and the beautiful old man with long silky beard and sea-blue eyes. They must have perished at the hands of the Germans, the jokes stifled in their gas chambers. Of 3,500,000 Polish Jews, less than 300,000 remained after the German butchery.

Eventually my path, if not my course, became clear. I determined to swim alone in the terrible waters preceded by no pilot fish. This may make me, in orthodox eyes, a sinner condemned to hellfire everlasting. Yet, with all respect due priests, preachers, rabbis, dervishes, mullahs, shamans, wardens, deacons, sextons, and seminarians, I submit that the final judgment lies without their province.

12

Small-Town Daily

As a writer, David Cohn freely acknowledged his debt to Will Percy, Carrie Stern, and several other enlightened Greenvillians, but Cohn also made a major contribution to Greenville's reputation as a relatively tolerant and intellectually dynamic community when he played the key role in bringing Betty and Hodding Carter to the town where, in Carter's words, "Main Street meets the river." [1]

The *Delta-Times,* published daily in Greenville, ranks high among American small-town newspapers, although Mississippi ranks low in many of the indices of progress. The shadowing forth of one man, it is published and edited by Hodding Carter, who was born in Louisiana and educated at Bowdoin College and Columbia University. Sometimes denounced by the northern Negro press as anti-Negro, he won the Pulitzer Prize in 1946 for his editorials on racial and religious tolerance.

How this soft-spoken man now nearing fifty came to Greenville, how its citizens helped him start his newspaper, and how he was morally supported by most of the townspeople although they differed with him sharply about things that most deeply concerned him is, I believe, a heartening American story.

In 1932, young and recently married, Carter was a reporter for the Associated Press in Jackson, Mississippi's capital. There he was fired for "insubordination," and his chief said he was not "cut out for newspaper work." This assessment was belied by later events, but it then seemed valid, since the young reporter had recently angrily quit the United Press. Now jobless in the depression, he took his wife and $367—his capital assets—and went to Hammond, Louisiana, his hometown. Sixty miles north of New Orleans, the energy and skill of Italian immigrants had made it the "strawberry capital of the United States."

Here two men were publishing a mimeographed, throwaway sheet, containing advertising and news in the ratio of nine to one. Carter's mother suggested to him that the town was big enough for a daily newspaper and her son took the plunge.

In New Orleans he bought a job press from a junkyard for $75, got a hand-

---

1. Hodding Carter, *Where Main Street Meets the River* (New York, 1953).

out from a foreman of the *Item* (where he had worked as a $12.50-a-week re-porter) in the form of slugs and old type, and brought the material to Hammond. He and his printer built some tables and, having no typesetting equipment, tried to set the newspaper by hand. This task proving impossible, they farmed out the typesetting, at backbreaking expense, and the *Daily Courier* came into being.

It was run from an improbable business-editorial office: a chicken coop space in the foyer of a movie theatre, the rental paid in advertisements. Here the edi-tor-publisher talked with callers, thought his thoughts, wrote the makings of the next edition. As he did so his fellow townsmen laid down their money for cel-luloid dreams at an adjacent ticket window while a lady pianist inside pointed them up with "appropriate selections."

When it became clear that setting his own type was the condition of sur-vival, Carter wangled a $600 loan from a local bank and bought the needed equipment. Then he began to run on a full head of steam generated by his own enthusiasm and stoked by the hams, eggs, chickens, and other produce that many of his subscribers gave him in lieu of cash. His wife, Betty, young, pretty, and recently graduated from Sophie Newcomb College in New Orleans, gathered the all-important "society news," was features editor, and served as advertising manager of the newspaper. But since it was a morning daily got out at night, when the husband was coming home to go to bed, the wife was leaving home to go to work.

Hammond is the parish (county) seat of Tangipahoa Parish, then notorious in Louisiana as "Bloody Tangipahoa," because of its constant shootings, stabbings, and other mayhems. There violence might flare momentarily. Once on a sum-mer evening, Carter at work in his office ran into the street when he heard gun-fire and saw a grisly tableau. A man lay dead on the pavement, pistol still in hand, while a policeman advanced upon him with drawn gun. Nearby another po-liceman was clubbing the shotgun-carrying companion of the dead man. But when Carter lifted his eyes from the scene, he saw an unexpected sight. Hud-dled in a doorway, where she had fled for shelter from the gunfire, stood his wife who was soon to have a child. On her way to a movie, she had walked into the battle and narrowly escaped a bullet.

This was the day when Huey Long, governor of Louisiana, "owned" the state. His thugs beat up people, his word was law, and as one man put it feelingly and not without admiration: "If Huey Long don't want you to pee, brother, you don't pee." And Hammond and Tangipahoa Parish had their share of violent Long sup-porters who had behind them the massive apparatus of the Long-dominated state.

Carter put his face against all this. Risking his life daily, jeopardizing his liveli-hood, banging his typewriter, a shotgun to hand nearby, he fought the Long tyranny from the moment he started his newspaper. Long's followers fought back in their way. They threatened Carter's life. They broke his windows. He answered by putting a pistol in his pocket and another by his bed and writing what he wanted to write. (He even ran for the legislature on an anti–Long ticket but was, of course, overwhelmingly defeated.) So doing he was in a vanishing tradition of American journalism.

It was a journalism in which the editor's opinions and personality were of the essence, and men might buy a newspaper primarily because they hated or admired its editor. ("What you doin' readin' *that* paper?" "Well, I just want to see what that ole sonofabitch Henry Watterson is shootin' his mouth off about," men used to say of the famous Kentucky editor.) It was of a day when editors fully exercised their function, when editorials were written out of a man's guts instead of being extruded by a committee. It was of a time, also, when editors had not handed over their editorial function to remote, nationally syndicated columnists "whose opinions are not necessarily our own," when the editor's name was at the masthead so that he who ran could see it.

The tradition of this journalism dictated that editors should not bow to threats of physical harm, to advertisers, or group pressures. The editor wrote what he wanted to write, took personal responsibility for it, and sometimes killed, or was killed, in defense of his right to say what was on his mind. How far that tradition has degenerated is clear. Journalism is now as safe as growing birdseed. Up North, editors have long died in bed surrounded by their families and public relations men. Down South, no editor has been shot within the memory of living men.

Carter, writing what he wanted to write, continued to fight Long and tote his pistol. Unable to silence him by threats, Long, shortly before his death, had the subservient legislature strike a deadly blow at him. His was the official journal of his town and parish for the publication of legal notices, a highly important source of revenue. Long changed the rules. A board would pass on the eligibility of printers, and Carter's chance of meeting this test was that of a blind man at a skeet shoot. He took his troubles to court, and while his case was pending, we met in Baton Rouge, Louisiana's capital.

I had known Carter for some time through his mother-in-law, Mrs. Philip Werlein of New Orleans, an old friend. I knew that he was making a courageous struggle against great odds in Hammond. It was obvious also that while he was physically courageous—a not uncommon quality—his larger virtue—one of uncommon rarity—was moral courage. For this is a quality whose exercise may expose one to pains and perils greater than those of physical injury or even death: isolation among one's fellows, "unpopularity," social ostracism from the community, the stigma of being "different."

On a hot summer's night we met at a party being held in the Hotel Heidelberg, and I suggested that we retire to the balcony for a bit of breeze blowing from the Mississippi River. There we talked. I found myself saying that Carter ought to leave Hammond and come to Greenville. Huey Long was now dead. Hence he no longer had an important function in Hammond and could certainly leave the field with honor. My hometown needed him. It would offer him a wider opportunity than he had, and he would find there, I believed, financial help for the enterprise. Why not come to Greenville, survey the situation, and then make a final decision? Carter agreed to do this, and I returned to Greenville.

I described Carter to Will Percy and said that in my opinion the town needed him. It was rapidly growing. "New people" were arriving. The older citizens, who had largely run the town out of a sense of noblesse oblige, were dying. New problems were arising. They included the hitherto novel problem of political corruption that nearly always arises when the population and wealth of a town increase. Greenville now needed a courageous, incorruptible, intelligently edited newspaper, and I felt that Carter was the man for the job. Percy agreed with these premises and invited the Carters to town as his guests.

It was not that Greenville lacked a daily newspaper. As far back as 1868 the Greenville *Times* had been launched, to be succeeded eventually by the *Democrat*. A dreamy, easygoing journal, it contented itself with reporting the vital statistics of the town such as deaths, births, and weddings as well as society news, church news, news of local group meetings, and brief press association accounts of the outer world. Its editors and publishers were gentle, honorable people whose gentleness was reflected in their newspaper.

Against sin, it was for the Democratic party and the Mississippi River flood control. It took no sides in local political battles or in hotly contested local issues. It had no point of view, spoke ill of no man, shed no light, gave off no heat, and, of course, made no new enemies. But neither did it, for the same reasons, have strongly devoted friends. As such it was representative of hundreds of other newspapers throughout the United States and inadequate to the needs of the growing community. It did, however, to its honor, oppose the Ku Klux Klan in the dangerous days of the 1920s.

Sometimes its point of view in reporting the news was quaint. During the plow-up campaign of 1933 when the federal government decreed that one-third of the growing cotton crop should be uprooted, a *Democrat* reporter went to the river to interview Roark Bradford, who was coming to Greenville on the *Tennessee Bell*. He found the writer on (as the British say) "the thunderbox." "Mr. Bradford," said the reporter, "what do you think about the plow-up deal?" "I'm for it," he replied. "Well, I'm sorry, but we can't print that," the reporter said. "We're against it."

One of the great needs of our national life—the more so as the simple, artless America of the past gives way to an increasingly complicated society—is a vigorous, intelligent, courageous, small-town journalism. The reasons are clear. We take it for granted—this is indeed a cliché of our national life—that a well-informed people is essential to the healthy functioning of democracy. But many rural and small-town people, rightly or wrongly, distrust metropolitan journalism. Since it is remote from their daily lives, corporately disembodied, anonymously edited, and "big business" by its very nature, non-urban people are likely to view it skeptically. Metropolitan journalism, moreover, is edited for metropolis. It does not, and cannot, deal with the daily affairs of outlying communities. Yet these affairs are the daily life of men. They are of the deepest interest and concern to the townsman, not only because he knows the personalities and questions involved but also because they affect him at every turn.

One reason why the small-town editor may be valuable to his community is that he cannot escape its assessment of him. It knows what kind of a man he is: strong, weak, intelligent, stupid, principled, opportunist. Whenever he takes a stand on any matter, or fails to do so, the community assesses his action in the light of its knowledge of him. The editor can rarely dissemble his motives under the circumstances. If, therefore, he is a man of character, he may have much influence in his community. He will be trusted—if not always followed—because he has been tested by the test of daily life lived with his fellows, a test obviously inapplicable to the metropolitan editor.

The Carters came to Greenville and decided to throw in their lot with the Delta. I had, the while, told local leaders that a considerable sum of money would be needed for the projected newspaper, the enterprise was necessarily precarious, and the chances were that they would lose their money. If, therefore, they should go into the venture, they must do so more as a contribution to community welfare than as an investment.

Second, I said, Carter must have editorial control entirely within his own discretion and be permitted to say what he wanted to say whether or not stockholders or the public agreed with him. These terms meeting with their approval, Percy called a meeting to raise the sum needed to augment the capital that Carter was bringing to the enterprise through the sale of the *Daily Courier*.

Greenville is not rich. It has always been innocent of millionaires. Yet here was Percy asking businessmen to put up sums considerable in relations to their means—money they would probably lose—for a newspaper to be run by a stranger to the community who was editorially an unknown quantity. Percy, however, vouched for Carter's intellectual integrity. He stated the financial risks of the venture and weighed them against the town's need for a courageous newspaper. Putting himself down for a substantial contribution, he was followed by Colonel Alexander Fitzhugh of Vicksburg (a wholesale grocer with interests in the Delta), W. T. Wynn (lawyer), Edmund Taylor (wholesale grocer), Joe Virden (lumber dealer), Frank England (automobile dealer), J. S. and J. Q. Strange (Coca-Cola agency), Mrs. Paul Gamble, a civic-minded woman, and a modest sum of my own.

Soon the *Delta Star* was competing with the established local daily. Carter often took the unpopular side of the case. He was occasionally, in his youthful impetuosity, intemperate. He ruffled feelings as he thrust at long-held concepts. His stockholders sometimes sharply disagreed with him, but they stuck to their word. No one of them attempted to dissuade him from his course or asked him to advocate or abandon any cause.

After a struggle of nearly two years' duration, the old newspaper sold out to Carter, and the *Democrat-Times* came into being. An enlightened newspaper of wide influence, a high percentage of its readers are Negroes, who are the poorest and least literate members of the community.

By 1946—ten years after Carter had come to Greenville, he had won the Pulitzer Prize for editorials on racial and religious tolerance, and his newspaper had achieved something approaching national fame.

If this achievement reflects creditably upon him, it also reflects credit upon the community, whose achievement perhaps is not less than that of Carter's. Recognizing the salutary role of a vigorous press in our democracy, it took him to its bosom almost sight unseen. It tried to impose no point of view upon him or to impede him when he expressed points of view that ran counter to its own. This is not mere "tolerance," a begrudging bow to decency. It is rationality married to open-mindedness, the more striking in that Carter came a stranger to a long-settled southern community that does not quickly embrace strangers. And, moreover, he was a "liberal" among deeply conservative people. One wonders, if the shoe was on the other foot, how many liberals would morally and financially help a conservative start a newspaper.

Nor is this all. Local issues often take on an intensity of feeling among small-town people—and the more so among emotional southerners—that is rarely approached in cities. But such issues, however important, take second place to attitudes, customs, prejudices—the definable and often indefinable elements that compose the index called "way of life." Among these none is more burning in the Delta than Negro-white relations.

It is easy enough to be a passionate liberal advocating racial change in the South when you are living at a distance from the scene in New York, say, or Boston. But strangely, when it is suggested to such liberals that they go South and state their convictions to the people involved, they reach for another martini and stay rooted in their chairs.

Carter, however, is no remote-control Tom Paine. He is a liberal in his community, a liberal among conservatives. Yet in a county whose population is more than half Negro and in a state where "white supremacy" is taken for granted (by the whites), he could write, "One half of Mississippi's population received in general less consideration than a smart planter gives to a mule." Speaking of his attitudes toward race relations in his *Where Main Street Meets the River,* Carter also reviews the march of his editorial opinions:

> Wasn't ready. . . . That was another shibboleth. Maybe Greenville hadn't been ready, fifteen years before, when we published a news picture of Jesse Owens, who was coming to the Delta to demonstrate, at a little all-Negro town's seventy-fifth anniversay fete, the co-ordination that had just won him four Olympic firsts.

The next day I was told, violently and often, that Mississippi newspapers didn't print pictures of Negroes. But we kept on printing such pictures . . . and now nobody bothers to mention it.

Carter discusses other "wasn't ready" items:

> Some had cautioned us that our people weren't ready when we urged the extension of the ballot to qualified Negro citizens and the removal of the poll tax; when we bespoke the equalization of education in Mississippi and the rightfulness of the Supreme Court's orders to admit Negro students to Southern graduate schools; and the wisdom of employing Negro policemen in our town, as we now do; and of spending tax money, dollar for dollar, to build Mississippi's first Negro public swimming pool and Negro hospital facilities and schools and playgrounds.

In retrospective mood, he continues:

> I looked back over each debatable issue, and I remembered some people had said we Mississippians weren't ready; and Bilbo braying . . . that I was a mongrelizer, a lymoculous (it means "mud-dwelling") liar, and telling my fellow Deltans that I ought to be skinned and put in a basket and toted out of town. But nobody had skinned me . . . nobody had ostracized me or promised economic retaliation; only a few had threatened me, and they anonymously.

Carter, therefore, had the support of the greater part of the community. Lacking it, he could not have gone on. In the Delta, as elsewhere, men's opinions change, if slowly. But they do change. Yesterday's radicalism becomes today's conservatism. The community has therefore caught up with Carter, and over wide areas of opinion, the editor and town go along together.

If he accelerated change in the community and so was its benefactor, he has also been a beneficiary because of change taking place within it. This is a process not uncommon in men's affairs, and the principle applicable to it has been put by Whitehead in his *Adventures of Ideas*. He writes:

> The final introduction of a reform does not necessarily prove the moral superiority of the reforming generation. It certainly does require that that generation exhibits reforming energy. But conditions may have changed, so that what is possible now may not have been possible then. A great idea is not to be conceived as merely waiting for enough good men to carry it into practical effect. This is a childish view of the history of ideas. The ideal in the background is promoting the gradual growth of the requisite communal customs, adequate to sustain the load of its exemplification.

Conducting a strongly personal journalism, Carter's personal qualities have also played their part while he met the test of daily living with his fellows and readers of his newspaper. His honesty unquestioned, it became apparent that while he is a man of opinions he is not opinionated, and unafraid of controversy, he does not seek it for its own sake. Nor did he flout the community's attitudes in search of cheap sensationalism or conduct himself editorially as a common scold.

Successful, his greatest test lies ahead of him. He must now avoid the pitfall of success that has brought him to ownership of a monopoly newspaper. Given the costs of starting a newspaper in even a medium-sized town such as Greenville, it is unlikely that his monopoly will be challenged by a newcomer. But Carter must face the almost inevitable hazards of his position. For the tendency of newspaper monopoly—although there are exceptions—is to wither the monopolist's heart and harden the arteries of his mind and to induce a stifling fatness and an opiate indifference to the public welfare. These tendencies increase as the dollar value of the newspaper increases, and the owner may be moved more by his vested interest than by his sense of public responsibility.

[*Cohn's worries were unfounded. Hodding and Betty Carter went on to make the* Delta–Democrat Times *a beacon of reason and enlightenment in what historian James W. Silver described as the "closed society" atmosphere of civil rights era Mississippi.*]

13

Tinsel Belongs on Christmas Trees

Moving to New Orleans, Cohn quickly became a successful businessman, rising to the position of executive manager of Feibleman's, a successful department store located on Canal Street. In this chapter, Cohn reveals many of his misgivings about the business world, its practices, and the consequences of these practices. He shows his distaste for deception and high-powered advertising and reveals his compassion for the working people, who struggled to achieve job security and career advancement while retaining such dignity as they could. As he did on so many occasions, Cohn also bemoans the growing depersonalization that he saw invading not only the workplace and the marketplace but all of American life.

Cohn's career as a businessman was brief but impressive. The qualities that contributed to Cohn's success as an entrepreneur, especially his sensitivity to human feelings and perceptive assessment of human behavior, would become the defining and sustaining elements of his success as a writer as well.

As many a small-town young man before me, when I had finished my college "education," I migrated to the nearest large city to earn my living, in this case, New Orleans. There I became associated with a department store and ultimately was its executive manager.

The store with which I was associated was old-fashioned even for New Orleans, where apathy lay sickly sweet upon the air like the heavy scent of gardenias in a small enclosure. Old-fashioned, uncomfortable, architecturally hideous, oblivious to success rules of the chart-and-curve school of business, the store flourished.

Our store was a crazy, rambling, column-cluttered structure. Designed in the 1870s—perhaps the worst period of American architecture—by an architect who must have been driven mad by absinthe or unrequited love, it offended every canon of art and utility. Its upper floors sagged from weariness. Such were the vagaries of our two ancient elevators—sometimes skipping like lambs and sometimes mule-balky—no one could ever know what they would do. The timbers of the ground floor were constantly torn up, as we fought a losing battle with termites. Hot in summer, cool in winter, uncomfortable for employees and customers, the building was grossly inadequate for the volume of business transacted within its out-of-plumb walls. But the store nonetheless did well. Anyone could see that our store building was but a poor thing, our fixtures shabby, our business without "side," factors in which many of our competitors excelled us. Why not, then, capitalize on something we had in abundance: shortcomings? This I did by writing and publishing advertisements on the theme that "Tinsel Belongs on Christmas Trees."

I told the ladies what they had already learned through hard experience shopping with us. Yet few things are so flattering and reassuring as reiteration of the obvious, a platform that has made some men wealthy and risen others to the estate of United States senator or even president. I said we had no Buckingham Palace guardsmen to greet customers, no fancy wrappings for packages, no elaborate "powder rooms," or appointments suggestive of the Petit Trianon. If women wanted these things, they must not come to us but go elsewhere. The firmer one is with lady shoppers, the better.

We left nothing to the reader's imagination. When we drew a moral, it was drawn so large it could be read miles away. Hence, with the subtlety of a ten-ton truck lumbering down the road, we said TINSEL BELONGS ON CHRISTMAS TREES. You pay for it. But you can't take it home with you. And you can't do anything with a label. We reduced costs, we said, to reduce prices. A dollar saved is a dollar earned. Therefore a woman who shopped with us might thereby raise her husband's salary.

This, to be sure, was our sales talk. Yet we never made any pretense of subscribing to the national nonsense, garnished with a meringue of bathos, that the businessman is in business "to serve his fellow man." We were in business for one and only one reason: to make an honest dollar, and since this was the case, we never pictured ourselves as Samaritans out of the holy writ of Dun and Bradstreet. I agreed warmly with what Judge Learned Hand said about "service." He wrote: "More cant . . . is poured out to youthful ears in the name of serving mankind than would fill the tally of those papers on which Panurge passed his momentous judgment some three hundred years ago."

I also, it goes without saying, agreed with Sir Winston Churchill that in a free enterprise system the crime lies, not in making a profit, but in incurring a loss. Yet I was nonetheless bemused by the spectacle of one of our competitors. Narcotized by his own clichés about serving mankind, he had convinced himself that he had become a merchant to protect the innocent New Orleans public from the rapacity of other merchants. He became rich and lived in the warm glow of what he took to be his perpetual good works, the saved Scrooge forever bringing fat geese to the Cratchits on Christmas Eve.

Yet, whatever the moonshine in our sales talk, underlying it was a serious truth. It was that the department store was something of an economic monstrosity. The consumer paid it a high price—in terms of its high overhead—merely to compensate it for gathering many things under roof. ("Store" is simply an abbreviation of storehouse.) Then he paid it more for its profit. The price he paid was sometimes five times the manufacturer's price. We manufactured efficiently. But we distributed wastefully.

Ours was a "popular price store." The South—for many decades economically the American Orient—was the dumping ground for the nation's shoddiest manufactures. Its people wore shoddy clothes, used rickety furniture, ate poor food, drank raw whiskey. The reasons for all this do not concern us here, but folk language was illustrative of the compulsions of necessity among the people. One man might say to another, "I want me some new shoes for Christmas," and the reply might be, "Yes, and there's souls in Hell wanting water." Or, "Like they say in Arkansas, you can do without 'em."

New Orleans was one of the poorest cities of this poorest section of the country. Its economic middle class small, there was a tiny group of well-to-do people and a huge group of pay-envelope people. The city's fine residential streets were a facade that concealed "Cockroach Row" and other components of dreary slums where flush toilets were as rare as Rembrandts and tenants fought a losing battle with rats, roaches, and other wildlife. In the merchandise trade, New Orleans (along with Baltimore) ranked as one of the nation's cheapest markets, and most of its stores were, therefore, in the "popular price" category.

But whatever the drabness of their environment, our customers were not a grim lot. Largely Roman Catholic, they had the magnificent cycle of feasts, penances, and seasons of the Church while, as Latins—French, Spanish, Italian—they knew how to amuse themselves with small things. The warm climate of the city ruled out expensive items of clothing and heating essential in colder areas. Nearby fields and waters abundantly yielded fish and vegetables. Wine was made at home by men who knew its uses. Rent was cheap. Here was a cheerful, easy-going, pleasure-loving populace, and I came to have an especial place in my heart for a band of girls who appeared often in our store.

They toiled long hours for small pay sewing sacks in a big plant. (Their rich, stingy employer, whether or not irony was intended, once gave the local zoo a monkey cage.) On Saturday afternoons these girls would buy dancing slippers for $1.89 a pair, tendering in payment their weekly paychecks of $6 or $7. The slippers would be worn to the most glittering dance ever held since men first moved to music with women: the dance they would attend that very evening. The dancer's slippers, therefore, had to match the dancer's dress; a dress, one knew, that was fairy woven even if its wearer had sat up three nights making it. The slippers, of poor quality, would be danced to shreds by the time morning came and the dancer went with her beau to the French Market for coffee and doughnuts and thence to make her devotions at St. Roch's before going home through sleeping streets. What of it? There would be another paycheck next week, another dance, another pair of slippers, and joy singing in the heart. Ah, youth!

I was enriched by my relations with the store's employees. Through them I came to understand Thoreau's melancholy dictum that "most men lead lives of quiet desperation." But I also came to understand that many of them lead lives of stoical courage.

One day I stopped at the hosiery counters to chat with Mamie Logan, a fairly young widow who supported herself and her young daughter. She was an old and valued employee. I observed that she was haggard, her eyes sunken within rims of darkness, her voice a whisper. But when I asked if she were not sick and ought to go home, she said she had a cold and would be all right.

Unconvinced and shaken by the apparition with whom I had just spoken, I asked a salesgirl to tell me the truth about Mamie's health. Reluctantly, she said that Mamie had tuberculosis of the throat but feared that if this became known she would lose her job and could no longer support herself and her child. She was dying upon her feet while standing to her task.

We sent Mamie home with the assurance of pay for a year, and at the end of that time we would see what could be done. I still remember with pleasure that this brave woman recovered her health and came back to us.

There was Jules Kling, our drapery buyer, who, soul of honor, had gone into bankruptcy in his youth as owner of a country store. Then, his debts legally expunged, he worked for three years in a sawmill until his debts had been paid. And there was Joe Hurst (this is not his right name), a trusted employee of the drapery department, who had been caught stealing. Now Jules Kling, soul of honor, pleaded with me not to fire Joe. He had stolen, Jules said, to pay medical bills for a succession of costly illnesses in his family. We kept Joe and reposed a trust in him that he never afterward violated.

There were women who year after year rose shortly after the sun, did their housework, cooked breakfast for themselves and theirs, and came long distances to the store, where they worked for eight hours six days a week. They returned home to cook, wash, clean, and sew before going to bed. Some of them, widowed, divorced, or deserted by their husbands, supported children. Others took care of parents or bedridden relatives. Some of our male employees, daily touched by physical pain, went quietly about their tasks because others depended upon them for bread. These things I learned only by indirection or from the lips of those concerned. Courageous, they were starred with dignity.

As many middle-aged women fear losing their jobs, so wage earners feared losing their jobs. The fear increased as a man's family increased and he grew older. It was fear that approached panic in bad days, especially when, as in my day, there was no unemployment insurance, and the wage earner's throat might tighten at the sight of the foreman, only to be relieved when that god smilingly said, "Good morning."

(In the present day of "full employment" all this may seem unreal, but full employment is a phenomenon of recent origin. Let us hope that the spectacle of jobs chasing men endures.)

I, too, once knew this fear that descended a chilling god on the spirit, for several people looked to me for aid. It is a fear that can spiritually emasculate a man, make a liar and toady of him, pulverize that "dignity of the individual" about which we prate so much.

We praise intellectual integrity. But is it not, for many of us, a luxury we can seldom afford? Rural Negroes, living close to harsh reality, put the case neatly. "A man's as honest as the times can stand," they say.

When a store buyer asks saleswomen how they like his recent purchases, they are likely to say, "Wonderful!" But, his back turned, they blurt, "Phooey!" The buyer, king of his little domain, wants "yes men" and gets them. On the campus, in banks, in the pulpit, wherever men's bread or chances of promotion depend upon the good will of other men, "yes men" abound and intellectual integrity is often corroded.

One of the more repulsive aspects of this is toadyism, the "yes, sahib" aspect of our culture. Some time ago I read the advertisement of a proud young man in the Hollywood (California) *Reporter* who, after describing his qualifications for the job sought in the movie industry, ended with a meaningful phrase: "No osculation." Throughout much of our business world executives toady to those above them while demanding toadyism of those below them, each giving and receiving according to his kind.

(In this field, Mr. Darryl Zanuck, haranguing his underlings, is credited with saying: "Don't say 'yes' until I have finished.")

"Yessing" is not only degrading to the yesser and the yessed but is also economically wasteful since it inhibits men's best efforts. I therefore determined that if I should rise in business, I would not demand yes men around me. And when I became general manager of our store, I told our executives I wanted their honest opinion, that I would weigh it, and while I would make the final decision, no one would suffer because he had disagreed with me. At first the men did not believe it. But when they saw that I was in earnest, they strongly voiced their views, gave the company the best they had, and made me their debtor for whatever success may have come to me.

I found that, aside from continuity of employment, men are so avid of economic security that they will often refuse a promotion if it entails executive responsibilities. They might then be more largely rewarded, but they would also be subject to the risk of being fired if they failed on the job.

I once offered the job of assistant buyer to a senior salesman. A young married man with family, his modest wages enabled him to support his family in simple comfort, and as long as he did not commit a nuisance, he would have his job for the rest of his life. I told him the road to advancement was now opened, and eventually he might become a buyer or manager of the whole business. These arguments failed. The salesman declined the promotion.

His reasoning was clear. As a salesman of proved ability, he had much economic security even if at a comparatively low level. As an executive he might succeed and gain large rewards. But if he failed, he would be out of a job.

If it be said that this man lacked enterprise, the reality is that few men seek leadership, only the bolder and more aggressive. Such men are relatively rare and hence, as businessmen say, there is always room at the top.

I learned that men working prize one thing above all. They want to feel they are needed, that they are human beings. They do not want to be regarded as interchangeable parts of a machine. Yet there is an ever increasing automatism of business.

In the remote time of twenty-five years ago, when I wanted to dictate a letter, I called in Miss Sylvia, our secretary, and got the job done. Today I might not see her successor for I could talk into a machine, and she could transcribe my words from it.

Factory workers are fractional fathers of a blind fruition. They rarely see the end product of their labors because the parts on which they work are combined into a whole at a distance from them. In the distributive trades, it is part of the cunning, calculated "simplicity" of our times that retailing relies more and more upon advertising to sell branded goods. I do not doubt that this makes for "efficiency." But neither do I doubt the validity of Whitehead's aphorism: "Seek simplicity and distrust it."

The process tends to transform the clerk from an individual dealing with individuals into a robot handing out goods to a faceless public, advertising having "sold" the goods to the customer before he bought them. Intelligence and initiative on the clerk's part are ruled out, and he is become a robot on sufferance until vending machines shall completely displace him.

Consider the supermarkets. These are dehumanized, colorless, odorless, humorless, prepackaged, cellophane-wrapped, metered, and measured bazaars in whose hospital-sterile atmosphere there is neither human warmth or human touch. Here, unlike the old-fashioned grocery stores, there is no cat dozing in the cracker barrel nor any droppings of midnight mice upon the shelves. But here there is no one with whom to discuss the merits of cheeses, the qualities of apples, the flavors of coffees. Here there are no butchers, wearing battered straw hats and pencils behind their ears, but only men behind glass partitions attired as surgeons for an operation.

Here vending machines dispense soft drinks, insurance, stockings, books, and there is a machine, naturally called "changette," that changes big coins into little ones. Here, too, when you write a check, you may do it before a camera that automatically photographs you and the check. Then if it should "bounce," your photograph may be sent to every policeman in the country, and you yourself will have sat in advance for a portrait of yourself as a criminal.

Here even—our equivalent of the Buddhist prayer wheel spinning at the pressure of an abstract thrum—is the abode of faith, not necessarily made manifest, but mechanized. A legend on a machine reads: INSERT ONE DIME AND ONE PENNY IN SLOT AND PUSH SLIDE ALL THE WAY IN. For your eleven cents the machine regurgitates a copy of the Lord's Prayer.

The supermarket customer, lonely amid the cart-pushing crowd, takes it or leaves it, the advertisement-preconditioned mind reaching compulsively for the prepackaged product.

The mood of these temples of economic determinism is totalitarian. "Order" is above all worshipped. The warm amiability, the give and take between friendly Americans that once characterized shopping in this once puppy-friendly country has been banished. In this place of robots, one is almost frightened by an occasional glimpse of a man restocking the shelves, one of the myriad of troglodytes of business who live and die anonymously behind the scenes. I do not know whether such men are "happy," but many authorities hold that the constant dehumanizing of wage earners poses the essential dilemma of management-labor relations. It is a dilemma we did not have to face in our New Orleans store.

Ours was a small, family-owned business with four hundred employees. They were "people" to the management, the management was "people" to them, and we were always accessible to one another.

14

I Leave the Business World

Although he sang the praises of the "mom and pop" atmosphere that prevailed at Feibleman's, Cohn was instrumental in convincing Sears and Roebuck executives to acquire the store. He then served briefly as national sales manager for Sears. Even as he did so, however, Cohn was already planning to abandon his business career, which despite his meteoric rise and the material well-being it provided, had left him troubled and unfulfilled. On a visit to Greece in 1929, he had made the decision to "leave the business world," later confiding to a friend that he was "tired of chasing dollars." [1]

In the summer of 1929, I was in Greece. Many of my countrymen remember that year as one of the unhappiest of their lives, for it marks the beginning of the great economic depression of our times and inaugurated a long season of suffering for most Americans. I recall it, too, for this reason. But it comes back to me the more sharply for quite another reason.

Then a young businessman in New Orleans, I had no cause to be unhappy about my material state. I was earning considerable sums of money, I had a comfortable house in the French Quarter, and, best of all, I had a number of friends who brought light and affection into my life. As a bachelor, I was traveling light. My health was vigorous, and I fell within the grouping of those who have at least "as much sense as the law allows." The world was very much with me.

Under these circumstances, on a late afternoon in the year 1929, I was standing on the hill of the Acropolis. Far below me was the temple of Theseus. It had been constructed twenty-five hundred years ago of white Pentelic marble. Time, working its alchemy upon stone, had changed the structure to gold. I made the not uncommon observation to myself that eighty generations of men and women had lived and died within the shadow of this temple: poets, bankers, thieves, sailors, shipping magnates, prostitutes, painters, sculptors, musicians, priests, actors, playwrights, businessmen, laborers . . . Then, for no perceptible reason, I began to query a central fact of my own existence, an existence whose brevity was pointed up by the centuries that lay piled up on the ground far below me.

1. Lee Lewellyn Jordan, "A Biographical Sketch of David L. Cohn" (M.A. thesis, University of Mississippi, 1963), 46.

I had long been deeply and inchoately disturbed despite my estate of material well-being, and I now suddenly knew that I would leave the world of business. It is as honorable a world as any other. The businessman is no less useful to society than many a writer who derides him. But I knew that I would cease being a businessman because it was a life that gave me no inner peace, because I felt I must proceed hereafter according to my own lights even if I had to wander in the desert until the lights should come on.

Thus it was that, young, "successful," and with an assured business career of some proportions before me, I returned to New Orleans and so arranged it that within eighteen months thereafter I was "free." What I was free to do, or would do, I did not know. Sometimes, it seems to me, it is the part of wisdom— despite the maxim to the contrary—to leap first and look afterward. In any event, that is what I did "midway in this mortal life."

I traveled widely, I fell sick, and I returned to my native Mississippi to recuperate under the sun in the company of beloved friends. There, with a shock of novelty, I began to see with fresh eyes the scenes of my childhood, and having little else to do, I noted on paper the things I saw. These notes became chapters and the chapters a book that, to my surprise, a publisher was willing to publish. And so it came about that I wrote a number of books and many articles for magazines. If I should ever succeed in writing one paragraph with high survival value, I'd be content.

15

Eighteenth-Century Chevalier

After traveling widely and falling ill, Cohn returned to Greenville and tested the Delta's vaunted hospitality to the fullest, staying for two years as the houseguest of William Alexander Percy. The effect of this visit was reciprocally beneficial. Percy provided information, advice, and support as Cohn produced God Shakes Creation, *while Cohn managed to dissuade Percy from abandoning the autobiography that would become* Lanterns on the Levee.

I first came to know William Alexander Percy, the author of *Lanterns on the Levee* and of several volumes of verse, when I was a high school student in our hometown of Greenville. A recent Harvard Law School graduate, he was practicing law with his father, who was leader of the Mississippi Bar. Already somewhat traveled and in my eyes a cosmopolitan, Percy was then also writing verse. My senior by about ten years, we were brought together by Miss Carrie Stern, our mutual teacher friend, who counseled with Will about verse writing and gave me invaluable aesthetic guidance.

Percy embodied many factors that drew me to him. He was a lawyer, and I aspired to the law. He was a poet, and I loved verse. He talked well, and I admired good talk. He was a companion warm, whimsical, humorous, generous in act and attitude, and I had need of a more mature companionship than I could find among my contemporaries.

Shortly after our first talks, he gave me several volumes of the Gilbert Murray translations of Greek dramatists that were then appearing. They brought me glimpses of an unsuspected beauty and implanted within me an affection for the classical world. The gift also marked, in my eyes, the beginning of a lifelong friendship that enriched me and leaves me greatly indebted to the donor. Soon the gulf of age and experience between us was so unobtrusively bridged by Percy that I was little conscious of it while, as I grew up, it was closed and it was as if we had always been contemporaries.

He passionately loved his own soil. Yet, his soul seeking a repose it never found, at home everywhere he was nowhere at home. He seemed to be of the community and yet withdrawn from it, a bright transient out of another time

A version of this chapter appeared as "Eighteenth-Century Chevalier," *Virginia Quarterly Review* XXXI (Fall, 1955), 561–75.

and place and a guest of indeterminate stay who would, so far as he could, render unto his host all that is seemly in the guest. Small, slender, finely drawn, forehead broad, eyes gray-blue, mouth generous, chin stubborn, abundant hair prematurely silver, he had an antique beauty suggestive of the Greece he loved and poet he was.

In him a marked fastidiousness and delicacy of manner, combined with a certain reticence and aloofness, recalled what Dumas said of the French poet Alfred de Vigny: "What most amazed Hugo and myself was that Vigny seemed utterly free of the gross necessities of our nature, necessities that some of us— and both Hugo and myself were of that number—satisfied not only without shame, but even with a certain sensuality."

Percy seemed to stem from an insubstantial world of light and air. Yet he was a lawyer, soldier, planter, poet, traveler, Red Cross worker, Rotarian, gardener, and bachelor parent to three adopted sons. He entered actively into the life of his community, suffered fools, comforted the distressed, caused iris to grow where iris had never before grown.

He had many friends, white and Negro. (He also had venomous enemies. These were white.) But, the loneliest man I have ever known, the companion of his heart was loneliness. Writing of a youthful stay in Europe, he says in his *Lanterns on the Levee*, "I was sick for a home I had never seen and lonely for a hand I had never touched. So for a year I walked and lived and slept with loneliness, until she was so familiar that I came not to hate her but to know that whatever happened in however many after years she alone would be faithful to me. . . . What must be learned at last had as well be learned early."

Loneliness sat with him when he played the piano, watched over him as he pruned a bush, sometimes hovered an aura about his head as he presided at his dinner table bright with laughter. Often on summer nights, as though keeping a lover's tryst with loneliness, he would pace up and down on the sidewalk before his house, his small figure dwarfed into tininess by the huge oaks under which he walked; he paced with head bowed, lost in thought or dreams, while sometimes lightning flickered, thunder growled, and an evening thrush sang an evening song from blue-entangled wisteria.

All this was clear to the inward eye. But to the outward eye he was the gayest of companions, the quickest to kindle and to be kindled by laughter, the most thoughtful of hosts, the most welcome of guests, the readiest to enliven the company with animated, mirth-provoking talk.

No one knows, or can know, or ought to know, the innermost being of his fellows. (Hell must be a place filled with fiends plucking at your sleeve and saying, "Now, tell me all about yourself.") Yet it was evident to those who knew Percy that this saddest of men felt sharply the agonies of the world, its beauties, its exaltations. The gods had endowed him with a heightened intelligence, a too-seeing eye, a too-sensitive ear, and he paid for their bounty in the one acceptable coin: pain.

His was a high heart, an engine mightier than his fragile body, that drove him into the trenches of the first world war, although at training camp he was often too weak to march under the hot Texas sun. It was a courageous heart that made his face granite toward injustice however obscure the victim or however much he risked his life seeking justice; it was a compassionate, stubborn heart that encompassed much and compromised little.

His infantry company was under orders to attack German positions at dawn on November 11, 1918. The attack would have had to proceed across a river against strongly held enemy positions. It seemed senseless since the guns would stop firing under the armistice at eleven o'clock that morning. Men would die for no reason. (Many did die, some at 10:59 A.M.) Then the compassion and the stubbornness in Percy rose in his throat. A mere junior officer, he saw his commanding general and, risking court-martial, this man who had already been decorated for bravery in action, pleaded so convincingly that the projected attack was abandoned.

In keeping with his spirit, Percy recommended to the young that they read not only the Gospels but also the meditations of Marcus Aurelius. "The self-communings of the Emperor," he wrote, "though often cold to clamminess, convince a man he never need be less than tight-lipped, courteous, and proud, though all is pain. It is saving to rest our eyes on nobility, severe and unalloyed, such as a god might pattern after."

Throwing himself into some of the great struggles of his day—the poet in action as poets have so often been—neither spiritually nor intellectually did Percy belong to his times. Spiritually he was of the thirteenth century, and in a sense, going home. He was more than once a pilgrim to Mont-Saint-Michel and Chartres and was one with Henry Adams in this respect if no other. The Age of Faith and its raising of great cathedrals, its crusades to Palestine (especially the almost inexplicable Children's Crusades), its singing pages and troubadours, and Blondel walking the roads of the world in search of his lost master—all manifestations of the morning time of the Renaissance—deeply moved him.

He also had an equal adoration for pagan Greece: for the immortal beauty created there in such a moment of fruition as men have never since known, for the hosts that stood before Troy, for the violet-crowned Athens that died in the sea off soft Syracuse, and for the Twelve upon Parnassus, the more appealing in their divinity perhaps because they sometimes committed the follies we call human.

Percy traveled twice throughout Greece, brought her image home, and gave it a hallowed place in his heart and his house. He also often visited Italy and Sicily where Catholicism and paganism remain in many places inextricably mingled, and although he left the Roman Church early in his youth, he continued to believe in its greatness while loving pagan Greece. In his bosom, Saint Francis of Assisi and cloven-footed Pan dwelt harmoniously together.

Percy's departure from the Church, and his membership thereafter in no organized religious group had, he bemusedly observed, a strange effect upon local Ku Kluxers, who hated him. They reviled him as a Catholic. But since he belonged to no church, they also reviled him as an "atheist."

His father, LeRoy, was of the Episcopal faith, but he was hardly a practicing member. His mother, Camille, was a Roman Catholic but was not excessively pious. Yet, in his early youth Percy became, he wrote, "intolerably religious, going to early Mass . . . racking my brain to find something to confess once a month, praying inordinately, and fasting on the sly. . . . I wanted so intensely to believe in God and the miracles . . . and the Church."

Doubt assailed him: "To be at once intellectually honest and religious is a rack on which many have perished and on which I writhed dumbly." A young student at the University of the South, in Sewanee, Tennessee, there came an apocalyptic change in his life. He describes it in terms of his essentially austere personality:

> Once a month I would ride ten miles . . . to Winchester to go to confession, hear Mass, and take communion. I had been thinking . . . I was determined to be honest if it killed me. So I knelt in the little Winchester church examining my conscience and preparing for confession. As I started to the confessional I knew there was no use going, no priest could absolve me, no church could direct my life or my judgment, what most believed I could not believe. . . . It was over, and forever.

(How blow the winds of revelation. Reading this passage from Samuel Butler's *Notebooks,* I was struck by the similarity of his religious experience with that of Percy's:

> I dropped saying them [prayers] suddenly . . . once for all. It was the night I went on board ship to start for New Zealand. . . . [Butler was then twenty-four.] The night before I had said my prayers and doubted not that I was always going to say them. . . . That night the sense of change was so great that it shook them quietly off. . . . I felt no compunction of conscience . . . about leaving off my . . . prayers—simply I could no longer say them.)

"Unable to believe what most believed" and yet deeply religious, Percy found Paul an unsympathetic figure. He was, he wrote, neither fool nor saint but "one of intellect that has somehow caught fire and so misleads when it is shiningest." In his Epistle from Corinth, he causes a Greek to say, "Paul, Paul, I'd give my Greek inheritance, my wealth and youth to speak one evening with the Christ you love and never saw and cannot understand!"

(Several years after Percy's death, Lucien Price in *Dialogues of Alfred North Whitehead* quoted the English philosopher as saying "The man who, I suppose, did more than anybody else to distort and subvert Christ's teaching was Paul. I wonder what the other disciples thought of him—if anything. Probably they didn't understand what he was up to, and it may well be doubted whether he did himself. It would be impossible to imagine anything more un-Christlike than Christian theology. Christ probably couldn't have understood it.")

Percy was not an "intellectual," nor was he, of course, anti-intellectual. His tastes in the arts were sound but conventional, although he permitted himself a wide range in music, being devoted to it, playing the piano himself, and annually going to New York to hear concerts. His Sunday afternoons were given over to radio broadcasts of music, and then his usually humming household was muted during an hour or two of symphonic music programs.

In his library were rows of translations from Greek and Roman classics, and many volumes about painting, sculpture, architecture. But the hair-splitting of metaphysicians engaged him not at all, nor did the metaphysical poets move him. He admired Donne. He loved Keats. Yet the symbolists were not alien to him, and he made translations from Verlaine and Mallarmé, whose pages drip with sad autumnal rains. The frosty beauty of mathematics was not him, neither were the marrowless data of economics, nor the many-chambered mansion of the physical sciences. So, too, he was little drawn to the social sciences except insofar as their conclusions sometimes illuminated problems of his community. Not even the law, although it was his profession and he practiced it successfully, if somewhat wearily, entered into his inner being but was always a thing apart.

Worldly, traveled, widely read, no denizen of an ivory tower, Percy nonetheless was marked by the naïveté and credulity that are nearly always the mark of the spiritually superior and truly sophisticated man. "If within the sophisticated man," wrote Thoreau, "there is not an unsophisticated one, then he is but one of the Devil's angels."

Travel refreshed and stimulated Percy, and he went far afield. The Rocky Mountain country, France, Italy, Spain, North Africa, Greece, Egypt, Turkey, Japan, all knew him. In Tahiti and Bora Bora he found happiness among a simple people living amid incomparable beauty. I had gone to the islands and chattered so much about them that Will's father visited them, and later Will.

He was delighted by an incident of his Japanese travels. Wherever he walked in Nikko, he was followed by laughing children. Percy was less perturbed by this than puzzled, for to his eye he seemed merely an ordinary white man where white men were no novelty and therefore no mirth-compelling phenomenon. But when he recounted the incident to a Japanese journalist friend for explanation, he laughed. Then he explained that to the Japanese a man with white skin, blue eyes, silver hair was so impossibly ugly that the children were moved to laughter.

A many-sided man and a romantic, Percy was primarily a poet. Puzzled men, understanding little of these priesthoods, dismissed him as incomprehensible or called him a mystic because they did not know what else to call him. Some cast him outside pragmatic society by terming him "impractical."

Others contemptuously called him an "idealist," one amiably weak-minded.

Percy said of his verse: "What I wrote seemed to me more essentially myself than anything I said or did . . . the results were intensely personal."

If, then, the writing in this case is the man, Percy was most himself, I feel, in the intensely personal lyric entitled "Overtones":

> I heard a bird at break of day
> Sing from the autumn trees
> A song so mystical and calm,
> So full of certainties,
> No man, I think, could listen long
> Except upon his knees.
> Yet this was but a simple bird
> Alone, among dead trees.

Once, when I was at loose ends, Percy said, "Come and stay with me." It was a stay that lengthened into more than two years.

In the Delta, where hospitality was not dispensed with an eyedropper, by old custom "visits" might extend from a few days to a few years, and apparently the Percys had been hosts to such visitors for decades. Once, Mr. M. R. Valiant, an elder citizen, speaking of visits before 1861, said, "Mrs. Walker Percy told me of an old lady who came to her father's to take dinner and stayed the rest of her life. I knew a gentleman who was invited to stay a few weeks at the Percys' and stayed eighteen months; he probably would not have left then if the war had not broken out."

On my first evening in Percy's house three gathered for dinner. They were my host, myself, and Will's Aunt Nana (Mrs. George Pearce), the elderly widowed sister of his mother, who ran the household. A large, gay, pleasure-loving woman of charm and tireless energy, born and brought up in New Orleans and member of a family of French descent, she remained essentially French however long she lived among outlander Anglo-Saxons (including her husband), who had such barbarous notions concerning food, drink, and other pleasures. I had taken French lessons from her as a boy, dreamily walking the summer-leafy streets to her house, my way a processional illuminated by bird music.

Aunt Nana, who seemed to be dressed by Paris dressmakers of the Second Empire although attired by Washington Avenue stores, welcomed me warmly and said, "David, now that you are here—and I hope for a long time—you will be a member of the family." Thereupon I rose, and making to my hostess what I took to be a continental bow, apologized to her for what I was about to say. I refused family membership because, in my opinion, few things were more overrated than the joys of family life while, more important, family membership implied that I would help with the Sunday night supper dishes when the servants were out.

Then Will arose. Bowing to Aunt Nana, he eloquently defended my right to remain in the house and enjoy the unfettered pleasures of the pampered guest. It was upon this note of laughter, warmth, and affection—a note characteristic of it—that I settled down to my long stay in the Percy household.

I had not been long in the house when I rescued Aunt Nana from a grave dilemma. She belonged to a ladies' card club, most of whose members had long been widows—evidence that in survival, as in other weighty matters, women have more sense than men. Since she and others of the group were of French descent and numbered thirteen, the club was given the elegant name "Le Club de Treize." If its members were not always hungry, they clearly liked to eat vigorously and to eat well, so much so indeed that their card playing seemed to be but a penitential detour to arrive at the excellent supper served at midnight.

It was coming on to be Aunt Nana's turn to be hostess to the club, and every evening at dinner Will and I heard in detail what she would serve for supper. The main dish would be turkey. The bird would be sacrificed in the bloom of its youth to appear golden-brown with oyster dressing after a New Orleans recipe. It would have to be, of course, a fresh-killed turkey. No store-bought fowl would do that had lain who knows how long in the icy vaults of some distant corporation.

But Aunt Nana could not find the bird of her heart in town, and as the time neared for the club's meeting her distress grew until to me it became unbearable. Then, on an autumn night of storm, the great day forty-eight hours distant, I decided to play knight errant and get a turkey for my unhappy hostess. Will said feelingly, "You're a bigger fool than Aunt Nana," but I went out nonetheless into the darkness. Two hours later, through the good offices of a Negro friend, I had the surety of a proper turkey on the morrow.

The next morning I suggested to Will that we should celebrate my success with appropriate ceremonies. I would appear at his door with the turkey around six o'clock in the evening. When I knocked, he would start playing Chopin and that would bring Aunt Nana to join him.

On a mournful afternoon of rain I knocked at the door, soon heard Will at the piano, and entered the great hall of the house with a big gobbler on a leash. The noise of its struggle brought pianist and audience to see what was happening and when Aunt Nana saw the gobbler she welcomed me warmly between tears and laughter. But, ever practical in all that pertained to the table, she tolled herself back to earth, called Lige, ordered him to imprison the bird carefully and off with its head at dawn.

So it was that the members of Le Club de Treize dined well and heartily as was their wont, and thus was Aunt Nana's prestige as a hostess preserved. I never did tell her, however, that I had paid a high price for the bird by perhaps jeopardizing my soul for it. For it was miraculously procured, and whatever my thoughts may have been, I did not ask my friend how it was that he, turkeyless at eight o'clock on a night of storm, had procured a big gobbler two hours later.

Immoral it may be, but if one is wise one does not always inquire too closely into the sources from which one's blessings flow.

Prominent in the household was Lige Collier. An elderly Negro, his nominal duties were such that he would have had to be the seven-handed Siva to discharge them. Nominally he was butler, gardener, handyman, valet, chauffeur, and benevolent tyrant to the three young Percy boys: LeRoy, Walker, Phinizy. But no one took this seriously, Lige least of all. A lesser man might have been crushed even by the contemplation of the weight of such duties, yet he regarded them calmly. Preoccupation with one's occupation is the mark of the unimaginative.

There were also in the household Arciel, the fat, middle-aged, kindly Negro maid, and Louisa (pronounced Lou-eye-ser), the presiding genius of the kitchen. She was a monumental, ebon-black woman, of such lofty demeanor and such palace mannerisms that Will had dubbed her the Queenly Woman.

The way in which Delta families acquire and lose Negro servants eludes precise definition. There are no employment agencies in the area. References are unknown and are indeed superfluous. If you wanted to hire a cook, some of your colored friends were sure to know whether the prospective employee was "triflin' " or steady. The cook, on the other hand, knew whether you were—as Negroes classified whites—"po' white trash," "mean," "kindly," or "quality." The act of employment was surrounded by an amiable vagueness on both sides. It was not unusual that one got a servant whether or no one wanted a servant. So it was that Lige had come into the service of the Percys.

Years ago, when Will's Birmingham cousins—LeRoy and Mattie Sue Percy—were building a house, Lige was night watchman on the job, hired by the builder. He became devoted to the Percys. Why not then, regardless of invitation, work for them when the house was completed? Lige did. What if he was ignorant of what are called "the domestic arts"? He possessed instead, in full measure, loyalty, good humor, honor, and that quality which is the universal passport nearly everywhere—charm. The more pedestrian attributes—such as competence for the task—he could acquire in time.

(In this context it is amusing to hear the convoluted grumblings of Henry James when he visited Charleston nearly forty years after The War. He found the "apparently deep-seated inaptitude of the negro race at large for any alertness of personal service," a "lively surprise. One had remembered," he said, "the old southern tradition, the house alive with the scramble of young darkies for the honor of fetching and carrying; and one was to recognize . . . its melancholy ghost. Its very ghost had . . . ceased to walk . . .; the old planters . . . were the people . . . the worst ministered to. I could have shed tears for them at moments, reflecting that it was for *this* they had fought and fallen.")

Few Delta people expected efficiency of their Negro servants or hankered for it. And besides, what was one to do with Lige? Here he was in the Percys' new house—had he not watched over it in the building?—grinning and never doubting he was welcome. And there he remained for several years while his employers had three sons upon whom he alternately discharged his affections and the lightnings of his wrath when they would not "behave."

Then one day their father died. Whereupon his cousin, Will Percy, a bachelor nearing fifty, asked Mattie Sue Percy to bring her boys and make their home with him in Greenville. They came and Lige came too without waiting upon so empty a form as an invitation.

Soon, Mattie Sue Percy died. Will Percy adopted the boys as his sons. This threw an additional burden upon Lige. He granted that Mistuh Will was a smart man. But he strongly felt that the boys also needed his guidance, and although they grew up and went to college, his supervision of them was surrendered only at his death.

Small, wiry, gray-haired, with bright chinquapin eyes, good mannered, good humored, a bachelor courtly yet dashing, Lige was both a delight to his employer and a weariness of the flesh. Whether because he found the world hard to bear or was merely emulating distinguished white gentlemen he had known, he not infrequently sought refuge in the otherworldliness of the whiskey bottle. These occasions, however, sometimes coincided with evenings when Will was giving a large dinner, he at one end of the table and Aunt Nana at the other. Then Lige, as butler, walking with glazed eyes and rolling seaman's walk the tightrope between intoxication and steadiness, desperately trying to be dignified and sweating from every pore, would stand uncertainly by Will's side as he carried and "helped the plates." The host, painfully conscious of Lige's condition and fearful of nameless calamities, would give his faithful servant black looks designed to kill him on the spot and so end all; or, that failing, sober him sufficiently to avert disaster. The while Aunt Nana, to whom grace was as godliness, looked, as the word is, mortified.

The plates helped, Lige made vagrant circumlocutions in time and space, moving like a sleepwalker but saving the honor of the house by never dropping anything. He nearly always saw the evening through and maintained an air of guardsman's correctness, whipsawed though he was between the withering glances of his employer and the Queenly Woman's imprecations when he went to the kitchen: "Lige, you jes ought to be ashamed of yo'self."

Once, however, the honor of the house was dragged through dust or, more accurately, through duck gravy. Will was giving a dinner for a northern lady visitor who turned out in her best dress, as did the local ladies present. The dinner, however, as dinners sometimes do, was going heavily, and Will, attempting to lift it, talked his charming best as he carved the wild duck. Then occurred the calamity. The mallard shot from under the carving things as though still alive and fell into the lap of the guest of honor. Lige, full of Old Rack and Ruin, bursting into laughter and going to the lady said, "Please, ma'am, us needs the duck, 'cause us ain't got no more out in the kitchen," and retrieved it upon a silver platter.

[*Another somewhat more amusing version of this story has Lige plucking the errant duck from the bosom of Mrs. Phillip W. Werlein.*][1]

The next morning, as upon so many similar mornings, he appeared repentant before his employer. Will, as usual, then read him a lecture upon his shortcomings and threatened to banish him from town if there should ever be a next time. Lige bowed his head beneath the blast and swore that he would "never tech another drap; I don't know what come over me, Mr. Will," while both men, possessed of the mellow wisdom that all that changes is the same, knew in their hearts they were just enacting the lines of a stylized ritual. The lecture over, they discussed the roses near the garden gate and talked no more of transient frailties. And so it was that, although Lige teetered uncertainly around the dining room on other occasions and several times wrecked his employer's cars in gin-induced carnival moods, he kept his job and the affections of the members of the household until he died and was tenderly buried by them. The Percy women and the Percy children cried. The men raised their eyes to the oaks in the front yard.

The Queenly Woman's fate was otherwise. A huge figure reminiscent of Swinbourne's line, "the solemn slope of mighty limbs asleep," rather humorless, but possessed of a magic way with beaten biscuit, she presided over the kitchen with massive hauteur.

It is part of the creeping barbarism of our times that it is a period without style, a form of degeneration against which the Queenly Woman valiantly struggled. On summer Sunday afternoons when dinner was over and the sun hottest, she would put on her palace dress. Short sleeved and primly décolleté as becomes the dress of a woman who is conscious of her charms yet modest, it was made of red upholsterer's plush. Invariably worn with it was a rope of coral beads that Will had brought her from Naples, an ornament literally rope-size in harmony with her monumental body. Regally attired, she would place a chair on the treeless sidewalk near the street, convenient of access to pedestrians and motorists. There, copiously sweating, she gave audience for her admirers throughout the blazing afternoon until, in the cool of the evening, she left her court, attired herself in clothes more seemly for worship, and went to church.

I record with some melancholy that shortly after I came to the household this admirable woman, through what malady of the spirit one never knew, went into a precipitous decline. Once proud of her noble craft, she became slovenly in its practice. Her beaten biscuit, a miracle of confectionery, seldom came to the table. Instead there was baker's bread, corpse-pale dough impregnated with chemicals. The breakfast coffee, formerly strong and aromatic, no longer

1. Lewis Baker, *The Percys of Mississippi: Politics and Literature in the New South* (Baton Rouge, 1983), 159.

smote pleasantly upon palate and nose. The bacon lay soggy upon the plate, and the grits were lumpy.

These are important matters to all except the cheerless fanatics of gulp-and-gallop who eat but to live. Will, therefore, without invading the Queenly Woman's right to privacy tried, as artist to artist, to toll back her spirit to the workaday world. This failing, he laid down the law. But it was all to no avail. The sauce of love in its preparation remained absent from the fried chicken. Yet one could not discharge an old employee; such an action belongs to the category of things not done. The household continued to endure what the kitchen brought forth until one day, alas, the Queenly Woman, forgetful of her high estate, committed a deed quite unworthy of her, and Will was forced to act.

The next morning at table, having thought over his course during the night, he gravely said to me, "I shall call the Queenly Woman in after breakfast and fire her when I can do it with dignity and without passion." And so it was that this once majestic figure, a canker at her heart, left the household. She was replaced by the gentle Theresa, who remained as long as Will lived.

Once Percy and I fell into conversation about some aspects of American Jewish life. Of Greenville's Jews he had written that they were "too much like natives to be even overly prosperous." His eyes twinkling, he said to me, "I have a great grievance against southern Jews. It is that they have fallen to the level of Gentiles." Twenty years before, he went on, there had been a local rabbi—a man of cultivation—with whom he had often discussed music. Ten years before, the town had had a Jewish tailor of Russian origin who had read Pushkin aloud to him in the Russian tongue. "But now," he said laughingly, "our local Jews are just like everybody else—nice people and rooters for the home team. I never did expect to be able to talk to many Gentiles, and now that I can't talk to the Jews, I sit here a lonely man."

Percy was rebelling, of course, against the nation's passion for conformity that was squeezing the once diverse elements of its population into the same mold. The town's Jews, responding to it and anxious not to be thought "different" by their neighbors, were neither distinguished in business nor learning. They had not even clung to the many items of cookery gathered by their forebears during their peregrinations through Russia, Rumania, Hungary, Poland, Germany, and the Baltic states.

Thus they were not "different" from their neighbors. But neither did they enrich the community with cultural contributions they might have made to it. Percy argued that if a Frenchman settled in Greenville and gave up his pot-au-feu for canned tomato soup, the town did not benefit by the change.

Yet this process was at work throughout the country—the process admiringly described as the "melting pot." But Percy understood how difficult it was for small minority groups to escape the crushing pressures of majority-group conformity, pressures abhorrent to the poet whose eye sought color and variety, whose spirit loved the infinite diversity of mankind.

Will's house, a big, rambling, two-story structure built by his parents, stood in an unfashionable, low-lying part of town that became a shallow lake in our sometimes torrential rains. In order to find occasional refuge from its teeming life—three young adopted sons, their companions, friends who came unannounced, and vagrants like myself—he had a wing for himself containing piano, books, and cherished art objects. Here he could retreat by closing his door.

There was a blessed quietude in the neighborhood. It was broken only by the soft voices of passing Negroes, the cries of schoolchildren, the occasional whistle of a riverboat, the singing of birds. In this seeming abode of innocence, evil, one thought, could scarcely enter.

But evil did enter. One evening in summer, Ellen Murphy, a Birmingham cousin of Will's, then visiting him, said to Roger Generelly (another cousin) and me, "My it is so quiet in Greenville. I do wish something would happen."

She did not have long to wait. About midnight I was awakened by the sound of pistol shots beneath my window. A moaning voice said, "Lawd Jesus." By the time I had got downstairs, the police had come. Across the street, Will's neighbor and friend, Julia Gratsy, called to the officers to ask whether they wanted any whiskey (to revive the wounded). "No'm," shouted one of them. "They don't need no whiskey." Then he added in a superb anticlimax, "—and besides they're dead."

Two Negro women lay in bloody pools upon the Percy lawn. It was quickly established by the capture of their murderer how they had come to their death. The women had been dancing at a nearby Chinese grocery–dance hall and there had aroused the jealousy of another woman who had recently been released from the state penitentiary after serving a term for manslaughter. Hiding behind the oaks in front Will's house, she shot her victims as they passed.

In the morning, sun bright, church bells ringing, Lige gingerly washed away evidence of blood on the sidewalk. But for sometime thereafter the tide of traffic shifted from our sidewalk to the sidewalk across the street.

The Percys were not unaware of the existence of evil, but they never locked the doors of their house. They felt somehow that to lock doors was to reveal a lamentable parsimony of spirit, while it never occurred to them that anyone would try to murder or rob them. Will's father narrowly escaped murder at the hands of a Ku Kluxer, but no attempt was ever made to rob the house although it stood open to enterprisers in this field.

It was also open to "decorators." Yet no member of that clan, with the prestige upon him of St. Louis or Chicago, had ever entered to transform the house into a replica of the Peabody Hotel lobby in Memphis or Lady Forster's chalet at Lucerne. But Will did have occasional grave consultations with ladies whose taste he trusted concerning the ways of chintzes. It is indeed inevitable, if you are a bachelor as Percy was, that ladies, as unbidden as evening moths, will come to you reeking with the lore of the decorator and vibrant with a passion for order no matter how much you, as a male, love the amiabilities of domestic disorder. None of these had their way. The house remained warmly lovable, comfortable, innocent of "antiques," slightly disorderly. Moroccan rugs, Persian vases, Mexican wood screens, Japanese prints, Victorian oddments, old-fashioned mahogany furniture, and brass beds somehow achieved a harmony that defied the rules and escaped analysis.

In his latter years Percy succumbed to the narcosis of gardening and was thereafter a changed man as are all who fall prey to it or to the frenzies of fly fishing. The fever upon him, he constructed a walled garden, installed iron gates brought from Spain, erected a fountain that made a tinny music, dug a small pond for ornamental fish, grew shrubs and flowers. He and Lige planted, sprayed, pruned, and fertilized so that there were flowers for the house and for friends while, if some plant for which the dealer promised much turned out to be but a poor thing, what did it matter? The gardener, I perceived, loves his garden not for what it is but for what it may become. So it is like to him in happiness who lifelong pursues in the woman he loves the remote, impossible Helen.

Many American novels, plays, and movies have so long exploited the theme of degeneration under the magnolias, that it has become stale and hackneyed. The "story," with a few variants, is always the same: Father is a slobbering drunkard; Mother, an ineffectual dreamer living in the past; Sister, an apprentice nymphomaniac; Junior, a reckless youth having a love affair with a Negro girl (his father's daughter and therefore his half-sister) in the bottoms below the white-columned house crumbling to ruins. In the attic live two crazy aunts. On moonlight nights they dress themselves in the finery of their ancestors, steal out on the mangy lawn, and do a wild ballet.

There have been, and still are, degenerate old southern families. This is not unnatural. Decay, as well as growth, is a constant phenomenon in nature, among men and societies of men. There is nothing novel in this. But some of our writers annually discover it anew with a shock of surprise as others, standing upon a peak in Darien, Connecticut, discover what most men have always known and regarded as unworthy of comment: namely, that the organs of excretion are also the organs of generation.

There are also fallen families of ancient origin and whilom distinction in New England, and I myself have encountered members of them moldering quietly amid the frangipani of South Sea islands. But our writers largely depict their southern counterparts. Decay under the magnolias seems a better box-office attraction than decay under the elms.

But what of the numerous southern families that have retained a continuing vitality? They maintain their traditions, live by their code, have a lively interest in the life of mind and body, and are free of the corrosions of inferiority that scarify the hearts of so many pushing members of our great middle-class society. Will Percy was of such a family. Yet there are few plays or novels about families of this group, and for discernible reasons.

First, nothing is so little wanted or so unfashionable in this Age of the Lout as the gentleman. Even the term itself, if not obsolescent, now has about it an odor of denigration. Second, a novel about a sound southern family of continuing vitality might raise disturbing questions.

Is it the Percys (to use them as a symbol) or the society around them that has decayed? What indeed are its values? Is it not concerned more with a standard of living than with a standard of life, with success rather than achievement, bigness rather than greatness, price rather than value, comfort rather than civilization?

In keeping with their code, Percy's father had urged, at a time when such views were rare and "radical," that southern Negroes be educated. Addressing the Mississippi Bar Association at Vicksburg about fifty years ago (1907), he denied the current concept that education "ruined" Negroes and urged that the South accept the burden of educating them. Negro education was a matter of right, he believed, but there were other considerations in his mind.

The Negro who knew arithmetic would be no easy prey for cheating plantation owners, white and Negro. "Justice, self-interest, the duty which we owe to ourselves and those who follow us, all demand that we should not acquiesce in the erroneous idea that the Negro be kept in helpless ignorance," concluded the speaker.

Such opinions did not endear the Percys to exploiters of Negroes. However callous to humane impulses, they were exquisitely sensitive to money. Many of them had become tetchy. Risen by toil and chicanery from humble beginnings to high economic estate, they had panoplied themselves with kinship to Old Virginia. Sometimes they endowed their mythical ancestors with antebellum plantations and, emerged as synthetic First Families, resented having their way indicated by others. But of noblesse oblige they knew no more than their shoats knew of Guy Fawkes Day.

(Members of the same group in Virginia itself had gone 'way back to Queen Anne's time to prove their "quality." In Thomas Nelson Page's *Red Rock,* the conniving overseer who takes over the old place pretends that his family, the Stills, are descendants from Sir Richard Steele.)

They did know one thing: what was "good for niggers." They insisted that beyond primitive necessities, Negroes needed money no more than turtles. Money corrupted them. It drove them to drinking, gambling, whoring. If they had money, they would not know what to do with it. It was therefore part of the white man's burden to see that farm Negroes had little money, even if he had to deprive them of it by fraud or duress.

Helpless Negroes sang about it as they so often sang under other sorrowful circumstances of their lives:

> Niggers plants de cotton,
> Niggers picks it out,
> White man pockets money,
> Niggers does without.

Enraged by the attitudes of the Percys and their kind, who stood against them in defense of the Negro's rights, white exploiters of Negroes called them—behind their backs—"nigger lovers."

(We have always had men who believed that money was bad—for the other fellow. In 1914, when Henry Ford raised his workers' wages to $5 a day, the New York *Times* and the *Wall Street Journal* said that such wages would ruin the country as other manufacturers tried to meet them. The wage scale was not only "unscientific." It was also un-Christian. For the man who earned $30 to $35 a week would drift into a life of sin. Therefore . . .)

Will Percy would risk his life or exert himself at whatever cost in time, money, comfort to see justice done a Negro. I was living in his house when there arose the case of Jim.

One day there came into his office a young Negro with bandaged head. Awaiting trial in the local jail for a minor offense, the sheriff had ordered him to assist in building a gallows. While working—whether by accident or design was never established—a timber had fallen upon his head and injured him. Then the sheriff, aware that he had illegally made the prisoner work and fearful of a scandal if he should die, sent him home.

Incensed by this recital, Percy sued the sheriff for misconduct in office under his personal bond.

This would seem to be a routine lawsuit, but it became violent. The sheriff, a big, burly man, who despised Negroes and liked Percy all the less because he befriended them, came to his office when suit was filed. There he posed the issue as he saw it: "You aren't going to take a nigger's word against a white man's, are you?" Percy said that he would if he believed the Negro was telling the truth. Whereupon the enraged sheriff made vague threats against him and stalked off.

Percy then, for fear that the sheriff and his friends might harm Jim or run him out of town, brought him into his household where, as a servant, he could have protection. It was now springtime, and Will left for Greece, intending to spend several weeks there. But Jim's case being called, he returned to Greenville for the trial.

By this time feeling was running high—on the sheriff's side—and Will thought it a wise precaution to go into court with a pistol in his pocket. By his side stood his law partner, Hazelwood Farish, a slender, gentle, fearless man. The accounting up to this point was that the firm of Percy and Farish had devoted much time to an obscure case from which it could not possibly financially profit, that both members had risked their lives to see it through, while Percy had taken on himself the personal burden of protecting his client and had given up his vacation in his dearly beloved Greece to appear at the trial.

The case never came to trial. It was compromised for a small amount of money damages. Jim remained a part of the household, and I went to Memphis to spend a few days. There, a police sergeant told me a man had been picked up and some of my things had been found in his possession. The thief, to my distress, turned out to be Jim. He had stolen all manner of belongings from the Percy household and things of my own. He was returned to Greenville by the Memphis police but was never brought to trial. We were all sick of the whole affair.

In the early 1920s the Percys and men like them suffered a terrifying ordeal. Then the Ku Klux Klan came to the Delta as it had come to other sections of the country including the Middle West. In Indiana it assumed an especially venomous form, evidence that no section of the United States is immune to racial and religious hatred and "fasism" [*sic*]. People of the Delta, Will Percy had written, had "broken every law except the law of kindliness." Now this law was broken as hatred and bigotry flamed under the bed-sheet banner of the Klan.

When a "Colonel" Camp appeared in the local courthouse to organize a Klan, he spoke to an inflammable, dangerous crowd of armed men. Percy noted Camp's words: "Who killed Garfield? A Catholic. Who assassinated President McKinley? A Catholic. Who had recently bought . . . land opposite West Point and . . . Washington? The Pope. Convents were brothels, the confessional a place of seduction, the basement of every Catholic church an arsenal. The Pope was about to seize the Government. To the rescue, Klansmen!"

The Klan organizer having spoken, there was a stir in the crowd as LeRoy Percy arose, hated, unwanted, unbidden. (His son, Will, called him the most dangerous man he had ever known.) Handsome, vigorous, impeccably dressed, eloquent, he began by shaking his finger under Camp's nose and loudly asking, "Who is this itinerant scoundrel that comes among us to set brother against brother? Upon what field of honor did he win his title?"

Warming to his task, his words scarifying acid, his eyes challenging, his posture contemptuous and defiant, he recounted the Delta's history. It was a land, he said, that had been made by all the people: Protestants, Catholics, Jews, Negroes. Together they had endured yellow fever, malaria, floods, hard times. Together they had drained the swamps, felled the forests, built the schools and churches. And here, he repeated, was an itinerant scoundrel come among them to set brother against brother.

At the conclusion of his speech—such was its power and such the unpredictable vagaries of crowds—the group that had met to organize a local Klan passed a resolution condemning the Klan! The while, Colonel Camp had scuttled out of the courthouse and was given safe conduct to his hotel by an Irish Catholic deputy sheriff.

The Klan struck back. Defeated in the light, it sought revenge in the dark by making an abortive attempt to kill LeRoy Percy in his own house. Thereupon Will Percy went to see the local Cyclops, a lawyer who had been a lifelong friend. Although he was physically fragile, looking a picture-book poet, his firm jaw and eyes that could be steel marked him as a dangerous man when aroused. He quietly told the Cyclops that if any ill should befall his father or any of their friends, he would be killed—by Will Percy. The Cyclops gave these words full faith. While the Klan raged elsewhere, it committed no atrocities in Greenville and never marched beneath its bed-sheet banner.

Throughout Percy's youth, a constant stream of men came to his house to talk to his father—politicians, dreamers, doers, levee engineers, planters, characters, houseguests. From the lips of vanishing men of a vanishing civilization, he heard much talk of the Old South and conversation about things that always engaged men's attentions: the river, politics, hunting, cotton. Among the visitors Will found John Sharp Williams especially engaging.

The last of Mississippi's "planter-statesmen," he had been anti-imperialist at the turn of the century when "manifest destiny" stirred the American air. He opposed our annexation of the Philippines and denounced as hypocritical our so-called "moral obligation to the little brown brother."

"There never yet," Williams said, "was tyrant or conqueror who did not proceed upon the theory that his government was better for the conquered than their independence."

Williams, whose home was on a cotton plantation near Yazoo City, was for many years congressman and senator despite the disability of having been educated, not in Mississippi, but at the University of Virginia and Heidelberg. Famous for his wit and a lifelong devotion to toddies, he was once challenged in the Senate by the notorious Senator "Tawm" Heflin of Alabama, who said to the senator from Mississippi, "At any rate, I always come into the Senate in full possession of my faculties."

"What difference does that make?" Williams retorted.

His debating skill received perhaps its most severe test in his own house where he had returned late one night after attending a bibulous stag party. Stumbling in the darkness of the bedroom, he awakened Mrs. Williams, who switched on the light.

"What time is it?" she asked.

"It's ten o'clock," her husband replied.

Mrs. Williams burst into tears, and he asked her what was the matter. "Well," she tearfully said, "we've been married ten years and this is the first time you've ever told me an untruth."

"What untruth?" asked Williams.

"You said it's ten o'clock. But the clock says it's two in the morning."

Williams looked sadly at his wife. "You wouldn't," he asked her, "take the word of that damnyankee clock in preference to mine?"

A constant stream of visitors later poured into Will Percy's house. Sociologists sought his views on race relations and studied him the while, as did students from many sections of the country and the merely curious come to see what manner of person was this twentieth-century man who was in so many ways an eighteenth-century chevalier. Aspirant writers sought his advice. Poor people came for money and got it. Men about to leave their wives, wives who had just left their husbands, young men who wanted to enter business or were about to lose the business they had, people crazed with fear or worry dropped in for comfort and counsel. There were youngsters he was sending to school and adults who were his pensioners, candidates for public office, members of the school and library boards, poetesses of the Confederacy bearing sheaves of bad verse, the worthless who knew that Mister Will was a soft touch, and an unending flow of Negroes. None was turned away.

Often Negroes came furtively at midnight, wounded, fleeing from the law after a brawl. (One of them, making what seems to be a somber commentary upon our times, said, "Mister Will, life ain't nothin' but livin' and killin'.") They, too, were received despite the hour and sent on their way aided if not rejoicing. Once at midnight, awakened by sobbings in the great hall, I went downstairs. There I found Will in his dressing gown with two Negroes. One was a young and gentle boy, David Scott, who had brought his friend Alvin Fowler to the only person in town who might save him. Will spoke comfortingly to the hysterical man racked by sobs as he trembled on the verge of suicide and sent him away restored. He later took David into his household and lent Alvin enough money to set up a grocery store. The store was soon lost. Then Alvin, as his father before him, killed himself.

Sometimes Percy brought visitors upon himself. Once the *Atlantic* published an article concerning a lynching that had occurred near Greenville. Percy concluded the author had been wrong about his facts and wrote Ellery Sedgwick, the magazine's editor, saying that the publishing of misinformation about the Delta made it difficult for decent men to do their best in race relations. Then he suggested that, if Mr. Sedgwick wanted to see things for himself, he might come to Greenville and be the guest of the Percys.

The editor, moved by a high sense of responsibility, traveled fifteen hundred miles to Greenville and stayed with the Percys. They gave him a car and driver and sent him alone to make his investigation. Mr. Sedgwick made it, and the *Atlantic* thereafter made no mistakes of fact in its discussions of the Delta.

I once thrust visitors upon Percy. I was lunching in New York with Dorothy Thompson and Raymond Gram Swing as the two were about to write on the alleged miseries of southern sharecropping. Neither had ever been on a cotton plantation or talked with a planter or with a sharecropper. I said that since this was the case I would suggest they study the Delta before writing even if this should commit them to the heretical doctrine that writers know something of the subject matter they discuss. The three of us shortly left for the Delta accompanied by Gordon Selfridge, Jr., of London, who was Swing's guest.

The Negroes of Percy's Trail Lake Plantation have forgotten the eminent journalists, but they remember Selfridge, tailored by Savile Row and wearing a bowler and a reserved air. I took him to visit a Negro sharecropper family where he insisted upon buying the "crazy quilt" off the bed to take to London. It was odd enough for a strange white gentleman to walk into old Ida's house and want to buy a "common ole quilt." Yet it was even stranger that, as she put it, "Hit 'peared like you could understand the gentleman, but when you got down to hit, you couldn't understand nair thing he said." I had to act as interpreter for these members of the English-speaking union, and ever since plantation folks have asked me about that "white gentleman look like he could talk English but couldn't."

The columnists investigated sharecropping unhampered by the presence of local whites. Then they came to the disturbing conclusion that not only were there many sides to the question but, confusingly for the space-limited writer, at least two sides. Swing and Selfridge soon left Greenville, but Miss Thompson remained for a few days to visit with Percy. They drank old-fashioneds, talked gardening, became friends.

Sometimes catalyst and sometimes spark, concerning himself with the lives of many people, one cannot know how many of them Percy affected. Indebted to him myself, I think of his wide-ranging heart in terms of Albert Schweitzer's meditation upon his childhood. Schweitzer said:

> I do not believe that we can put into anyone ideas which are not in him already. As a rule there are in everyone all sorts of good ideas, ready like tinder. But much of this tinder catches fire . . . only when it meets some . . . spark from outside . . . often, too, our own light goes out, and is rekindled by some experience we go through with a fellowman. Thus we each of us have cause to think with deep gratitude to those who have lighted the flames within us. If we had before us those who have thus been a blessing to us, and could tell them how it came about, they would be amazed to learn what passed over from their life into ours.

As Will inflexibly adhered to his code—call it noblesse oblige, romanticism, gentlemanliness, or what you like—the more his fragile strength declined. Tired himself and sick, when his friend Tommy Shields became fatally ill, he sat by his bedside for six weeks until he died. Tommy, in a coma, could recognize no one, yet Will stayed with him fifteen hours a day, and when a friend asked him why he did so, he replied, "Tommy needs me."

Hating totalitarianism, loving Britain and France, and fearful of his country's security, he vainly offered his services to Washington before we entered the second world war. Failing, he tried to arouse others to the dangers and obscenities of the Nazi dictatorship, going, despite ill health, wherever people would listen to him. Few listened. Few wanted to listen: an agony of disappointment to this high-hearted man and the source of a disillusionment that ate into his soul. He wrote of all this with unwonted bitterness: "The North destroyed my South; Germany destroyed my world. In the dog-days of 1914 the mad dog of the world broke loose. After 1918 the world forgot that hydrophobia is curable only by death and it is paying for the oversight now. Again the mad dog is loose. (He was writing when the second world war had started, but we had not yet entered it.) His victims clutter the roadside, but still my own people, with the mentality of priests and tradesmen, prefer to pass by on the other side."

Percy now understood with an iron finality what he had long believed to be true, namely, that there was little place left in society for men of his kind. He accepted it as an immutable fact and mentioned it only when, facing death, he wrote his autobiography.

He had long toyed with the notion of writing an autobiography, but he was deterred because, a modest man, he felt he had done nothing distinguished that would warrant an account of his life. "One by one," he wrote, "I count the failures—at law undistinguished, at soldiering average, at citizenship unimportant, at love second best, at poetry forgotten before remembered . . ."

Discussing the question of an autobiography with him, I said the point was not whether he had acquired special distinction in any field. It was, rather, this. His recorded life to some extent would reflect the lives of all men. It would afford a glimpse into the mystery of personality and partially illuminate man's life on earth. In this sense every man has the "right" to set down an autobiography, and I reminded him how Montaigne had put it. "Every man," he said, "carried within himself the whole condition of humanity."

I do not know what effect my words had upon Percy. But soon, unsure of himself as a writer of prose, unconvinced of the validity of his task, and plagued by bad health, he began to write his book. He sent several chapters to (as he called them) his "highbrow friends." They advised him to abandon the book because, they said, he could write verse but not prose. Convinced they were right, he stopped writing. Then chance, using me as its instrument, intervened.

I had left Greenville for some months and upon my return asked Percy about his book. He told me what he had done, and when I asked to see the abandoned chapters, he said he did not know where the chapters were, nor did it matter. We were talking in his library on a hot day, and squirming upon the sofa, I heard a rustling of papers. There, under the cushions, were the missing chapters. I went out on the gallery to read them.

Then I urged Will to complete the task. He did so, and there emerged a sad, wise, poetically luminous book, the author's spirit instinct in its pages and the shadow of death upon them. He entitled his book *Lanterns on the Levee* and was astonished by its critical and popular acclaim. It gave him great comfort, I believe, and a year after its publication he died.

Percy was of the small, dark, dangerous brotherhood of the romantics, one with those who have been "half in love with easeful Death, call'd him soft names in many a mused rhyme." But, by a curious degradation of the term, "romance" to many of us connotes the tryst of a soap-opera couple in an atmosphere of moonlight and poison ivy. The romantic, however, as typified by Percy, is otherworldly, austere, given to gaunt convictions, and, when persuaded, immovable though heaven trembles. He may be compassionate and woman tender. Yet defiance sometimes sits upon him like a dagger lightly worn, while his seeming apathy in the face of fate is no apathy but, rather, a form of active communion with cosmos—the end implicit in the beginning.

Musing upon the local cemetery where lay his parents, his only brother, many of his friends, and fellow townsmen and knowing he would soon join them, Percy wrote:

> Here among the graves in the twilight I see one thing only, but I see that thing clear. I see the long wall of a rampart somber with sunset, a dusty road at its base. On a tower of the rampart stand the glorious high gods, Death and the rest, insolent and watching. Below on the road stream the tribes of men, tired, bent, hurt, and stumbling, and each man alone. As one comes beneath that tower, the High God descends and faces the wayfarer. He speaks three words. "Who are you?" The pilgrim I know should be able to straighten his shoulders, to stand his tallest, and to answer defiantly, "I am your son."

The Rounded Man as Writer

For all his productivity and the breadth of his interests, David Cohn remains best known for his first book, the one that grew from his decision to return to Greenville, where during his two-year "visit" with Will Percy he began "to see with fresh eyes the scenes of my childhood." Brimming with vivid detail and keen insights, *God Shakes Creation* presented readers with a striking human and environmental portrait of the Mississippi Delta. While making it clear that the Delta was the undisputed domain of a high-living and sometimes heavy-handed white elite, Cohn also understood that blacks played a key role in shaping the pattern and setting the tempo of Delta life. For example, he drew his title from a sermon delivered by the Reverend Kid Scott, a black minister, who reminded his flock that "Gawd sends us His rain in de summer time so de cotton and corn will grow. De fall brings de cool of the evening. Snow drops from His shoulders in winter tell de mountain tops is covered and snow veils de face of de valley. De seeds dey sleeps in de ground and de birds dey stops dey singing. Den Gawd shakes creation in de spring." [1]

Cohn described the Delta at the time of white settlement as a land that had sprung from "the loins of the river. Untold centuries ago," he wrote, "it began to deposit here the rich detritus of mountains and plains borne on its bosom as it flowed from the north to the south to sea. Accretion by slow accretion, without foundation of rock or shale, it laid down this land. . . . pure soil endlessly deep, dark and sweet, dripping fatness." [2]

Drawn by rumors of the inexhaustible fertility of the soil, in the late 1820s planters and sons of planters abandoned the rapidly deteriorating lands of the eastern cotton-planting states for the black dirt of the Delta, where they quickly established a regime of the "wealthy well-born planter" who owned large numbers of slaves. Cohn then proceeded to delineate between the inhabitants of the Delta and those of the Mississippi hills, pointing out that the Delta was a society of "gentlemen, overseers, and slaves" and that "it still remains true that neither then nor now has the Delta ever welcomed the so-called 'poor white.'" These latter creatures—usually portrayed by Cohn as both pitiful and despicable—

---

1. David L. Cohn, *Where I Was Born and Raised* (Cambridge, Mass., 1948), x.
2. *Ibid.*, 26.

"took to the sterile hills of Mississippi," where they raised "large crops of children and meager crops of cotton. . . . worshipped a fierce God, hated aristocrats and Negroes, dwelt in poverty and darkness," and awaited their opportunity to descend on the "fat lands" of the Delta. The hill people were particularly incensed by what Cohn described as the "church-going and whiskey-drinking society" of the Delta where "that which is due to the church and to the bootlegger is offered up with such smooth harmony that the life of the body and the life of the spirit go happily in mystic marriage."[3]

To Cohn, most Deltans seemed largely oblivious to these contradictions: "Year after year the Delta functions in almost complete detachment in the land of the radio. All kinds of 'isms' come and go beyond its borders, but it hears little of them or, hearing, little heeds. The roaring sounds of revolution in a changing world dwindle in this far distance to tiny whispers. Change shatters itself upon the breast of this society as Pacific breakers upon a South Sea reef. . . . Disturbing ideas crawl like flies around the screen of the Delta. They rarely penetrate. It is only when the price of cotton is affected that the Delta takes cognizance of the outside world."[4]

Cohn's book offered both keen insight and pithy phraseology—"The people of the Delta fear God and the Mississippi River"—and an occasional misstatement—"Here there is no great wealth and no great poverty." The planters of Cohn's era were not by any means the nation's wealthiest people (as their ancestors perhaps had been in 1860), but their relative affluence was striking indeed in a region where, as Rupert Vance observed, "the Negro is to be found at his lowest levels in America."[5]

In her review of *God Shakes Creation,* black anthropologist Zora Neale Hurston praised Cohn for producing a book "full of brutal and hideous truth," one unlikely to "call forth any loud clamor of approval from Negroes or Southern whites" because "it too rudely brushes aside the traditional magnolias and roses that shield the pig pen." The primary weakness Hurston detected in Cohn's work lay in his treatment of "the internal life of the Negro. It is here," Hurston believed, "that he suffers from the disability of being white," but she hastened to add that the distortion in this section of the book "was surely due to lack of understanding rather than dishonesty."[6]

Hurston's criticism was certainly valid, although there was no white man or woman in the Delta who observed blacks more closely or sympathetically than Cohn. Still, his discussions of blacks and the so-called race problem in the Delta were laced with contradiction. In his foreword, Cohn conceded that his book

3. *Ibid.,* 25–27, 15.

4. *Ibid.,* 41.

5. *Ibid.*, 43, 46; James C. Cobb, *The Most Southern Place on Earth: The Mississippi Delta and the Roots of Regional Identity* (New York, 1992), 153.

6. Zora Neale Hurston, review of *God Shakes Creation,* in *Books,* November 3, 1935, p. 8.

would be "but a pale tract" had it not been for the assistance of "hundreds of Delta Negroes," who "with complete frankness, . . . bared to me their sorrows, their aspirations, their way of life." Yet less than forty pages into the book Cohn acknowledged that all Delta blacks adopted "the language of caution and secretiveness in the presence of the white man." Despite this admission, however, Cohn confidently assured readers that "the present relatively untutored Negro of the Delta harbors no feelings of resentment or bitterness or revenge against the whites unless the disabilities under which he labors are too cruelly pressed upon him. If he is able to earn a living and seek happiness among his own people, he is content."[7]

Elsewhere, Cohn bemoaned the absence of frugality among Delta blacks, whom he described as a "thriftless mass," although he observed that "when money is plentiful, the planters and townsmen commit the same crimes against economy that the Negro does, differing from him only in kind." In fact, echoing a theme expressed by William Alexander Percy, Cohn found it admirable that the average Delta black did not "burn with the white man's passion for acquisition" but possessed instead "a high capacity for the artless employment of leisure" because "the wellsprings of his being have not been poisoned at their source by the white man's virus of let us then be up and doing."[8]

Though clearly sympathetic to blacks, Cohn identified closely with Delta whites, and he also took great pains to explain their racial dilemma. His explanation, however, presented another tangle of contradiction. For example, he noted the dishonesty and deceit that marked white behavior toward blacks in the North and gave thanks that "the Delta is free at least of that kind of hypocrisy and chicanery." On the other hand, however, Cohn also conceded that the Delta's racial order was hardly free from other kinds of hypocrisy. Explaining that fear of sexual aggression by black men was responsible for many of the offenses committed against blacks, Cohn also pointed out that in the Delta "white men have not hesitated to pour their blood into the veins of Negroes" and noted that "the history of miscegenation in the Delta is interwoven with dark threads of blood and grief and pain." Through it all, however, there remained in the Delta one "great and inflexible taboo": "There shall not be, under any circumstances whatsoever, a sexual relationship between a white woman and a Negro."[9]

Nowhere did Cohn's views seem more conflicted and contradictory than on the question of black education. The superbly educated, widely traveled, and well-read Cohn was clearly a believer in the kind of schooling that produced a "rounded man." Yet he nonetheless worried that the typical black youth was being encouraged in the classroom to harbor expectations "which he can never

---

7. Cohn, *Where I Was Born and Raised*, x, 37, 159. *God Shakes Creation* was expanded into *Where I Was Born and Raised*, published in 1948.
8. *Ibid.,* 34–36.
9. *Ibid.,* 152, 66–67.

hope to realize so long as he lives in the section where he was born." Bemoaning the well-intentioned efforts of those who sought uplift for Delta blacks through education, Cohn explained, "There is room and welcome in the Delta only for the Negro who 'stays in his place'. . . . The delicate balance of harmony between the races rests squarely upon this basis. If it is lightly disturbed without first preparing a counter-equilibrium, both races may suffer grievously." [10]

In his summary of the racial viewpoint of enlightened Delta whites, Cohn also revealed his resentment of the criticism they had received from whites living in the North: "We are at all events as just and as fair as it is given to us to be. We live among tens of thousands of Negroes. You who live far from the Delta live among whites. You may meet an occasional Negro. Your life is not bound up with them as our lives. Your economy does not rest upon their shoulders. You do not see them morning, noon, and night. We spend all our days with Negroes and yet we know them so little. Is it possible for you to know them better?" [11]

As a white paternalist, Cohn had little use for race baiters of his own color, but his reaction to blacks who expressed anger or bitterness toward whites also showed the limitations within which southern moderates of his era operated. Still a literary fledgling in 1921, Cohn reviewed W. E. B. Dubois' *Darkwater,* which he described as "a bitter book" that attempted to convey the "essentially false" impression "that all the negroes of the South lie under a monstrous shadow and are deeply depressed by a burning sense of inferiority that the white people will never for a moment permit them to forget." Cohn depicted Dubois himself as a tragically alienated figure: "His values are not those of his people, his aspirations are not theirs and his voice is scarcely audible above the voices of the cotton fields which sing the paean of the negro's joy in life." [12]

"The Southern Negro" was making great progress, Cohn argued, "carving out for himself a worthy place in the empire of the South, of which he is so great a part and to which he has made such a mighty contribution." Cohn lamented the emergence of a militant spokesman like Dubois, concluding that "the work that is being done by the educated and understanding white men of the South toward the adjusting of the Negro problem is seriously hampered by Northerners who are familiar only with the school of thought that Dubois represents, and who know nothing of the saving sanity of Booker T. Washington." [13]

Nearly two decades later, Cohn was still sounding much the same theme

10. *Ibid.,* 158, 159.
11. *Ibid.,* 161–62.
12. David L. Cohn, review of W. E. B. Dubois' *Darkwater,* in *The Double Dealer* I (June, 1921), 255–56.
13. *Ibid.,* 256–57.

when he described Richard Wright's *Native Son* as "a blinding and corrosive study in hate." As Cohn saw it, "The preaching of Negro hatred of whites by Mr. Wright is on a par with the preaching of white hatred of Negroes by the Ku Klux Klan."[14]

Cohn focused on Wright's use of a Jewish lawyer to plead the case of his black murderer-protagonist Bigger Thomas, and he found considerable irony in the lawyer's contention that "white society drove Bigger to crime by repressing him." If repression was justification for violent retaliation, Jews, of all people, would have ample justification for taking such action, although Cohn noted that only a few Jews had followed such a path. "Over the whole sweep of two thousand years of dark Jewish history," Cohn wrote, "the mass of these people, enduring greater oppression than Negroes knew here even in slavery, created within the walls of their ghettos an intense family and communal life and constructed inexhaustible wells of spiritual resource. They used their talents and energies as best they could, serene in the belief that a Messiah would ultimately come and deliver them out of bondage into the Promised Land or that justice would ultimately triumph."[15]

As he had in 1921, Cohn contended that "the Negro's lot in America is constantly being ameliorated," insisting that "nowhere . . . save in the most benighted sections of the South, or in times of passion arising from the committing of atrocious crime, is the Negro denied the equal protection of the law." Again stressing the gravity and complexity of the race problem, Cohn concluded that "Mr. Wright obviously does not have the long view of history. He wants not only complete political rights for his people but also social equality and he wants them now." Cohn reminded Wright, however, that "men are not gods." Hence, "justice or no justice, the whites of America simply will not grant to Negroes at this time those things that Mr. Wright demands" and, Cohn warned, "Hatred and the preaching of hatred, and incitement to violence can only make a tolerable relationship intolerable."[16]

Cohn was but one of a host of southern writers who undertook the often painful task of regional self-scrutiny in the 1930s and 1940s. The most influential of these was Wilbur J. Cash, whose *The Mind of the South* appeared in 1941. Cohn's analysis of Cash's work was one of the most penetrating and gently skeptical treatments that the book would receive for the first twenty-five years that it was in print. Offering an insight that would recur in the analyses of literary

14. David L. Cohn, "The Negro Novel: Richard Wright," *Atlantic Monthly* CLXV (May, 1940), 659, 661.

15. *Ibid.*, 660.

16. *Ibid.*, 661, 660, 661. Contemporary observers will not only note Cohn's insistence that the historic suffering of the Jews was worse than that of American slaves but detect the ironic comparability of his positive treatment of the Jewish family and culture and the recent emphasis on the strength and viability of the black community in both slavery and freedom.

historians for several decades, Cohn observed that " 'The Mind of the South,' for all the author's heroic attempts at objectivity, is often a strangely embittered book. It is obvious that he is, in the Nietzschean phrase, a great despiser because he is a great adorer." [17]

Cohn praised Cash's courage in attempting to write such a book: "He is no pale and precious essayist distilling the thin essence of a thin theory in polite language, but one who has taken an empire as his province and tears open its belly with strong hands to show us its inner workings. Where he has succeeded, his success is that of one who has triumphed in a large and stimulating enterprise; where he has failed, he has failed because his reach exceeds not only his grasp but the grasp of anyone who may undertake the same task." [18]

Although he observed that "in a world moving apparently toward a drab uniformity, it is to be hoped that some differences between people will survive on this continent," Cohn also took issue with Cash's attempt to isolate "so-called Southern characteristics or failings from national characteristics or failings." Pointing to Cash's caricature of the "skyscraper" craze that seemed to sweep Piedmont towns in the post–World War I era, Cohn asked, "Were not skyscrapers built all over the country in boom days? . . . Is elephantiasis of the ego common only to the South?" Moving to a more serious question, Cohn asked, "Is the exploitation of labor a Southern, a national, or an international phenomenon? You may conceivably show that exploitation was worse in the South than elsewhere, but this is a difference of degree and your end proof is that men everywhere tend to exploit their fellow men unless restrained by law." [19]

Although his overall reaction to the book was clearly positive, Cohn was one of the few initial reviewers to challenge Cash's insistence on the distinctiveness of southern society. A few years later, however, Cohn sounded a different note as he observed the rise of racial tensions during World War II and appeared to offer an earnest reaffirmation of Cash's argument for the existence of a distinctive southern mind:

> This society is almost primitively simple on the surface and almost incomprehensibly complex underneath. . . . Here each white is deeply affected by the Negro, just as each Negro is deeply affected by the white. The one is a problem for the other. If there has never been a free Negro in the South, it is also true that there has never been a free white in the South since the Civil War—free, that is, in the sense that the Vermonter is free—because the southerner's whole society and way of life are conditioned by the presence of the Negro. Consequently no one knows what a free Southerner might be like, since the Southerner now functions in an environment of which he is a prisoner. [20]

17. David L. Cohn, "Tissues of Southern Culture," *Saturday Review of Literature* XXIII (February 22, 1941), 7.
18. *Ibid.*
19. *Ibid.*, 17, 7.
20. David L. Cohn, "How the South Feels," *Atlantic Monthly* CLXXIII (January, 1944), 48.

Cohn also expressed his concern about the passage of an older generation of whites, "many of whom are almost the last exemplars of the tradition of *noblesse oblige*," and the disappearance of an older generation of blacks who had at least established "a workable—if perhaps far from ideal—relationship with whites." In their places on both sides of the color line came a younger and angrier generation less inclined to tolerance or patience. Cohn realized that this "generation gap" would only make interracial communication more difficult, but he insisted that any effective compromise would have to be reached through "conviction rather than compulsion." [21]

As racial tensions rose even more rapidly in the postwar era, Cohn expanded his analysis of his native Delta in an updated version of *God Shakes Creation,* entitled *Where I Was Born and Raised.* In the latter book, Cohn described the cumulative economic forces that had swept across the Delta since the mid-1930s. The acreage-reduction programs of the New Deal and the dislocation of labor resulting from World War II had spurred the rapid mechanization of agriculture. Meanwhile, with federal funds pouring in for roads and bridges, local industry grew as well. The war brought an air base, and "thousands of men and millions of dollars poured into the community." The overall result was prosperity, which proved, as always, "not an unmitigated blessing." [22]

Because it incorporated Cohn's observations on the Delta as of the mid-1930s, as well as his insights into the region as it entered the post–World War II era, *Where I Was Born and Raised* also offered readers an opportunity to assess the ideological, psychological, and demographic changes wrought by four years of global conflict. In 1947, Cohn saw a Delta that no longer functioned in "complete detachment" but now confronted instead all "the changes and fears of the world":

> Since the first section of this book was published in 1935 . . . many changes have occurred in the life of the Mississippi Delta as elsewhere. Whether for that small spot upon the American earth, or a Pacific atoll, there is not in our times "any hiding place down there." We had scarcely emerged from a shattering economic depression following upon the First World War, before we were plunged into man's most catastrophic war. The foundations of our faith are severely shaken. We no longer devoutly believe, as we once did, in the inevitability of progress. Our compass is aberrant; our course erratic. We are more than a little fearful that we shall not make our landfall. [23]

In a perceptive chapter entitled "Vanishing Mules and Men," Cohn agonized over both the regional and national consequences of the revolution in the Delta's agricultural economy. He predicted, for example, that "large operating units under a single management will continue, but in the coming farm-factory the old

21. *Ibid.,* 49, 51.
22. Cohn, *Where I Was Born and Raised,* 225.
23. *Ibid.,* x.

paternalistic relationship between management and labor will go. It was a relationship that, whatever its defects, was often marked by human tenderness, understanding, and enduring friendships. As such it was without parallel in our national life. Sharecropping will go, and all those things that were the essence of an economic and social system that had become a distinctive symbol of a traditional agrarian way of life in the Delta." [24]

Cohn estimated that two-thirds of the plantation labor force would be displaced, and he hoped that the ensuing reduction of the Delta's black population would ease racial tensions and make life better for those blacks who remained in the Delta. For those uprooted by farm mechanization, however, the outlook was not nearly so bright. Most of them were "totally unprepared for urban, industrial life." Nor, Cohn feared, were the northern cities where they were likely to wind up prepared to receive them. Cohn's concerns were more than a little prophetic:

> Will the Negro problem be transferred from the South to other parts of the nation who have hitherto been concerned with it only as carping critics of the South? Will the victims of farm mechanization become the victims of race conflict?
>
> There is an enormous tragedy in the making unless the United States acts, and acts promptly, upon a problem that affects millions of people and the whole social structure of the nation. [25]

Although Cohn continued to insist that the Delta's racial situation was "almost without counterpart in the United States," he also realized that "the Negro question, as it exists in the United States" was "without counterpart elsewhere." Deeply concerned about the future of American blacks and the future of race relations in general, he observed that "it is more than two hundred and fifty years since the ship *Hannibal* of London brought a cargo of Negro slaves to Barbadoes. When and where," he asked, "shall their descendants and the descendants of all the others who came in other slave ships, find a permanent home on the American earth?" [26]

Cohn's writings on the South and on race relations quickly won him considerable attention, but as a "rounded man" he pursued a variety of other interests, and his analyses of American society and values and world affairs soon gained him an even wider audience. In 1936, Cohn published *Picking America's Pockets,* in which he launched a withering attack on the protective tariff, noting that "for one hundred and fifty years the United States tariff—a law affecting the national interest—has been written on nearly every basis save that of the national interest. It has been the plaything of politics, the instrument of privilege, and the weapon of monopoly." [27]

24. *Ibid.,* 327.
25. *Ibid.,* 330.
26. *Ibid.,* 356.
27. David L. Cohn, *Picking America's Pockets: The Story of the Costs and Consequences of Our Tariff Policy* (New York, 1936), 239.

"In the making of the tariff," Cohn wrote, "section has been arrayed against section; capital against labor; industry against agriculture; importers against exporters; and the insular possessions of the country against the continental United States." The tariff seemed to Cohn "a living and vital relic of the infamous days of railroad rebating, the wasting and stealing of national resources, and the prodigal despoiling of a prodigally rich country for the benefit of the few and the impoverishment of the many." [28]

In Cohn's view, no section of the country had been more cruelly victimized by the tariff than his native South. He effectively blamed the tariff for the Civil War and insisted that because it forced southern farmers to sell their crops in a depressed export market, while buying their consumer needs in an artificially inflated, protected one, the tariff had helped to keep the South poor, diseased, and degenerate—an "American India," as Cohn called it. [29]

Wherever he went, Cohn preached the merits of both economic and political internationalism, insisting that throughout human history free trade and human progress and enlightenment had gone hand in hand. As the prospects of war in Europe grew throughout the 1930s, Cohn condemned "isolationism," equating it with "feudalism," which at its essence was nothing more than "localism." To Cohn, isolationism meant "treating the wireless, the radio, the four-day transatlantic ship, and the airplane as though they did not exist." Not only would the triumph of isolationism mean exchanging "the broad life of the world for the narrow life of the village," but its overall long-term consequences were even more tragic: "For just as capitalism was the death of feudalism and the genesis of democracy, so will a recrudescent feudalism—I don't care what modern name you call it—mean the end of capitalism and of its concomitant democracy." [30]

Shortly after the war began in Europe, Cohn bemoaned a Gallup poll showing that 96 percent of those questioned were opposed to American involvement in the conflict. He observed that the prevailing consensus that "we will not . . . fight unless our vital interests are attacked" seemed to imply that "the possible disappearance of Britain and France, along with their empires, is not a vital interest of America." [31]

Such a position was utterly nonsensical to Cohn, and he found America's policy of not-quite neutrality equally ludicrous, noting that "while we devoutly desire the victory of one side, seeing something of our own ease and security in the victory of that side, we extend it only our good wishes and our willingness to sell goods for cash." As a result, Cohn noted that for all the complexities and interrelationships that had brought matters to this point, the situation had actually been reduced to one of terrifying simplicity: "The whole vast structure of

28. *Ibid.*
29. *Ibid.*, 244.
30. David L. Cohn, "Isolation: The DoDo," *Atlantic Monthly* CLXIV (August, 1939), 161.
31. David L. Cohn, "The Road Not Taken," *Atlantic Monthly* CLXV (March, 1940), 299.

the British and French empires, and with them a certain concept of life and living, rest ultimately upon seventy or eighty skinny cylinders of metal called naval rifles, installed upon fourteen floating platforms called capital ships of the British Navy. . . . Destroy those platforms, put those rifles out of action, and a cataclysmic crash of empires will convulse the earth for generations. Hitler knows this, too, and in order to destroy his enemies he must first destroy the handful of long-nosed cylinders on which they rest." [32]

Cohn was pleased but not surprised that his fellow southerners were considerably less isolationist than other Americans. He expressed his irritation with his northern "intellectual" acquaintances who looked down their noses at the "hordes of shoeless yahoos dunking their hoecake in pot likker who now want to get out and fire their Long Toms at Germans and may drag the rest of the country with them." Cohn understood the desire of southerners to stop Hitler in his tracks. The South, after all, was "the only section of the country that has ever been invaded, trampled upon, and occupied by a hostile army." Hence, he reasoned, "the South dreads another invasion as only a people who have once been invaded can dread it" and southerners preferred to "go into action on foreign battlefields rather than at home." Cohn found it strange "that the millions of persons who saw Atlanta burned in the movie version of *Gone with the Wind,* should wonder why Southerners prefer to do their fighting abroad rather than at home." (Ironically, nearly two decades later, southern-born historian C. Vann Woodward would cite the South's experience with humiliation and defeat as one of the reasons why southerners should offer a skeptical ear to those who preached the militant internationalism and interventionism espoused by Cohn.) [33]

Cohn continued to fret about American isolationism even after the United States had entered the war. He described his countrymen as "volatile but not tenacious," adding that "the fact that it took thirty million years for the Eohippus to evolve into the horse bores us," while "the Biblical story that the Lord made the earth in six days and rested on the seventh appeals to us. It is evidence of a big job well and quickly done." As a result, he worried that the United States was "as likely to retreat from the whole mess as we are to remain and clean it up." [34]

As World War II drew to a close, Cohn embarked on an extended tour of Europe, the Middle East, and the Orient as a special invited correspondent with credentials provided by the United States Army. The result was Cohn's most intriguing "non-southern" book, *This Is the Story.* Although Cohn's subject

32. *Ibid.,* 302.

33. "Why the South is moved . . . to fight Hitler," typescript, David L. Cohn Collection, J. D. Williams Library, University of Mississippi, Oxford, Miss.; C. Vann Woodward, "The Irony of Southern History," *Journal of Southern History* XIX (February, 1953), 3–19.

34. David L. Cohn, "Tariff or No Tariff," *Atlantic Monthly* CLXXI (February, 1943), 87–89.

was ostensibly the American soldier abroad, he managed not only to provide valuable insights into the culture and society he was visiting but to offer a new perspective on life in the United States as he encountered the American G.I., who for the first time "saw his country plain and seriously discussed it with his fellows." Although he confessed that he was "in this respect an older campaigner than the G.I.," Cohn also "looked anew at my native land" and used his book to present "certain home thoughts from abroad." [35]

Cohn visited Great Britain, France, Belgium, Corsica, Italy, Egypt, Palestine, Iraq, Iran, India, Burma, and China, and at every stop, he immediately immersed himself in local culture and values. A great admirer of the French, Cohn believed that "if this were a wise world, it would preserve France as a living example of how to live." Recalling his earlier observation in a French bistro of a heated and protracted argument about whether a *fruit rafraîche* should be made with maraschino or kirsch, Cohn reflected on the meaning of the incident: "This was my last glimpse of France before the deluge. It was a France which knew the importance of both sauces and symphonies, that life is to be lived joyfully if possible; food may be of a kind which will merely nourish the body, or, nourishing it, also water the soul; and that, in the words of the wine-growers' chamber of commerce, a meal without wine is like a journey without sun." [36]

Reiterating a point that he would make again and again about life in the South and the United States as a whole, Cohn reminded his readers that "civilization is more than the statistics of trade and bank clearings; more than air-conditioning and electric refrigerators and trains running on time. It also has to do with the making of a *fruit rafraîche* and, above all, of being able to become passionate about the manner in which it should be made." [37]

For all his apparent cosmopolitanism, Cohn not only retained but reveled in his southern identity. (For example, he delighted in telling and retelling the story of his dinner with the Maharajah of Jodhpur, who had his personal orchestra play "Dixie" in Cohn's honor.) As he skipped about the globe, soaking up local culture and assessing the spirit of the people in various locales, his thoughts often returned to his native Delta. In the Air Transport mess in Goose Bay, Labrador, the ringing of the cash register triggered memories of cash registers back home in Greenville, especially the one operated by "Carter," a "small, plump, quiet, unsmiling, heavy-lidded mulatto Negro who owned and ran Carter's Stationery Store on Washington Avenue." Cohn recalled his fascination as a ten-year-old boy in visiting Carter's establishment where one could buy not only stationery but agates, books, and baseball bats and mitts as well. Cohn also recalled the cash register in the shop of "the London Tailor" who measured men for suits made in Chicago ("which fitted to a 'T'"). The London Tailor was actually a

35. David L. Cohn, *This Is the Story* (Boston, 1947), v–vi.
36. *Ibid.,* 24.
37. *Ibid.*

Russian Jew who had fled the terrors of persecution for a new life in America. The tailor's daughter, Anna, was a schoolmate of Cohn's, but after she died of consumption, the tailor moved away. As for Carter, when Cohn returned from college, Carter's shop had become a dime store. "Since that time," Cohn realized, "no Negro has had a store in the white part of town." [38]

Elsewhere, Cohn likened the antiquated credit system that financed pearl diving in Bahrain to the one that supported sharecropping in the Deep South. He also compared a successful New Delhi businessman to a Greenville grocer (whose wife was said to be "a secret paregoric drinker"). In Corsica, Cohn encountered "a corn field Negro from Arkansas," and the two grew homesick together as they reminisced about the life, death, and protracted funeralizing of the Reverend Kid Scott, whose sermons had provided Cohn with the title for *God Shakes Creation*. [39]

The overall tone of *This Is the Story* was upbeat enough. Cohn wrote that he came "back from the wars profoundly impressed by the greatness, realized and potential, of our people. . . . No American moving among his countrymen at war could but be filled with exaltation and a solemn pride in their achievements as he witnessed the display of their courage, their dedication to the task, their electric energy, their Yankee ingenuity, their humor by turns ribald, corrosive, tender, and, novelly, their patience." [40]

Such praise notwithstanding, Cohn foresaw a postwar world in which the United States would find global leadership unavoidable, and he wondered if his countrymen would be up to the task. Consequently, as the high-stakes postwar geopolitical struggle that would become the cold war began to take shape, Cohn urged Americans to support generous assistance programs for underdeveloped or war-ravaged nations. "You can't eat democracy," he reminded his readers, pointing out that in many of the lands in question "enormous hordes" of people lived their entire lives in "a twilight zone between sleep and hunger—hungry, naked, diseased, illiterate, housed as miserably as beasts of the field, they darkly breed and darkly die." "Hunger is revolutionary," Cohn warned, "and while we offer these people democracy, it was the Russians who offered them bread. As between democracy without bread or bread without democracy, it is not hard to guess which a hungry man will choose." [41]

Citing the poverty and maldistribution of wealth that prevailed in Iraq, Iran, or India, and noting as well the inclination of the United States, in the interest of global stability, to support "debauched" regions with no commitment

---

38. "The Maharajah's Band Played Dixie," typescript, Cohn Collection; Cohn, *This Is the Story*, 3–5.

39. Cohn, *This Is the Story*, 189, 348–49, 405.

40. *Ibid.*, vi.

41. David L. Cohn, "You Can't Eat Democracy," *Atlantic Monthly* CLXXVII (June, 1946), 59–60.

to human uplift, Cohn asked, "Does anyone doubt, moreover, that the land-less, poverty-stricken peasantry of these regions are not hearing how the Russians divided the great estates of Eastern Europe among the landless peasants of Germany, Poland, Russia, and Hungary?"[42]

Cohn drew a sharp contrast between American impatience and the willing-ness of the Russians to "plod" toward their goal, although in a particularly in-sightful passage, he noted that the Russians "have performed the feat of jump-ing from the oxcart into the airplane within one generation" in large part because "Western technology enabled them to skip the transitional processes that the West itself endured." As a result, "this enemy telling the centuries upon his beads, glacier obdurate, fanatically possessed, goes with the secrets of nuclear fis-sion in his head and a piece of black bread in his hand." In the face of such Russ-ian determination, Cohn remained deeply concerned about whether the United States, which he described as "a capricious colossus," was "temperamentally fitted" to pursue its own policy of containment, a policy that required a consist-ent long-term commitment and carried no guarantee of success.[43]

Cohn's misgivings about his own countrymen's willingness to remain stead-fast in the struggle against Soviet expansionism was in sharp contrast to his ad-miration for the Finns, with whom he visited during the summer of 1949. Faced with the prospect of a Soviet invasion, the Finns refused to be intimidated. Not-ing that they had enjoyed only two decades of independence after "seven cen-turies of servitude to Sweden and Russia," Cohn praised the Finns for their courage: "Their population small, their resources slender, their burdens huge, the odds against them great, they daily stare into the eyes of an unrelenting en-emy." He lauded the willingness of the "iron-willed" Finns to "die in the effort" to keep their freedom, a freedom they had thus far retained through "a con-junction of the high heart and the stubborn mind." In Cohn's eyes, the Finns "presented to all who desire to remain free a miracle of the human spirit."[44]

Throughout the early years of the cold war, Cohn consistently expressed his belief that economic isolationism and political internationalism were wholly in-compatible. On December 12, 1957, he appeared before the Subcommittee on Foreign Trade Policy of the House of Representatives Committee On Ways and Means to talk about tariff policy. Always adroit in his use of humor, Cohn com-pared the warnings of American industrialists that their firms were about to be ruined by competition with "foreign pauper labor" to the "supremely corny" jokes dealing with the traveling salesman and the farmer's daughter and poked fun at those who "whine that we are about to be overthrown by Japanese-

42. *Ibid.*, 60.

43. David L. Cohn, "Inventory of America," *Saturday Review* XXXIII (August 26, 1950), 18; David L. Cohn, "The American Temperament," *Atlantic Monthly* CLXXXV (September, 1951), 65.

44. David L. Cohn, "Finland Under the Guns," *Atlantic Monthly* CLXXXV (April, 1950), 38.

made falsies, Hong Kong shorts, Swedish clothes pins, Dutch cheese, Chilean tuna fish." [45]

He then moved quickly from ridicule to melodrama, casting the tariff question in the context of the cold war and nuclear age: "Today the signals of the Russian-made satellites above us may be sounding the horns of mankind's impending doom. Today, one-third of our strategic Air Force is constantly aloft to strike if we are stricken. This is indeed a moment when, in a flash, there could come such catastrophic change that all of man's history to date would thereafter seem to be but a footnote to history." [46]

Cohn cited free trade as the key link in a "fragile chain of interdependence that binds us to other friendly nations, some of whom control the military bases that are the forward bastions of our perilous security. Upon this chain," he warned, "we hang suspended above the abyss." [47]

Cohn grew up with the feeling that a sense of "doom" hung over his native Delta, and as his congressional testimony indicated, whenever he commented on world affairs, he excelled at—and seemed almost to revel in—conveying a sense of impending disaster. Writing in 1953, he began, "We are living in the night of total crisis. . . : Two global wars have brought men not to their senses, but to the brink of penultimate disaster." The only hope for avoiding a world dominated by a single ruthless force (in the form of the Soviet Union) was the recognition on the part of citizens of the United States that they could not "escape history" by "shrinking from reality." [48]

As a Jew, Cohn knew something about the difficulties of escaping history. Despite his refusal to embrace orthodox Judaism, he nonetheless clung to his Jewish heritage as a vital part of his identity. As World War II drew to a close, Cohn bemoaned the rise of anti-Semitism in the United States, noting "the fantastic irony that the American Army is battling its way into Germany to fight the Hitler fanatics who rose to power through the use of anti-Semitism." Cohn observed that the United States had long had a tradition of "genteel anti-Semitism" manifested in the exclusion of Jews from certain resorts, hotels, or clubs or the maintenance of a quota system in certain private and professional

45. Statement by David L. Cohn before the Subcommittee on Foreign Trade Policy, Committee on Ways and Means, December 12, 1957, typescript in Cohn Collection.

46. *Ibid.*

47. *Ibid.* On the CBS News that evening, Eric Sevareid reported that the House subcommittee had heard some "low tariff testimony from Mr. David Cohn, ex-merchandiser, expert on tariffs, love, good places to eat, books, and the general condition of mankind." In Sevareid's view, Cohn had "left the congressmen in a state of flabby flabbergastedness," and he suggested, tongue-in-cheek, that "the Committee for an Effective Congress is reportedly considering subsidizing Mr. Cohn to stay in Washington and freshen up the place." Lee Lewellyn Jordan, "A Biographical Sketch of David L. Cohn," (M.A. thesis, University of Mississippi, 1963), 111–12.

48. David L. Cohn, "The Great Turning Point," *Saturday Review of Literature* XXXVI (May 16, 1953), 10, 37.

schools. He pointed out as well that "Great Britain has had a Jewish Prime Minister and Viceroy of India, but no Jew may aspire to become President of the United States; during our entire history only four Jews have ever sat in the Senate, and a somewhat larger number in the House; while it is almost as difficult for a Jew to enter the State Department as for a Baptist to become Pope." [49]

A few years later, Cohn renewed his attack on anti-Semitism, explaining why, unlike some American Jews, he had found that "keeping my name, far from complicating my life, simplifies it. . . . Bearing an unmistakably Jewish name, I am spared the crude comments of virulent anti-Semites, for even they retain a modicum of manners in my presence; and, there being no possibility of mistake, I am not asked to join groups that do not 'take' Jews. I am accepted by my fellows as a human being, or I am rejected as a Jew." He conceded as well that with a new name—"preferably one suggesting kinship with a high-church bishop—I might even be asked to dine with some newly minted family that having gouged the government during the first World War, is now almost as pedigreed as a grand champion bull." This option Cohn rejected out of hand: "We already have an over production of social climbers in this country; folks who, in the telling and contemptuous rural Negro phrase, have 'got above their raisin'.'" Nor did he desire to become one of the "pet Jews" who had their "Gentile keepers." Cohn described the United States as "the kindliest of countries," but he vowed that if this situation should ever change he would cling to his Jewish identity rather than "reject the fifty centuries' history and tradition of my people in order to gain a hotel room at Newport." [50]

Cohn conceded that his attitude might be a product of a personal experience largely free of encounters with blatant anti-Semitism. In this regard he expressed particularly warm feelings about his native Greenville: "I was born and raised in a good world. It was far more Gentile than Jewish, but I never felt alien there, nor was any attempt made to make me feel alien. . . . In Greenville neither I nor any of my co-religionists, to my knowledge, suffered any indignity or lack of opportunity because of being Jewish. Gentiles and Jews rejoiced together in happiness and mourned together in sorrow. There were bigots in the town, it is true—Jews as well as Gentiles—but they were a tiny minority looked upon commiseratingly by the majority as unhappy aberrants." This observation was more than a little ironic. Certainly, Delta blacks could hardly have agreed that bigots constituted a "tiny minority" within white society. In fact, they might even have numbered in that sizable group of bigots some members of the local Jewish community. Even as Cohn wrote, a study of the attitudes of southern Jews suggested that, perhaps as a means of securing their identification with

49. David L. Cohn, "What Can the Jew Do?" *Saturday Review of Literature* XXVIII (January 27, 1945), 8.

50. David L. Cohn, "I've Kept My Name," *Atlantic Monthly* CLXXXI (April, 1948), 42.

the local white population, southern Jews seemed to have embraced whole-heartedly the racial views of their Gentile counterparts.[51]

Referring to his own experiences, Eli Evans observed that he had "inherited the Jewish longing for a homeland while being raised with the Southerner's sense of home." Cohn revealed almost identical sentiments whenever he wrote about Israel. In 1946, Cohn noted the desire of so many Jews to return to Palestine: "These people are witness to the wonder, the pity, the terror, the mad-miracle of so much Jewish life-in-death. Unforeseeable, unfathomable acts in time and space drive the despised to Palestine, and armor with iron resolution the mystic-desperate logic of Zionism."[52]

Hoping to explain why Zionists wanted their own state in Palestine, Cohn related a story told him by Dr. Chaim Weizmann, who became the first president of Israel:

> I was thinking today of an old Jew who lived in my village. There is a prayer which pious Jews recite when they have been delivered from an extraordinary period, thanking God for their deliverance. But every day the old man went to the synagogue and recited the prayer which most men would not have occasion to use once in a lifetime. Asked why he did it, he said, "Every morning when I go to make my devotions, I see the woodchoppers going to the forest with their axes. They also see me. They can kill me, perhaps they would like to kill me, and some day they may kill me. Every day, then, that I live through the day, I am delivered from peril."[53]

Cohn also saw Israel playing a key role in furthering the internationalist foreign policy aims of the United States. Specifically, he saw Israel as an enlightened Western outpost in a sea of Arab medievalism. Cohn believed that "western technology and a square deal at home might 'whisk' the Arab states from the twelfth century to the twentieth," and it was here that he saw the potential importance of Israel, "a fragment of the West set down in the East" and peopled with a large number of "scientists and technicians" capable of offering much advice and assistance to their Arab neighbors. Not only would Israel itself be better off—as "a tiny island in an Arab ocean" Israel could certainly profit from the "warm friendship of Arabs"—but the efforts of the United States to promote political stability through economic uplift would benefit enormously. In hindsight, Cohn's wishful vision of Israel's role and its relationship with its Arab neighbors seems hopelessly naïve, but it nonetheless illustrates the comprehensiveness and complexity of his world view, in this case, specifically, the

51. *Ibid.,* 44; Mannheim S. Shapiro, "A Report on Southern Jewish Opinions," American Jewish Committee, typescript in Cohn Collection.

52. Eli Evans, *The Provincials: A Personal History of Jews in the South* (New York, 1974), x; David L. Cohn, "Chaim Weizmann: Zionist Statesman," *Tomorrow* VI (December, 1946), 14.

53. Cohn, "Chaim Weizmann," 17.

manner in which he managed to integrate his identification with Israel with his commitment to American internationalism. [54]

Despite his almost obsessive interest in international affairs and foreign policy, Cohn proved himself a keen observer of American domestic life and customs. Though he would soon become stridently critical of American materialism, as an emerging writer, he realized that material culture offered key insights into the changing patterns of American life. Given to perusing back issues of the *Sears and Roebuck Catalog* when he was employed by that company, Cohn began to realize that "they constituted an invaluable record of American life . . . a diary of the times created by the people; a measure of the desires and ambitions of millions." [55]

Taking an approach that would not be widely adopted by American social historians for several generations, Cohn wrote *The Good Old Days,* published in 1939, using the pages of the catalogs to discern "how men lived, and what they lived by, for nearly fifty years." For example, Cohn saw illustrated in the catalog's pages the long-term impact of technology on American life: "In edition after edition, we note the liberation of the housewife through the coming of labor-saving devices; we observe the drudgery once done by her hand transferred to machines; we see the means by which even the servantless woman in the United States has come to have a higher degree of leisure than any other woman of her kind in the world." [56]

In addition to chronicling economic and technological change, the catalog also served for Cohn as a "social barometer":

> Here we find the development of countless new attitudes—toward reading, the use of cosmetics, the virtues of fresh air and of bathing, and the pleasures of sports. We note how the luxuries of one generation become the necessaries of the next generation, and how the clothing of the middle class tends to approximate that of the rich in fashion and materials, even if inferior in design and workmanship. The catalog as a chronicle of change and a panorama of American life through fifty dynamic years reveals diversity, and by implication, countless forces of many kinds that are constantly at work in a virile, restless civilization such as ours. [57]

As would be the case with some of his other books, several academic reviewers charged Cohn with practicing history without a license. In reality, however, although Cohn offered his readers more than a few highly subjective and sweeping generalizations, *The Good Old Days* was as valuable a contribution to

54. David L. Cohn, "Can Israel Help the Arabs?" *Atlantic Monthly* CLXXXII (August, 1948), 34–35.

55. David L. Cohn, *The Good Old Days: A History of American Morals and Manners as Seen Through the Sears, Roebuck Catalogs, 1905 to the Present* (New York, 1940), xxiii.

56. *Ibid.,* 58.

57. *Ibid.,* xxvii–xxviii.

American social history as one could expect to encounter from many professional scholars in 1939. [58]

Cohn was also intrigued by the social impact of technological change. In *Combustion on Wheels,* he described the impact of the automobile on American life: "The car became as intimately and pervasively a part of American life as the horse had never been. . . . It touches us somehow at every turn, whether in our play habits, our home life, or our method of earning a living, our sex attitudes or our church attendance; its meanings range from the sacred to the profane, the utilitarian to the pleasurable." [59]

Noting that the automobile now served as "a chief cornerstone of our economy" and transformed Americans into "an automobile-intoxicated people," Cohn found it difficult to arrive at "a balance sheet of the automobile as a factor for good and evil in American life," but, he added, "It is plain that no mechanical instrument could achieve so dominant a place among us, and indeed so often engage our affections, if it did not respond to our deep-seated needs." Cohn made this final point effectively by concluding his book with a description of the sense of drama and uncertainty about the future that marked the war-induced suspension of automobile production at the General Motors assembly plant at Flint, Michigan, in January, 1942. [60]

Cohn did not own a car, and his book suggested a concern about how quickly and completely Americans had become dependent on and obsessed with the automobile. Actually, Cohn's worries reflected a larger concern that he often expressed about the destructive effects of materialism on American society. (After Cohn's death, James W. Silver, a longtime friend, recalled that "one of the charming qualities of David Cohn was his careless unconcern for material things.") Even as a businessman Cohn had been critical of high-pressure advertising that encouraged people to buy merchandise for which they had no need. In 1944, Cohn offered a tongue-in-cheek confession that he was "an enemy of society" but not "an ordinary enemy such as a murderer, a sponsor of soap operas, a monopolist or an interior decorator." Cohn's great offense against society was his well-nigh heretical advocacy of thrift and financial responsibility: "I walk through the valley of the five o'clock shadow without fear and am the despair of advertisers, however skilled. If the Joneses want to get ahead of me, more power to them." [61]

Although Cohn did not own an automobile, he wondered about the

58. Jordan, "A Biographical Sketch," 71.
59. David L. Cohn, *Combustion on Wheels: An Informal History of the Automobile Age* (Boston, 1944), 264–65.
60. *Ibid.,* 266.
61. James W. Silver, "David L. Cohn, Friend of the University," typescript in Cohn Collection; David L. Cohn, "I Am an Enemy of Society," *Saturday Review of Literature* XXVII (May 13, 1944), 12.

consequences should Americans stop trading cars every few years or begin to have their shoes resoled or engage in similar exercises in frugality. Such behavior could be extremely destructive: "We cannot, I am told, exist unless we have a constantly expanding economy in which people buy more things whether or not they need them. . . . Suppose that when an advertiser leered at us and asked, 'Is Anything Too Good for YOUR Wife?' we leered right back and honestly answered, 'Hell, yes'?" [62]

As he saw the nation emerge from the horrors of World War II and dive head-first into an orgy of materialism and conspicuous consumption, Cohn's tone became uncharacteristically caustic. He cited a New York *Times* headline proclaiming "Fashions of the Times Keyed to Gaiety of Land at Peace" and the newspaper's sponsorship of a fashion show suggesting that "although we have walked through the valley of the shadow of death we have come at last into the promised land of nylon stockings," and "real rubber girdles that contain as they give so that flesh and figure hitherto irreconcilable are made one." [63]

His words dripping with sarcasm and disgust, Cohn proclaimed, "This is indeed a time for gaiety and exuberance and fine frenzy shot through with filaments of Alanese." He went on to salute the soldier "eviscerated by a land mine" and the one who "died in a delirium of cerebral malaria at the Pongsau Pass," reassuring them that "we haven't forgotten any of you, dead or living. It's just that in these busy happy days of peace when 'coats whirl out in gay colors and dresses have a more romantic sweep,' we can't quite do all the things we'd like to do." Conceding that "it may seem churlish," Cohn closed this, his most bitterly satirical piece, with the observation of Santayana that "fashion" is "that margin of irresponsible variation in manners and thoughts which among a people artificially civilized may be larger than the solid core." [64]

Although he remained a bachelor until he was nearly sixty, Cohn was a keen observer of male-female relationships, and much of what he saw troubled him. He observed that marriage all too often seemed the path to automatic happiness in a society where happiness was seen as the natural, God-given right of every individual: "Few people pursue happiness with such demoniac energy as we, briefly pausing at one roadside stand of illusion before rushing to another." "We reject the austere truths that human life is tragic and its destiny dark; that frustration and pain are of the world as well as fruition and joy." A national obsession with material comfort only made matters worse. Instead of anything approaching a realistic portrait, young men and women were fed a vision of married life as "a perpetual Christmas Eve with Tiny Tim passing double martinis

---

62. Cohn, "I Am an Enemy of Society," 12.

63. David L. Cohn, "Styles of a Nation Glorying in Victory," *Saturday Review of Literature* XXVIII (November, 3, 1945), 22.

64. *Ibid.*, 63–64.

and saying, 'God Bless you, every one'" or a kind of "gumdrop heaven: soft, gooey, chewy, and oh, so sweet." [65]

In *Love in America,* Cohn provided an exhaustive analysis of the "basic relations between American men and women" and found that they were "far from satisfactory." He placed more of the blame for this situation on men than women. In fact, Cohn concluded that despite the prevailing impression, the "actual status" of American women (as opposed to their "alleged status") was low, and their influence, "both inside and outside the home," was anything but strong. [66]

In Cohn's view, men resented the fact that women were further constricting their space by preempting a number of formerly male prerogatives. Whereas men had once clung to an image of women, "desirable and inaccessible, gazing downward from the heavens," women had now descended to earth: "Now she is the woman seated on the next chair at the cocktail bar matching him drink for drink; the woman ahead of him on the golf links shooting in the low seventies; the woman telling *him* the off-color story; the woman doing a job as well as he can do it and doing it for half his salary." [67]

Cohn offered up a number of sweeping and stereotypical generalizations, but his insights were nonetheless unusual for a male writer of his era. As his analysis unfolded, he managed to set the problematic aspects of male-female relationships in the United States within the broader context of his concerns about isolationism, materialism, and the general emotional immaturity of the American people. In fact, on the first page of *Love in America,* Cohn offered a list of his oft-reiterated themes about trends in American life between the wars. These included: "We are an emotionally adolescent people. . . . From Versailles to Pearl Harbor, our national life has been marked by much shabbiness and vulgarity. . . . The conditions of that national life have brought us to believe that if you have the price, you can get the other fellow to do for you what you want done, with almost no effort on your part. Thus you may become cultured in six easy lessons or you may stand by while other nations keep the peace for you or, peace failing, they fight the wars with a minimum of disturbance to you." [68]

Cohn clearly believed that every woman was (or should be) seeking some male's total devotion, although he argued that attainment of this end was more likely if a woman developed her own aesthetic and intellectual interests so as to make herself a more interesting and satisfying companion to a man. Still, Cohn saw the world divided into distinctly male and female spheres. Nothing was quite

---

65. David L. Cohn, "Are Americans Polygamous?" *Atlantic Monthly* CLXXX (August, 1947), 32; "Moonlight and Poison Ivy," *Atlantic Monthly* CLXXXIII (January, 1949), 36. Cohn married Lillian Millner in 1954.

66. David L. Cohn, *Love in America: An Informal Study of Manners and Morals in American Marriage* (New York, 1943), 1.

67. *Ibid.,* 53.

68. *Ibid.,* 1.

so revealing of his attitude on this point as his unpublished sketch of "The Southern Belle" (also titled in other drafts "Nobody Likes Her But Men").[69]

Cohn saluted his stereotypical Southern Belle for her obvious belief that "it is glorious to be a woman" and lauded her conviction that "to be born a woman is to be born with such power over men that only a fool would dissipate it by aping them or competing with them." He also applauded her resultant willingness to let men run the world and remain content "merely to run the men who run the world." Hence, while men remained "earth-bound by the chains of the demonstrable," as an "unalloyed female" the Southern Belle was "free to soar."[70]

Having been "caricatured in books, plays, and movies," the Belle had "hostile critics everywhere." This, Cohn believed, was totally understandable:

> The Southern Belle is guilty of heresy in this age of women's rights. These include the right to abandon womanliness; to go mentally and physically attired in pants on the assumption that things equal to one thing are equal to one another. Even more heretically the Belle, insisting upon womanliness, tries to please men. She is taught by her mother to please them and does not deny or conceal her desire to do so. Her whole training indeed prepares her to collaborate with men rather than to compete with them. . . . Some of our more earnest ladies regard her, in her societal aspects, as an essentially seraglio soul with marshmallow outlook who is restrained from the harem only by the prevalent Presbyterianism, and so dead to social progress that she is not even interested in women's rights. Middle West housewives who can toss off the family laundry and bake a cake before getting breakfast, think of her as lazy and inevitably therefore enveloped in Original Sin. Indeed women generally—outside the azalea areas—dislike her and look upon her as a traitor to their sex, and this for a female reason that only men would find paradoxical: namely, that she glories in being a woman.
>
> Nobody, it would seem, likes her; nobody but men. Yet she is satisfied to languish in their adoration as President Franklin Roosevelt—who had more than a touch of the Southern Belle in his personality—was content that for many years no one was for him except a majority of the voters.[71]

Though he realized that despite the pedestalization of middle- and upper-class white women, their actual status was low, his plea for women to take the initiative in improving the quality of American life assumed that this initiative would properly begin in the home rather than the public or political arena. While he might well have been considered "progressive" or "liberal" for a male writer of his era, Cohn's generalizations about the intrinsic differences between men and women—for example, his insistence that men craved adventure while women craved security—would have incensed feminists of any era,

69. David L. Cohn, "The Southern Belle," typescript in Cohn Collection.
70. *Ibid.*
71. *Ibid.*

as would his habit of distinguishing between "Americans" and "their wives."

Never one to refrain from sharing (often more than once) his opinions, preferences, and prejudices, near the end of his life Cohn published two books on subjects dear to his heart. *The Fabulous Democrats* was a "natural" for one of the nation's most ardent Democrats, although Cohn insisted that he planned to give the Democrats "hell" at a number of points throughout the book. Surveying his party's history from Thomas Jefferson to Adlai Stevenson, Cohn noted that the Democratic Party had maintained its vitality despite long lapses of inept leadership and "intellectual laziness," but he also offered a warning that seems as appropriate in the 1990s as it was in the 1950s: "When the Democratic Party is merely a low-church version of the high-church Republican Party and its spiritual anemia makes it pale as the underbelly of a catfish, it has no appeal for voters and certainly does not deserve their support." [72]

Not surprisingly, critical reaction to Cohn's book broke sharply along partisan lines. Despite his obvious ardor for the Democrats, however, he was much dismayed by the direction his party seemed to be taking in 1956. Reflecting on the recent Democratic Convention, he wrote his friend James W. Silver, noting that "the big Southern vote for Kennedy was something. They don't like no Catholics. But they don't like Kefauver. And—the clincher—Kennedy, coming from textile-making Massachusetts, is for increasing textile tariffs. Hence the Ku Kluxers, looking at their pocketbooks, voted for a Catholic." [73]

Cohn went on to decry the "economically isolationist" Democratic platform in 1956, explaining this regrettable state of affairs by pointing out that "manufacturing has for the first time become a huge Southern interest." With both parties embracing such isolationist trade policies, Cohn woefully predicted "an economic fortress America," adding that "the millions of saps who'll be affected by it will never hear of it and if they hear of it, won't care because they're so goddamned busy buying things on the installment plan, life being a detour to arrive at a perpetual state of deferred debt." [74]

Always attentive to economic concerns, Cohn's examination of national tariff policy in *Picking America's Pockets* had also spurred his interest in the economic future of cotton. In fact, his persuasive speeches and lobbying activities played a key role in a movement that led ultimately to the founding of the National Cotton Council. Cohn's lifelong interest in cotton culminated in what

72. Jordan, "A Biographical Sketch," 107; David L. Cohn, *Those Fabulous Democrats* (New York, 1956), 109.
73. David L. Cohn to James W. Silver, December 12, 1956, in James W. Silver Collection, J. D. Williams Library, University of Mississippi, Oxford, Miss.
74. *Ibid.* Cohn's frustration with his party was apparently less serious than it seemed, for he had recently written "The Case for the Democrats," an article published in the *Saturday Evening Post* under the name of House Speaker Sam Rayburn. Sam Rayburn to David L. Cohn, August 31, 1956, in Cohn Collection.

would become his final book, *The Life and Times of King Cotton*. Making no pretense of detachment, Cohn explained almost proudly, "My book, suh, will be The White Rose of Memphis done to the music of Show Boat with many a hey nonny no and a fie fie to the Yankees. I have always prayed the good Lawd to prevent the blight of objectivity from descending upon me, and in this book he has answered my prayer." [75]

In his book, Cohn set out "merely to tell something of an agriculture that fashioned the life of a great region and profoundly affected the destiny of the whole American people." Yet, as he also explained, even this simple-sounding task was a demanding one: "As fibers of various lengths may appear in a bale of cotton, so the fabric of cotton culture is highly complex. It contains elaborately intermingled elements of politics, finance, business organization, social organization, soil and insect chemistry, race relations, and the politico-economic policies of the nation in its international relations with other people." [76]

Cohn began with Eli Whitney and the cotton gin, examined the growing market for cotton fueled by the textile revolution in England, and discussed slavery and the plantation system and the Civil War, as well as the problems of cotton agriculture in the late nineteenth and twentieth centuries. Yet, however ambitious the task that Cohn had undertaken, for the most part, reviewers were not terribly impressed with what historian Gilbert C. Fite described as an attempt "to write a popular account of cotton and its development in the United States since the 1790s." [77]

Historian Bennett H. Wall praised Cohn for making "high drama of King Cotton" and lauded his "remarkable talent for pin-point expression." Both Wall and Fite, however, challenged Cohn's reliance on a limited number of secondary sources. Fite concluded that although the book was "interesting and well-written" and thus "good for a pleasant evening's reading," it nonetheless lacked "depth." [78]

As his final book, *The Life and Times of King Cotton* was remarkably illustrative of the overall strengths and weaknesses of Cohn's writing. On the one hand, it was typically readable and entertaining; on the other, it was highly impressionistic and subjective, grounded but little in primary documentation or statistical data. Dedicated readers also knew that Cohn often reiterated certain "pet" themes regardless of whether he was examining international or domestic issues. Hence, as he had in his writings about United States foreign policy, as well as those about marriage and male-female relations, he worried about finding a

75. David L. Cohn to Walter Johnson, May 12, 1954, in Cohn Collection.
76. David L. Cohn, *The Life and Times of King Cotton* (New York, 1956), viii.
77. Gilbert C. Fite, review of *The Life and Times of King Cotton*, *Journal of Southern History* CXXIII (May, 1957), 236.
78. Bennet H. Wall, review of *The Life and Times of King Cotton*, in *Mississippi Valley Historical Review* XLIV (December, 1957), 547; Fite, review, 237.

206 • The Mississippi Delta and the World

solution to the cotton problem because "as a nation we are somehow committed to the naïve concept that we can solve difficult international, social, or economic problems by finding a sovereign remedy that will dispose of the problem for all time." [79]

A voracious reader who immersed himself in current affairs, the amiably opinionated Cohn also shared his views with the readers of the letters-to-the-editor columns of the New York *Times* and the Washington *Post*. As with his other writings, Cohn's letters to the editor often offered an effective mix of humor and satire. When cotton farmers called for greater federal assistance in 1951, Cohn expressed his sympathy:

> Some of these farmers are barefooted corporations, capitalized in the millions, tilling measly patches of 25,000 acres. Others scratch out a bare living on patches of 10,000 acres; hardly room enough for a protracted meeting, let alone calling it a farm. . . .
>
> This year, so big is the crop and so hardpressed the poor farmer, two Arkansans had to call their daughters home from Vassar to help with the picking. The wife of another, the rugged spirit of the pioneers coursing in her veins, just tucked up the dress she bought last year in Paris and waded in where bolls were thickest. Such people deserve our sympathy. They also deserve our cash. [80]

Anyone who felt that the farmers' calls for increased federal assistance amounted to nothing more than socialism was simply uninformed:

> It was hard for the farmer to ask the Government for help. He hates Washington. He believes it is rottenly socialist to the core. He wants no part of what his favorite orators call "this foul foreign doctrine." He is prepared to cut Mr. Truman's throat, if he should run again, because Mr. Truman is "socialist." Hence it's tough on him to take more handouts from Washington. . . . Besides, it wasn't socialism when F. D. Roosevelt bailed out the cotton farmer in the 1930s. And it isn't socialism now when Mr. Truman helps him; not even if his leaky skiff of the 30s has become the equivalent of the Queen Mary. Socialism, as any freshman congressman can tell you, is federal aid to everybody except one's own constituents. [81]

In July, 1951, Cohn reacted in the Washington *Post* to reports that a number of Senate Republicans were "secretly pleased" by Senator Joseph R. McCarthy's insinuations of disloyalty on the part of Secretary of Defense George C. Marshall and Secretary of State Dean Acheson. Cohn was especially incensed by indications that "Senate Republicans prefer to talk with Senator McCarthy in the privacy of their cloakroom," but few of them were willing to "sit near him on the Senate floor, or engage in conversation with him." Cohn considered such

79. Cohn, *King Cotton,* 272.
80. David L. Cohn, "Stockpiling Farmers," Letter to the Editor, Washington *Post*, September 19, 1951.
81. *Ibid.*

behavior "cowardly above and beyond the demands of pustular cowardice." Here again, he found an analogy in his Delta experience:

> Senators who connive with Senator McCarthy in the woodwork—blind but destructive as is the termite—yet who would no more be seen publicly with him than they would be photographed with Joseph Stalin at a covered dish supper, toll me back to the days when I was a boy in a Mississippi town. There, nice ladies walking on Washington Ave., our main street, pulled their skirts close about them when they passed a woman outrageously resplendent in ostrich-plumed picture hat, blue velvet high-top shoes, and blue velvet dress, a diamond-encrusted watch chain pendant from the shoulder. But men furtively smiled to her when she made her stately way down the street, the air for a moment faintly redolent of heliotrope. [82]

The witty and well-traveled Cohn was equally entertaining and amusing in his private correspondence. In July, 1949, he wrote Betty and Hodding Carter from Paris:

> Your powerful kind letter reached me here, and I'd be mighty pleased to join y'all were it not that I'm clawing Ole Satan right here in Paris where he has his headquarters. Over here he wears a shiny frock coat and speaks a language called French, but he can't fool me so I and him are going around and around. I've just come from a fascinating trip through Finland having gone way up to the North in Lapland to visit Santa Claus, and incidentally to see what them Roosians are doing. . . . I hope to see y'all this fall about the time the frost hits the persimmons and as usual, let me warn you I'll be hungry and thirsty. The while, suh and m'am, I hope y'all continue to grow in beauty and piety. Thanks ever so much for asking me up yonder to [*sic*]. [83]

After an essay from *Love in America* appeared in the *Ladies' Home Journal* with a photo of Cohn, the author received a letter from a reader who expressed his regrets that Cohn had supplied his picture, because he had such a grim expression and the reader was left to suspect after reading the article that Cohn's teeth had been mail-ordered from Sears and Roebuck. [84]

The response was classic Cohn:

> Crushed by your letter, suh, I have retired to the Deep South where I now am, licking my wounds, drinking good whiskey in the homes of friends, and awaitin' the end with calm dignity. . . . But it is only when you touch upon my personal appearance, that you wound me. For, suh, at various times I have thought of myself as an overweight faun, a mail-order Silenus, an installment-plan Casanova, and you demolish these illusions with hammer strokes. To destroy a man's amour propre is to filch from him his essential riches, for every gent fancies himself a guy

82. David L. Cohn, "The Popular Pariah," Letter to the Editor, Washington *Post,* July 8, 1951.
83. David L. Cohn to Hodding and Betty Carter, July ?, 1949, in Hodding and Betty Werlein Carter Papers, Mitchell Memorial Library, Mississippi State University, Starkville, Miss.
84. Jordan, "A Biographical Sketch," 81.

of shaggy charm irresistible, if he would be, to the ladies. . . . I, shorn of my illusions, see myself as a fat, embittered, frustrated bachelor. I should be completely bereft of hope were it not for the fact that homely gents—bald, shaky of teeth and capricious of blood pressure—I am told, work hard at the pleasant business of pleasing the ladies and thus achieve by artifice what has been denied them by nature. And so, suh, I leave you, bowed of head and dim of eye, to practice disappointment amid the moonlight and poison ivy of the Deep South.[85]

Cohn was every bit as appealing in person as he seemed on paper—Richard H. Estabrook of the Washington *Post* described him as "one of the most stimulating, amusing, and gentle souls I have ever known." Not surprisingly, Cohn was widely sought as a house or party guest. During the 1940s, he spent a great deal of time in Washington, D.C., living at the Mayflower Hotel, making the rounds of the city's vibrant party circuit and meeting a number of powerful political figures. Cohn was soon preparing statements and speeches for his friends. As early as 1948, Lyndon Johnson was preaching "Cohn-isms" from "Texarkana on the north to Port Arthur on the south." Cohn maintained his ties to Johnson, advising him on matters relating to the public image of the oil industry and praising Johnson's efforts to promote joint United States–Soviet exploration of outer space.[86]

In April, 1955, Adlai Stevenson noted a speech given by House Speaker Sam Rayburn at a testimonial dinner: "Rayburn's eloquent and philosophical speech not in character but very good—written by David Cohen" [*sic*]. Cohn also prepared a number of speeches for Stevenson, serving during Stevenson's 1952 presidential campaign as a member of his speech-writing team (called the "Elk's Club Group" because they were quartered in the Elk's Club in Springfield, Illinois), a cadre that included historian Arthur M. Schlesinger, Jr., economist John Kenneth Galbraith, labor expert Willard Wirtz, and journalist John Bartlow Martin, to name but a few.[87]

As might be expected from an aggregation of such talented and strong-willed individuals, the "Elk's Club Group" sometimes disagreed as to Stevenson's best course of action. Even the normally congenial Cohn, for example, found it difficult to work with Schlesinger and Stevenson aide Carl McGowan. Cohn insisted on handing speeches he had written directly to Stevenson, and he soon formed a rump group of writers, described with obvious disdain by McGowan

85. David L. Cohn to Bruce Gould, February 8, 1943, in Cohn Collection.
86. Richard H. Estabrook to James W. Silver, March 1, 1961, in Cohn Collection; Lyndon B. Johnson to David L. Cohn, July 30, 1942, in Cohn Collection; David L. Cohn to Lyndon B. Johnson, July 29, 1957, in Lyndon B. Johnson Correspondence, Lyndon Baines Johnson Library, Austin, Tex.
87. Walter Johnson, ed., *The Papers of Adlai E. Stevenson IV: Let's Talk Sense to the American People, 1952–1955* (Boston, 1974), 239; John Bartlow Martin, *Adlai Stevenson of Illinois: The Life of Adlai Stevenson* (Garden City, N.Y., 1976), 630–32.

as the "moonlight and magnolia team." McGowan later claimed that Stevenson rejected as "terrible" a speech that McGowan termed "just a lot of moonlight and magnolias by Cohn." Cohn's team usually prepared the speeches that Stevenson delivered in the South, and John Bartlow Martin observed that while Schlesinger had "highly developed political instincts," Cohn and his associates such as Louisville journalist Herbert Agar "were more interested in the prose of a speech than in its political effectiveness."[88]

Cohn later advised Stevenson on his 1956 campaign, urging him to hammer away at Richard M. Nixon's character and fitness to be "a heartbeat away" from the presidency. He also counseled the erudite Stevenson to counter his image as an "egghead" by delivering at least one major nationally televised speech to the American people without using a prepared text.[89]

Cohn went on to establish friendships with other powerful Washington figures such as Senators Stuart Symington of Missouri and George McGovern of South Dakota. His closest affiliation came, however, with fellow southerner J. William Fulbright of Arkansas. Cohn and Fulbright had much in common. They shared an intense commitment to a vigorously internationalist foreign policy aimed at containing Communism and a genuine concern that what they viewed as the ineptitude of Eisenhower administration officials would undermine public support for such a policy. Cohn wrote a number of speeches for Fulbright, including, for example, a 1959 statement by the senator concerning Chinese Communist oppression in Tibet. As he assailed Chinese attempts to suppress Buddhism in Tibet, Cohn seemed to reflect on his own experience as a member of an oft-persecuted religious group: "There is little we can do to succor a Tibet in agony. But our deepest feelings are engaged, for although we are not of the Buddhist faith, it is nonetheless true that he who lays rough hands upon the followers of Buddha lays rough hands upon all who believe in freedom of worship, independence of spirit, and the dignity of men."[90]

For all their agreement on world and national affairs, it was their common regional heritage—and racial dilemma—that led Cohn and Fulbright to work together most closely. Cohn had long realized that the region's racial inequities had to be eliminated, but he continued to resent the criticism his region received from politicians and the media in the North. Hence, in July, 1957, he wrote Fulbright, "I observed Senator McNamara of Michigan huffing and puffing on television about your Southern barbarisms and civil rights. So—when it becomes pertinent in the debate, you might ask him out loud for all the country to hear why it is that Dearborn, Michigan (near Detroit, that center of light), with

88. Martin, *Adlai Stevenson,* 632–33, 730.
89. David L. Cohn to Adlai E. Stevenson, September 2, 1956, in Cohn Collection.
90. George McGovern to David L. Cohn, June 16, 1960, and Stuart Symington to David L. Cohn, November 15, 1951, both in Cohn Collection. See undated tear sheet accompanying J. William Fulbright's letter to Cohn, April 11, 1959, in Cohn Collection.

55,000 population, has no Negroes, never has had any, and apparently won't permit any there."[91]

In February, 1958, the Little Rock School Board asked the federal courts to delay the implementation of the integration order in Little Rock on the grounds that, given the level of white hostility, orderly education on a desegregated basis was impossible. In June an Arkansan, Federal District Judge Harry J. Lemley, granted a delay until January, 1961. Lemley conceded the right of black students to attend white schools, but given the evidence of chaos and tension at Central High, he concluded that the time had not yet come for blacks to enjoy their full rights where school integration was concerned. The NAACP appealed this judgment, and the Eighth Circuit Court of Appeals set aside Lemley's ruling. The Little Rock School Board then appealed the circuit court decision to the Supreme Court, which agreed to hear the case in a special session in August, 1958.[92]

As the court prepared to receive arguments in the case of *Cooper* v. *Aaron,* Senator Fulbright submitted an *amicus curiae* brief for the court's consideration. Anyone familiar with David Cohn's writings and opinions, however, could have easily recognized the brief as his handiwork. In language drawn almost directly from Cohn's 1944 article "How the South Feels," Fulbright's brief warned that "it is a grave error . . . to fail to realize that there is a Southern Mind," adding that "history tells us that race memories long endure. They are perpetuated in myths, and monuments and a mother's lullaby. They are sentimental and emotional and when stirred up, they become irrational." In language that was vintage Cohn, the brief argued that "the whites and Negroes of Arkansas are equally prisoners of their environment" and that "no one of them has ever been free with respect to racial relationships in the sense that the Vermonter, say, has been free. . . . In Arkansas, one finds a relationship among men without counterpart on this continent, except in similar Southern states." (Readers will recall that many years earlier Cohn had written almost the same words about the Mississippi Delta.)[93]

The Fulbright-Cohn brief warned that if the courts were unwilling to support local school boards when they were acting in good faith, the boards might "fall into the hands of radicals and fanatics," the result being that "neither the process of justice nor education would be served." The brief further argued that the members of the circuit court who overturned Lemley's ruling were "not familiar with the tradition, the cultural patterns, the way of life of our Southern

91. David L. Cohn to J. William Fulbright, July 16, 1957, in J. William Fulbright Collection, University of Arkansas, Fayetteville, Ark.

92. Numan V. Bartley, *The Rise of Massive Resistance: Race and Politics in the South During the 1950s* (Baton Rouge, 1969), 274; "In the Supreme Court of the United States, August Special Term, 1958," *John Aaron, et al.* v. *William E. Cooper, et al.,* "Brief of J. W. Fulbright, Amicus Curiae," typescript, in Fulbright Collection.

93. "Brief of J. W. Fulbright," in Fulbright Collection.

states." Quoting former Supreme Court justice Louis D. Brandeis, Cohn insisted that "no law can be effective which does not take into consideration the conditions of the community for which it is designed." [94]

The court's refusal to review the Fulbright-Cohn brief was a symbolically appropriate fate for an argument that added little to what Cohn and other southern moderates had been saying for more than a generation. Much the same could be said of an article Cohn wrote for *Western World* in December, 1957. Sensitive to the geopolitical implications of the nation's racial problems, Cohn complained that "a favorite weapon of Communists" was the allegation of "mistreatment of the American Negro by his Caucasian fellow citizens." Conceding that "no American in his right mind" would deny that blacks continued to suffer from certain abuses and the denial of their full "freedoms" and "rights," Cohn nonetheless asserted—as he had been doing since 1921—that American blacks were now moving toward "the status of a first class citizen with racehorse speed." Likewise, he also insisted that "thousands" of American blacks lived "by luxurious standards," and he went on to conclude that "if as Communists and many non-Communist Europeans maintain, the American Negro is 'dispossessed,' then he must be the only man who has ever been dispossessed in his own country clubs, on his own golf courses, on his own riding horses, in his own automobile, in his bought-and-paid-for house, and in his own multi-million-dollar business institutions." [95]

However conservative, even reactionary, his rhetoric may sound today, like other southern moderates of his era, Cohn was often labeled a traitor by his less tolerant southern white contemporaries. After his 1944 article "How the South Feels," for example, he received a flood of hate mail, including an envelope filled with ashes and containing a note explaining, "This is what we think of your story . . . you bunch of Negor [sic] lovers." [96]

When the Mississippi legislature denounced his fellow moderate Hodding Carter for slandering Mississippi and selling out the South, Cohn wrote Carter, admitting that he was "horrified, but not surprised" and adding:

> We both knew, and both predicted long ago, that federal efforts to impose desegregation in Mississippi could succeed only through the use of force and, although I haven't been around the state for a long time, I guess that's still the case. You, however, suffer some sharp disabilities in your person, and therefore call out violent attacks:
> You actually believe in seeing justice done and would have Christianity work. Most folks ain't for that and they are deeply wounded when people like you make it to [sic] clear to 'em that they ain't for justice and Jesus no matter how loud they holler.

94. *Ibid.*

95. David L. Cohn, "Negro Advances on the Economic Front," *Western World* I (December, 1957), 52, 54–56.

96. "A Southern" [sic] to David L. Cohn, June 23, 1944, in Cohn Collection; Jordan, "A Biographical Sketch," 83–84.

Worse, perhaps, you are a gentleman. And this is the Age of the Lout. The gentleman in our times is here on sufferance and he may be permitted to live and die
obscurely if he keeps his mouth shut. Otherwise . . .[97]

Cohn went on to explain to Carter that after "thousands of interruptions" he
planned to "get out my little book about my life in the South." He promised to
include a chapter on the Carters and pledged as well to "do right by you in what
I calls the rounded way." As this volume attests, Cohn never saw this project
through. Although he produced numerous drafts, he was too busy with travel
and too distracted by what he viewed as the lamentable course of world and
national affairs to organize what he had written.[98]

On his way to pay yet another visit to his beloved Israel, Cohn suffered a heart
attack and died in Copenhagen on September 12, 1960, leaving a host of
mourners scattered about the globe. Reporting on the 1960 presidential campaign in Mississippi, George Carbone, a history professor at the University of
Mississippi, where Cohn was a frequent visitor, wrote Senator Fulbright that "we
all miss David something awful down here. The perennial pessimist was so very
good for us." Fulbright echoed Carbone's sentiments, describing Cohn as "one
of the most stimulating conversationalists I have ever known." Fulbright observed, however, that the fanatically partisan Cohn might "never have stood
the election in any case, so perhaps it is just as well."[99]

Cohn's passing was noted in the New York *Times* and a host of other newspapers around the world, but nowhere was he more fittingly eulogized than in
his hometown, where his old friend Hodding Carter wrote of the "brilliantly
versatile" Cohn: "He was scholar and writer and wit, urbane traveler, and con-
fidante of statesmen. His compassionate, far-ranging mind could discover social
meaning in mail order catalogues, world danger in tariffs on buttons, warning of
disaster in the glance of an Asiatic coolie. Successful at an age when most of us
are just getting started, he withdrew from business to win more meaningful success as a multi-faceted author and as an interpreter of our region, our nation, and
our times. And withal, he was as much at home and as happy at a catfish fry as
anywhere."[100]

Carter's tribute to Cohn not only sounded good, but it was true. In fact, not
only could Cohn attend a state dinner or a fish fry and enjoy them equally, but
he could also learn from both and relate what he learned at one to what he
learned at the other.

Like the "enlightened provincial" of whom he wrote so admiringly, David
Cohn showed great appreciation for the devotion of "alien" peoples to their own

97. Cobb, *The Most Southern Place on Earth*, 226; David L. Cohn to Hodding Carter, April 5,
1955, in Cohn Collection.
98. Cohn to Carter, April 5, 1955, in Cohn Collection.
99. New York *Times,* September 13, 1960; George A. Carbone to J. William Fulbright, October 27, 1960, and J. William Fulbright to George A. Carbone, October 29, 1960, both in Fulbright Collection.
100. *Delta-Democrat Times,* September 13, 1960.

customs and traditions. Unfortunately, however, for all the concern he expressed for the suffering and repression he saw both in his travels and in the historical and contemporary experience of his fellow Jews, Cohn was least enlightened in his attitudes toward the way of life with which he was most familiar. Hence, he refused to acknowledge the urgent need for—or even the possibility of—immediate and sweeping changes in a Jim Crow system whose inequities and abuses he readily conceded. Certainly, among contemporary southern whites and most whites elsewhere in the nation as well, the racial views Cohn expressed in *God Shakes Creation* were relatively tolerant and benign. On the other hand, however, Cohn was espousing essentially the same views more than two decades later.

Consequently, if it might be said that Cohn was once well ahead of his time on the "Negro question," it must also be said that his "time" was 1935. Cohn's position remained consistently moderate, but in the changing social and political context of the post–World War II years, his rhetoric of moderation, while quite a soothing contrast to the venom and rabble rousing of the massive resistance crowd, nonetheless began to sound increasingly like a defense of the status quo.

As time passed, Cohn's once relatively progressive views on male-female relationships and his endorsements of free trade and aggressive internationalism also seemed increasingly anachronistic. On the other hand, however, many of Cohn's warnings proved quite prophetic. Mechanization of agriculture did indeed result in a massive displacement of southern blacks, and the racial polarization of the urban North is now a long-recognized reality. Likewise, Cohn's oft-reiterated concerns about American materialism present thunderous "I told you so's" to a society now struggling to come to grips with the social and economic consequences of a half-century's addiction to self-indulgence and instant gratification culminating in the excesses of the Reagan era.

A thoroughly cosmopolitan (though somewhat less thoroughly enlightened) provincial, David Cohn might best be described as "a rounded man" with some rough edges. Cohn's southern heritage was responsible for some of these rough edges, but it was his ability to make that heritage the definitive component of his own identity while also using it as a lens on the rest of human society that enriched and distinguished his writing. Following advice offered by C. Vann Woodward more than four decades ago, scholars of all sorts are now busily engaged in making comparisons between the American South and other parts of the globe. That this research has produced such interesting and useful findings would hardly surprise David Cohn, who seldom missed an opportunity to contemplate the similarities between the larger world that fascinated him so and the tiny but equally intriguing one that lay between the Peabody Hotel and Catfish Row.[101]

101. For examples of this comparative approach, see Jonathan M. Wiener, *Social Origins of the New South: Alabama, 1860–1885* (Baton Rouge, 1978); Dwight B. Billings, Jr., *Planters and the Making of a New South: Class, Politics, and Development in North Carolina, 1865–1900* (Chapel Hill, 1979); James C. Cobb, "Southern Writers and the Challenge of Regional Convergence: A Comparative Perspective," *Georgia Historical Quarterly* LXXIII (Spring, 1989), 1–25.